W9-DBA-502

Automatic
Government

Automatic Government

The Politics of Indexation

R. Kent Weaver

The Brookings Institution
Washington, D. C.

Copyright (c) 1988 by

THE BROOKINGS INSTITUTION

1775 Massachusetts Avenue, N.W., Washington, D.C. 20036

Library of Congress Cataloging-in-Publication data

Weaver, R. Kent, 1953-
    Automatic government : the politics of indexation / R. Kent
Weaver.
       p. cm.
    Includes index.
    ISBN 0-8157-9258-1   ISBN 0-8157-9257-3 (pbk.)
    1. Indexation (Economics)—Government policy—United States.
2. Indexation (Economics)—United States.   I. Title.
HG229.5.W43   1988   331.2'15—dc19   88-10562
                                             CIP

9 8 7 6 5 4 3 2 1

Set in Linotron ITC Garamond
Composition by Graphic Composition, Inc.
  Athens, Georgia
Printed by R. R. Donnelley and Sons, Co.
  Harrisonburg, Virginia

For my parents

Foreword

In the past twenty years, the use of automatic inflation adjustments in federal programs has exploded. Many large and important programs, such as individual income taxes, social security, and food stamps, now have statutory indexing provisions. From the outset, indexing has sparked controversy. In the 1970s it was accused of fueling an inflationary spiral. In the 1980s it was criticized for contributing to the budget deficit. Despite this controversy, social scientists have devoted little attention to understanding how and why indexing came to be included in certain federal programs but not others. Nor have they paid much attention to the consequences of indexing or to possible reforms.

This book, by R. Kent Weaver, a senior fellow in the Brookings Governmental Studies program, is an inquiry into the politics of indexation. Equally important, it is an investigation into the objectives of policymakers. Weaver rejects the idea that indexing was a simple technocratic effort to reduce the effects of inflation on federal programs. Although inflation helped to put indexing on government's agenda, politicians and interest groups disagreed seriously about whether indexing should be used and if so how it should be implemented. In many programs, indexing deprived politicians of opportunities to claim credit for granting ad hoc inflation adjustments. In other programs, it allowed politicians to avoid blame for making politically unpopular decisions. These considerations played an important role in determining policymakers' decisions about whether to use indexing.

Understanding political incentives is critical also for analyzing the consequences of indexing, which can be powerful and sometimes perverse. In unindexed income transfer programs, for example, policymakers can refrain from action while inflation gradually erodes the real value of benefits. In indexed programs, however, politicians need to impose losses by openly changing the benefits. While critical of the effects of indexing, Weaver contends that it will remain an important part of the federal policymaking machinery. In the final chapter of this book, he offers some guidelines for its future use and some specific policy options.

The author received much help in conducting this research. D. Roderick Kiewiet suggested the topic. Steven S. Smith encouraged the author to expand the discussion of blame-avoiding motives that appeared in early drafts. Both he and Joseph White read many drafts of the manuscript, and their comments improved it in many ways. R. Douglas Arnold, Morris P. Fiorina, Thomas E. Mann, Paul E. Peterson, Paul Pierson, Robert L. Weaver, and Aaron Wildavsky also read the entire manuscript and made many helpful suggestions. One or more chapters were read by Henry J. Aaron, Ellen Broadman, Evelyn Brodkin, John E. Chubb, Timothy Conlan, Roger H. Davidson, Martha Derthick, Samuel Kernell, Joseph A. Pechman, James P. Pfiffner, Alice M. Rivlin, Harold Seidman, Gilbert Y. Steiner, and Sven Steinmo. The author suggests that if any of the aforementioned do not wish to be associated with the final result, they refer to the blame-avoiding strategies outlined in chapter 2.

The author also had the benefit of expert research assistance. Alice Keck Whitfield helped with the statistical analysis and wrote initial drafts of parts of chapters 7 and 8. Additional research assistance was provided by Kirstin Lundgaard, John Lee, Paul Pierson, Patrick Poulin, Maureen Weston, and Karl Knapp. Paul Pierson verified its factual content. Nancy Davidson edited the manuscript. Louis Holliday and Michael Doleman provided assistance in preparing manuscripts and research materials. Diane Hodges, Sandra Z. Riegler, Eloise C. Stinger, Vida R. Megahed, and Renuka D. Deonarain provided administrative and staff support. Diana Regenthal prepared the index.

The Brookings Institution is grateful to the Lynde and Harry Bradley Foundation for a grant to support the research of this book. Additional support was provided by an anonymous foundation and by the German Marshall Fund of the United States.

The views expressed in this book are those of the author and should not be ascribed to the persons whose assistance is acknowledged above, to the sources of funding support, or to the trustees, officers, or other staff members of the Brookings Institution.

BRUCE K. MAC LAURY
President

April 1988
Washington, D.C.

Contents

Tables

Figures

1

Indexation as a Policy Puzzle

One of the most remarkable public policy developments of the past twenty years in the United States is the extent to which policymakers have surrendered—at least formally—control over public policy decisions. The vehicle for this public policy revolution is indexation: automatic adjustment of public policy outputs for inflation. The scope of the change is evident in the statistics. The number of programs with indexing mechanisms grew from seventeen in 1966 to more than ninety in 1980.[1] About 30 percent of the federal budget was directly indexed to measures such as the Consumer Price Index (CPI) by 1980, and another 20 percent was indirectly indexed.[2] Indexing was applied to programs both large (social security benefits) and small (pensions of former presidents). And the dollar amounts involved were huge: a 1 percent increase in the CPI was estimated in 1981 to trigger more than $3 billion in additional direct and indirect federal expenditures.[3]

While indexing is best known for its application to benefit levels and eligibility standards in federal entitlement programs, it has also been applied to the revenue side of the federal budget (income tax brackets, medicare supplementary medical insurance premiums). It has also been used in a limited way in federal purchases of goods and services, notably in the fields of health care and federal employee pay. Limited use of indexing has also been made in regulation, for example,

1. Congressional Budget Office, *Indexing with the Consumer Price Index: Problems and Alternatives* (CBO, June 1981), p. xiii.
2. General Accounting Office, *What Can Be Done to Check the Growth of Federal Entitlement and Indexed Spending,* Report PAD-81-21 (GAO, March 1981), p. 16.
3. *Indexing and the Federal Budget,* Hearings before the Task Force on Entitlements, Uncontrollables and Indexing of the House Committee on the Budget, 97 Cong. 1 sess. (Government Printing Office, 1981), p. 1.

in campaign spending limits for presidential candidates receiving federal matching funds.

Burgeoning budget deficits in recent years have led to a serious reevaluation—and in some cases modification—of the built-in increases. Even before the advent of the budget-cutting Reagan administration, President Carter and Congress began curbing some inflation adjustments. But these cuts have been limited for the most part to tinkering (for example, small changes in indexing formulas). Once federal programs get indexed, they generally stay indexed.[4]

Much Ado about Nothing?

Indexing has clearly changed the way that government does much of its business. And this change appears to involve a substantial, long-term replacement of legislative discretion by automatic formulas. But some important questions about the causes and consequences of indexing remain unanswered. Why do politicians agree to index—and to index some programs but not others? Does politicians' discretion over indexed programs really decline? And if it does, should this be cause for concern?

One can offer simple answers to each of these questions, but these simple answers are inadequate. Politicians' willingness to index, for example, may be seen as resulting simply from decisionmaking overload: they have more tasks to perform than they can possibly handle and are always casting about for ways to make their decisionmaking easier.

Politicians' desire to reduce their decisionmaking load can clearly be seen in the budgetary process. According to Aaron Wildavsky's classic study, legislators and program administrators make adjustments to programs in large part by reference to previous experience. In the case of spending programs, the primary referent is the previous year's expenditures. Legislators and executive policy specialists seek to increase funding for their favorite programs; budget guardians seek to limit expenditures. But this conflict takes place within a carefully circumscribed set of expectations: in general, next year's program will

4. This stability of indexing provisions is very different from the experience in the private sector, where the number of workers protected by cost-of-living adjustments in their collective bargaining agreements has tended to fluctuate with the level and persistence of inflation. Stuart E. Weiner, "Union COLAs on the Decline," *Federal Reserve Bank of Kansas City Economic Review,* vol. 71 (June 1986), pp. 10–25.

differ only marginally from this year's. Congress employs these cognitive and normative rules in budgeting not only to simplify the decisionmaking process, but also to reduce the scope of political conflict.[5] If all budgetary outcomes are simply modest adjustments to last year's levels, no clientele group will feel unduly threatened, and all will realize that they must moderate their demands if they are to be taken seriously.

The high and persistent inflation that plagued the United States beginning in the late 1960s expanded government's agenda and made conflict management more difficult. The effects of inflation were especially severe on programs where certain standards—social security benefit levels, income tax brackets, minimum wage laws—were written into law in specific dollar amounts. Unless income tax brackets were altered, for example, the effective tax burden of individuals with constant real incomes would go up as they were pushed into higher tax brackets. Without inflation adjustments, workers employed at the minimum wage or pensioners dependent on social security would also find their income declining. Moreover, there was no tradition of annual marginal adjustments in spending levels through the appropriations process for many of the programs most severely affected by inflation, either because those programs were entitlements where benefits were guaranteed by statute (social security), or because they were not explicitly spending programs (the income tax, the minimum wage). Although regular adjustments would prevent the real value of these program standards from eroding, policy specialists in Congress had deliberately attempted to limit routine consideration of both social security and the income tax because they recognized that opening up policy debate on programs with such broad clienteles could lead to dangerous raids on the treasury.

Inflation certainly helped to pave the way for the huge expansion of indexing in the 1970s. Indexing allows politicians to reimpose limits on their decisionmaking load and to lessen conflict. If politicians' dominant concern was to lessen their decisionmaking load, however, they would presumably choose to exclude from their consideration the least important policy decisions while retaining control over the important ones. But Congress in fact spends a lot of time on relatively minor issues—for example, giving names to post offices and federal

5. Aaron Wildavsky, *The Politics of the Budgetary Process,* 4th ed. (Little, Brown, 1984), pp. 135–38.

office buildings, designating specific water and highway projects, designing detailed regulations for administrative agencies, and deciding which government officials can use chauffeur-driven cars. These issues pale in importance when compared with the issues of individual well-being and the federal budget that are determined by decisions about social security benefits and income tax brackets. Yet Congress has decided to give up routine reconsideration of the latter issues and retain it for the former. Clearly something other than decisionmaking overload leads politicians to index programs.

Moreover, indexing also takes away important opportunities for policymakers. Providing ad hoc inflation adjustments in social security benefit levels and income tax brackets in an election year is a perfect mechanism for politicians to claim credit for benefits they have provided their constituents. Any desire to index in order to reduce their decisionmaking load and stabilize the real value of programs is likely to conflict with the credit-claiming interests of reelection-minded politicians. Even if politicians are willing to give up discretion, there are likely to be conflicts over the level at which program standards are indexed. Just how politicians reconcile these conflicts needs to be investigated.

Simple conclusions about the consequences of indexing can be as misleading as those about its causes. Consider its effects on policymakers' discretion, for example. An economist's approach might suggest that "automatic government" is an illusion. In a world of stable prices, it is hard to imagine that Congress would require funding for some programs to fall automatically every year, by some amount unknowable in advance, unless Congress intervened annually to prevent it. But when prices are not stable, that is precisely what would happen to the real value of social security benefits and many other programs in the absence of indexing. At least in theory, indexing simply maintains real expenditures in the face of an unpredictable, unlegislated event: inflation. Legislators do not sacrifice discretion: they retain the power to change real program standards upward or downward whenever they wish. Indexing simply provides a more realistic base from which to make adjustments.

A political perspective, on the other hand, suggests that indexing may have powerful effects on the policy process (including politicians' discretion) and upon outcomes. In the absence of indexing, programs with inflation-sensitive provisions are almost guaranteed a place on the agenda; certainly their clienteles have a powerful incentive to press for their consideration. In the case of indexed programs, however, opponents of change—upward or downward—have a strategic advantage. There is no obvious claim for reconsideration of the program standard, as there would be if inflation were eroding it. And in the American system of fragmented power, it is always easier to block change than to enact it. For these reasons alone, the ability of policymakers to exercise discretion over indexed programs is likely to decline. Rudolph Penner, former head of the Congressional Budget Office, has argued that cost-of-living allowances (COLAs) "have greatly reduced the discretionary power [of Congress]. They may have used their discretionary power to do exactly the things they have done, but the point is that they would have had the choice."[6]

Just how much discretion declines can be determined only by looking at specific programs. But if the decline is substantial—if much of government has in fact become automatic—it raises important questions of democratic accountability. Should politicians cede to anonymous bureaucrats and their computerized formulas the authority over decisions affecting billions of dollars in federal spending and revenues and the income of tens of millions of citizens? When government decisionmaking becomes automatic, how can citizens hold their elected representatives accountable for those decisions? Is the potential cost in terms of democratic control over the policy process worth the added security to recipients of government transfer payments?

In short, there are major shortcomings in the simple explanations of why politicians index and what difference indexing makes. Important questions remain to be answered. At best, the simple explanations can serve as a starting point for inquiry; their adequacy must be tested, not merely assumed. That is what this study proposes to do.

How Indexation Works

The principle behind indexation is a simple one. There is a base, some program standard at a given point in time. The base may be a cash benefit to which an individual is entitled, an income eligibility level for a specific program, an income tax bracket, or even a program budget. Second, there is an index—a measure of changes in wages or prices (or both) since the time at which the base was set. The index

6. Quoted in Jonathan Rauch, "Congress, Worried About Huge Budget Deficits, Eyes an UNCOLA Strategy," *National Journal,* vol. 17 (January 19, 1985), p. 153.

may either be a very general measure, such as the Consumer or Producer Price indexes, or more sector-specific measures, such as the parity index used in setting dairy price supports. Indexing means simply that the base is automatically adjusted at regular intervals by multiplying it by the percentage change in the index in relation to its value in a prior period. Some programs may have several components indexed—and by different indexes. In the food stamp program, for example, the base for eligibility is linked to the poverty line, which is adjusted according to changes in the CPI. The base for food stamp benefits is the Department of Agriculture's thrifty food plan, which is adjusted for changes in food prices. Some programs are even indexed to other programs: inflation adjustments for veterans' pensions, for example, are triggered by increases in social security benefits, while increases in coal miners' disability payments are tied to the salary level of federal employees at the GS-2 level. Social security was seen by the clientele of many other programs as a particularly safe vehicle to which their benefits could be linked.

Use of indexing does not necessarily imply completely automatic changes in federal expenditures or revenues. It can be combined with discretionary mechanisms: in the case of federal civil service pay, for example, a plan is drawn up every year to keep each grade level comparable, on the average, with private-sector pay levels. But the president can submit an alternative plan to Congress. In every year since 1978 he has proposed a lower alternative to the full comparability increase, and Congress has gone along.[7] But if the indexing mechanism were purely advisory (that is, there would be no changes without positive action by Congress or the executive), then a program would not be considered truly indexed.

On the other hand, many programs have provisions that tend to grow automatically with inflation, but are not considered to be formally indexed. Open-ended grant programs like medicaid require the federal government to match state expenditures according to a specified formula (for example, one-to-one or two-to-one). Interest pay-

---

7. See Robert W. Hartman, *Pay and Pensions for Federal Workers* (Brookings, 1983), pp. 28–31; and *Pay Comparability System and Related Matters*, Joint Hearings before the Subcommittee on Civil Service and the Subcommittee on Compensation and Employee Benefits of the House Committee on Post Office and Civil Service, 99 Cong. 2 sess. (GPO, 1986), p. 18. For 1984, the president suggested and Congress accepted a 3.5 percent pay increase. Congress later granted an additional 0.5 percent pay raise, which was still far below comparability levels. See Advisory Committee on Federal Pay, *Report on the Fiscal 1988 Pay Adjustment under the Federal Statutory Pay Systems* (Washington, D.C.: The Committee, August 1987), p. 18.

ments on the federal debt also tend to rise with inflation, as do physicians' charges under medicare. These "implicitly" indexed programs will not be considered here.[8]

Pros and Cons of Indexation

The advantages and disadvantages of indexation have been widely debated. As noted earlier, indexing may provide a more realistic baseline for legislative decisionmaking. It also provides additional security and stability to the recipients of federal benefits. Similarly, indexing tax brackets prevents taxpayers from losing income to the government as inflation pushes them into higher tax brackets, and indexing eligibility levels for means-tested programs prevents low-income workers from losing benefits if their nominal income increases with inflation. Indexing also lessens the workload on government, relieving it of the necessity to make repeated inflation adjustments. On issues like congressional salary increases, indexing offers a way to lessen severe political pressures (in this case, legislators' reluctance to be seen by their constituents as raising their own salaries) that may work to the detriment of important national interests—namely, attracting and keeping the most qualified individuals in Congress.[9] Finally, indexing may remove real changes in benefits from the political agenda, making it easier for Congress to avoid the temptation to increase benefits during election years.

At the same time, indexing creates a number of potential problems. It certainly holds the potential for reducing discretion, even if it does not do so in all cases. And this in turn raises the important question of democratic accountability.

Automatic government also poses important questions of fiscal responsibility. Indexing places spending increases in entitlement programs beyond the routine purview of the congressional authorization

8. Programs can also have automatic provisions tied to indexes that are not inflation related: eligibility for unemployment insurance extended benefits, for example, is tied to the unemployment rate. This study focuses only on inflation-related indexing provisions. It includes programs with indexes that are both external (such as the Consumer Price Index) and internal (such as commodity production cost) to the program. On definitional issues related to indexing, see Vee Burke, "Inventory of Federally Indexed Programs," in Congressional Research Service, *Indexation of Federal Programs* (GPO, 1981), pp. 8–9.

9. See Roger H. Davidson, "The Politics of Executive, Legislative, and Judicial Compensation," in Robert W. Hartman and Arnold R. Weber, eds., *The Rewards of Public Service: Compensating Top Federal Officials* (Brookings, 1980), pp. 53–98; and chap. 6 of this study.

and appropriations committees in Congress. Many critics believe that as a result indexing has caused federal spending to be higher than it would otherwise be in a period of high budget deficits. And because indexed commitments are hard to break, automatic government may deny government needed flexibility in budgetary decisionmaking. Other critics argue that it is not fair for the recipients of indexed benefits to enjoy greater protection from inflation than wage and salary earners. For programs based on specific revenue sources (such as social security), indexing of benefit levels means that the actuarial soundness of long-term program decisions is very dependent on unreliable assumptions about future rates of inflation and economic growth.[10]

Indexing of federal programs has also been criticized as undermining the fight against inflation. It removes the pain of inflation from beneficiaries of federal transfer payments, so they do not have to adjust their consumption to avoid products that have risen especially fast in price (for example, oil after 1974 and 1979)—or they can enjoy real income gains if they do make those adjustments. In addition, COLA adjustments in social security benefits automatically trigger increases in incomes subject to social security payroll taxes, increasing labor costs for business.

Lastly, critics have argued that the specific indexes and bases used may misgauge inflation or simply be inappropriate for some or all of the specific programs to which they are applied. A few of the acknowledged shortcomings of the CPI—the most widely used index in the federal repertoire—illustrate the dilemmas inherent in any attempt to adjust programs based on a formula, especially when that formula was not designed for that purpose in the first place.[11] First, the CPI tends to overstate inflation because the market basket of goods it uses is changed infrequently. While it may be an accurate measure of changing prices for those goods and services, it is not a true cost-of-living index, because it does not accurately capture changing patterns of

10. On the politics of economic assumptions, see Paul Light, *Artful Work: The Politics of Social Security Reform* (Random House, 1985), chap. 5.
11. For a detailed discussion of the Consumer Price Index, see *Indexing and the Federal Budget*, Hearings, as well as CBO, *Indexing with the Consumer Price Index*; and Richard W. Wahl, "Is the Consumer Price Index a Fair Measure of Inflation?" *Journal of Policy Analysis and Management*, vol. 1 (Summer 1982), pp. 496–511. On the general problem of formulas in federal programs, see the testimony of Joseph Duncan, director of the Office of Federal Statistical Policy and Standards, in *Indexing and the Federal Budget*, Hearings, pp. 104–116; and "Demography and Discontent: Constitutional Issues of the Federal Census," *Harvard Law Review*, vol. 94 (February 1981), pp. 841–63.

consumer preferences—in particular, shifts to cheaper substitutes when the prices of some products go up relative to others. For example, if the price of oranges doubles due to a frost in Florida, consumers may substitute apples for oranges, minimizing their welfare loss.[12]

Second, some critics have argued that the CPI does not reflect the purchasing patterns of specific subgroups to which it is applied. The elderly, for example, tend to spend more heavily on medical care, and thus to be more affected by cost increases in that sector than the population as a whole. On the other hand, they are less affected by changes in mortgage interest rates than the general population.[13]

Third, the treatment of homeownership cost in the CPI was clearly defective for many years, causing a serious overstatement of the inflation rate. The CPI did not take into account the fact that some of the expenditure for homeownership should be considered as an investment in an appreciating asset. The heavy weighting given to mortgage interest rates in the housing component of the CPI also caused the index to be excessively volatile (and for several years, excessively high as well).[14] These problems were corrected in 1983, but benefit standards in indexed programs were not corrected for past overadjustments. The Congressional Budget Office estimated that if an alternative

12. For examples of substitution effects and their effects on the Consumer Price Index, see Charles Mason and Clifford Butler, "New Basket of Goods and Services Being Priced in Revised CPI," *Monthly Labor Review*, vol. 110 (January 1987), pp. 3–22. See also Christopher Jencks, "The Hidden Prosperity of the 1970s," *The Public Interest*, no. 77 (Fall 1984), especially pp. 50–52.

13. For contrasting views of the adequacy of the CPI as an index of living costs for the elderly, see the testimony of James Hacking, Rudolph Oswald, and Joseph Minarik in *Indexing and the Federal Budget*, Hearings, pp. 144–68, 130–43, and 27–33, respectively. Bridges and Packard find that differences in inflation rates between the elderly and the general population are small. Boskin and Hurd agree, but argue that different individuals within age cohorts may have very different inflation experiences. Baum and Sjogren argue that a lower rate of indexing would exacerbate both income inequality and rates of poverty among the elderly. See Benjamin Bridges, Jr., and Michael D. Packard, "Price and Income Changes for the Elderly," *Social Security Bulletin*, vol. 44 (January 1981), pp. 3–15; Michael J. Boskin and Michael D. Hurd, "Indexing Social Security Benefits: A Separate Price Index for the Elderly?" *Public Finance Quarterly*, vol. 13 (October 1985), pp. 436–49; and Sandra R. Baum and Jane Sjogren, "Alternative Social Security Indexing Schemes and Poverty among the Elderly," *Policy Studies Journal*, vol. 12 (September 1983), pp. 79–90.

14. On the other hand, a decline in mortgage interest rates can cause a drop in the CPI. OMB Director David Stockman opposed a shift in the CPI to a "rental equivalence" approach in 1981 because he believed that the administration's economic policies would cause interest rates to fall, and a change in the index at that point would lock in windfall gains made under the old indexing scheme (see Stockman's testimony in *Indexing and the Federal Budget*, Hearings, p. 206). The CPI also exaggerated shelter costs because it did not recognize lower true costs resulting from mortgage interest deductibility.

index, the Personal Consumption Expenditure Implicit Price Deflator, had been in place since 1975, federal spending on benefit programs would have been $12 billion lower in fiscal year 1981 alone.[15]

Finally, the CPI does not measure changes in the overall living standard of the population—notably general improvements due to productivity increases—as a wage-based index would do. Thus, if it accurately reflected living costs, it would hold beneficiaries of indexed benefits to a constant standard of living while that of the working population generally would increase over time.

The poverty-level guideline used to establish eligibility for many federal programs, including food stamps, head start, legal services, and the national school lunch program, has also been subjected to heavy criticism.[16] The primary criticism of the poverty standard by conservatives is that it includes only cash income. It excludes in-kind benefits (food stamps, medicaid benefits, rent subsidies) that raise living standards. It also excludes assets, although many federal programs have additional assets tests. And because the poverty line has been adjusted since 1969 by changes in the CPI, increases may have been overstated.[17] These restrictive definitions of income may lead to overcounting of the number of people living in poverty and expand eligibility for federal programs. On the other hand, the poverty line is based on before-tax income and thus includes income that is not actually available for consumption. It is based on an income standard that many feel is inadequate.[18] And the poverty-line measure does not allow increases

15. Testimony of Lawrence E. DeMilner in *Indexing and the Federal Budget,* Hearings, p. 8. The Bureau of Labor Statistics estimates that if the current treatment of housing costs had been in place earlier, the CPI would have increased 165 percent between 1967 and 1982, rather than the 187.8 percent actually measured. See "The Effect of Rental Equivalence on the Consumer Price Index, 1967–1982," *Monthly Labor Review,* vol. 108 (February 1985), pp. 53–55; and Robert Gillingham and Walter Lane, "Changing the Treatment of Shelter Costs for Homeowners in the CPI," *Monthly Labor Review,* vol. 105 (June 1982), pp. 9–14.

16. Eligibility is not always set at the poverty line, but may rather be some multiple of it—or both. The food stamp program, for example, has both a gross income limit of 130 percent of the poverty line and a net income limit of 100 percent.

17. See John C. Weicher, "Mismeasuring Poverty and Progress," *Cato Journal,* vol. 6 (Winter 1987), pp. 715–30.

18. The poverty standard was originally developed by multiplying the cost of the Department of Agriculture's economy food plan by a factor of three, based on a 1955 survey showing that the poor spent about one-third of their income on food. However, they may have to spend more than the value of the economy food plan to receive a nutritionally adequate diet. See chap. 5 on the shortcomings of the economy food plan. The poverty standard has not been adjusted to the fact that families now generally spend less of their income on food. On the development and revision of the poverty standard, see Mollie Orshansky, "How Poverty Is Measured," *Monthly Labor Review,* vol. 92 (February 1969), pp. 37–41; and Orshansky's testimony in *Census and Designation of Pov-*

in general living standards to be reflected in a more generous definition of poverty—that is, it is an absolute rather than a relative standard.[19] Nor does it reflect regional variations in the cost of living that
affect family need.

Program indexes and bases are inevitably imperfect. They are necessarily built at least in part upon inadequate data, incomplete and
possibly faulty assumptions and formulas, and value judgments by statisticians and the policymakers who guide their work. This does not
mean that indexing is undesirable, or that it produces worse policy
outcomes than does discretionary decisionmaking. But it does point
out another potential flaw in indexing: it may lock in policy mistakes
that might be corrected under a less automatic policy process.

Pieces of the Puzzle

Increased use of indexing by the federal government may or may
not be a desirable policy development, but it certainly is an important
one that poses some critical questions about policymaking. These
questions can be broken down into four areas of inquiry: the participants in indexing decisions and their objectives in making them; the
patterns of policy choice made in adopting and revising indexing; the
consequences of those policy choices; and the future of indexing.

Participants and Objectives

Which groups in and out of government dominate decisions to
adopt, reject, or modify indexing? Several groups would seem to be
likely candidates. Policy specialists within the executive branch (the
agency having jurisdiction over a specific program) will presumably

---

erty and Income, Joint Hearing before the Subcommittee on Census and Population of
the House Committee on Post Office and Civil Service and the Subcommittee on Oversight of the House Committee on Ways and Means, 98 Cong. 2 sess. (GPO, 1984), pp. 6–
18. See also U.S. Department of Health, Education and Welfare, The Measure of Poverty:
A Report to Congress as Mandated by the Education Amendments of 1974 (GPO,
1976); Gordon M. Fisher, "The 1984 Federal Poverty Income Guidelines," Social Security Bulletin, vol. 47 (July 1984), pp. 24–27; and Leonard Beeghley, "Illusion and Reality
in the Measurement of Poverty," Social Problems, vol. 31 (February 1984), pp. 322–33.

19. See Sheldon Danziger and Peter Gottschalk, "The Measurement of Poverty,"
American Behavioral Scientist, vol. 26 (July–August 1983), pp. 739–56; and S. Anna
Kondratas, "Poverty and Equity: Problems of Definition," Journal of the Institute for
Socioeconomic Studies, vol. 9 (Winter 1985), pp. 37–48. The poverty line fell from just
under one-half to around one-third of median family income in the United States in the
1960s, and it has remained near that level since then. Courtenay Slater, "Concepts of
Poverty," Journal of the Institute for Socioeconomic Studies, vol. 9 (Autumn 1984),
pp. 1–12.

have an important role in developing legislative proposals for the program. Policy specialists within the legislature (the House and Senate authorizing committees having jurisdiction over a program) have both expertise and a mandate from their colleagues to develop legislation and perform program oversight. "Budget guardians" in the executive branch (notably the Office of Management and Budget) and in Congress (notably the Appropriations and Budget committees) are also likely to be involved. While they may be less concerned with the details of the program, they will give considerable weight to the budgetary implications of indexing, with respect to both total spending and controllability. Policy nonspecialists in Congress (that is, members voting in floor votes),[20] and executive branch nonspecialists (notably the president and White House staff) are presumably somewhat less likely to be involved in developing policy proposals, but they may veto proposals made by others. Other potential participants are policy experts in and out of government (for example, academics, but also technically trained personnel within agencies and congressional committees). A final—and critical—type of participant is interest groups, notably the program's clientele.[21]

Not all of these actors necessarily participate in indexation policy decisions. Indexing could presumably result from pressure from only one of these actors, with the others passively acquiescing. On the other hand, indexing might require near unanimity of active support to overcome the procedural obstacles in the American system. What is important here is to discern which groups do in fact press for indexing and which combinations of support are most conducive to its adoption. It is also useful to know whether indexing has a consistent base of political support, or whether that support varies across programs.

A second question relates to policymakers' objectives in instituting indexation. These concerns may be policy oriented, political, or some combination of the two. With respect to the first, one can ask whether policymakers think that indexing increases government spending,

20. The implication here is not that some individual members of Congress specialize on particular issues while others do not (although this is true to a limited extent), but rather that on any given issue some members of Congress will be specialists while others will not.

21. The distinction between these groups, notably between policy experts and interest groups, is not always clear, however. See Hugh Heclo, "Issue Networks and the Executive Establishment," in Anthony King, ed., *The New American Political System* (Washington, D.C.: American Enterprise Institute for Public Policy Research, 1978), especially pp. 98–105.

INDEXATION AS A POLICY PUZZLE l 13

shrinks it, or is neutral in its effects on the deficit. For executive and legislative budget guardians, indexing may limit ability to respond to budgetary constraints. Are indexing decisions made over the objections of these important actors, or do they in fact support indexing for reasons different from those outlined here?

Indexing also has consequences for the power and prerogatives of policymakers. Above all, ad hoc increases in programs such as social security present an opportunity for politicians to claim credit with their constituents for increasing benefits (although these increases may be only nominal ones). This study will attempt to explain why policymakers are willing to limit these opportunities.

Explaining Policy Choices

This study will also attempt to draw generalizations about the scope of indexation—that is, why some programs are indexed while others are not. Programs that provide visible, measurable benefits to individuals have been indexed more often than those that do not. But there are some important anomalies even among benefit programs with similar clienteles. Moreover, some other types of programs (for example, income tax brackets, commodity price supports) have also been indexed. Is it possible to find a general explanation of why some programs are indexed and others are not, or is the pattern largely a result of historical accident?

The prospect that indexing will be confined to a set of programs with common characteristics is undermined by the diffusion of policy ideas across policy sectors.[22] Once policymakers and interest groups become familiar with the concept of indexing and how it works, they can adapt it to new program contexts, often very different from those where it was first used. Indexing is, in short, in the policy repertoire—the set of options that policymakers know about and are likely to consider. But just because it is part of their repertoire does not mean that indexing will make it onto decisionmakers' formal institutional agenda. For example, legislative specialists may attempt to exclude indexing from congressional agendas because it conflicts with their credit-claiming interests. In short, while diffusion of policy ideas may increase the scope of indexing, politicians' interests may decrease its scope.

22. Jack Walker, "The Diffusion of Innovation among the American States," *American Political Science Review,* vol. 63 (September 1969), pp. 880–99.

Two additional questions about the choice of indexation policy relate to modifications of indexing after it has been adopted. Why has it so rarely been eliminated once it is in place? As noted above, indexing may well face opposition from the budget guardians in Congress and the executive. The severe budget restraint pressures in the 1980s also might have been expected to contribute to a substantial backtracking from indexing, especially for programs that are either politically weak or have relatively weak claims to protection from inflation. Has this attack simply failed to materialize, or has it been beaten back? If the former is true, one must ask why. If the latter is the case, one must ask how and by whom.

Changes *have* been made in indexing, however. Although it has rarely been abolished, it has been modified in certain ways that have undercut its effects—for example, stretching out periods between adjustments and changing indexing formulas. Why has indexing been cut more in some programs than in others?

The Consequences of Indexation

A third set of questions concerns the consequences of indexing: does it matter, and if so, when, how, and how much? First, how does indexing affect individual programs to which it is applied? Does it really provide a firmer protection against inflation for program clientele than ad hoc policy changes? Second, how does indexing affect the overall federal budget? Does it cripple the federal government's ability to control and adapt its spending to changing fiscal constraints? Does it cause spending to be higher than it otherwise would be? Third, how does indexing affect the economy? In particular, by lessening the pain of inflation, does indexing make it more difficult to fight inflation? Finally, indexing raises some important questions about the policymaking process. Does it change the political agenda—for example, by taking changes in the program base off the agenda? And is policymaking for indexed programs fundamentally different from that in nonindexed programs, or is indexing simply a mechanism to adapt old policymaking procedures to the new challenge of persistent but uneven inflation?

Indexing has many possible effects. When applied to federal benefit programs, for example, it can help groups to maintain benefit levels that they might otherwise lose through inflation. Alternatively, it might prevent them from winning real benefit increases that they could otherwise have gained by exerting political pressure. Or indexing might have an effect similar to the phenomenon of wage stickiness—that is, making benefits susceptible to upward real adjustments but not to downward ones. With respect to user charges (such as medicare premiums and deductibles), indexing gives policymakers a way to allow prices to rise with inflation without having to bear the political costs associated with raising them.

However, if political outcomes are determined primarily by the constellation of political forces involved in a policy area rather than by the procedures used to make decisions, then indexing might be inconsequential. It might simply serve as a substitute for changes that would have been made anyway on an ad hoc basis. It must also be remembered that indexing is itself a policy decision that can be repealed or modified if it gets in the way of what powerful political actors seek. In short, there are sound theoretical reasons both for believing that indexing has a substantial effect on the policymaking process and outputs—or for believing it has no effect at all.

Assessing the consequences of indexing for individual programs and for the federal budget is a difficult task. Obviously, the effects vary depending on how much discretion program implementers have in administering the indexing provisions. If, as in the cases of federal civilian pay and dairy price supports, policymakers have some latitude in adhering to indexed adjustments, any possible effects on spending levels and budget controllability can be undercut.

But there are more serious methodological problems in making judgments about the consequences of indexing. Such judgments implicitly assume an answer to the question: what would have happened if this program had not been indexed, and how does this compare with what has in fact occurred? Too often, it is assumed that no inflation adjustment would have been made. But this is clearly an inappropriate standard for comparison with actual indexed expenditures. Before explicit indexing was enacted, there were ad hoc inflation adjustments that often outpaced inflation.

Knowing the magnitude of program adjustments that would have occurred without indexing is obviously impossible, which makes a precise understanding of the effects of indexing for either individual programs or the budget as a whole equally impossible. There are three ways to try to simulate an answer, however. First, spending trends can be compared for indexed and nonindexed programs that have similar clienteles and eligibility requirements. But this ignores a crucial problem: there are usually reasons why some programs are indexed and others are not. The effect of indexing is often difficult to distinguish from these underlying forces. For example, benefit standards in the indexed food stamp program have been relatively stable in real terms over the last few years, while nonindexed aid to families with dependent children (AFDC) benefits have declined much more. Clearly the existence of an indexing mechanism is not the only force at work here. The fact that AFDC is administered by the states has inhibited the institution of indexing. Severe fiscal stress within the states, compounded by state constitutional restrictions on budget deficits, has inhibited benefit increases. It is difficult to separate out the effect of indexing from the role played by institutional constraints in explaining these differing outcomes.

A second way to try to assess the effects of indexing is to examine the spending trends for individual programs before and after they were indexed (or deindexed). But for this to be a valid test, everything else about the world in which the programs operate must remain the same. Even if controls are made for economic fluctuations (for example, using individual benefit data rather than total spending data), it is difficult to control for other factors—notably the onset of severe fiscal stress—that may shape the effect of indexing.

A third way to evaluate the effects of indexing—best used in tandem with the others—is to examine changes that have been made in a program's indexing provisions (in either the base or the index) since the program was indexed. If indexing acts as a barrier to changes in real program standards, any adjustments that are made in those provisions are probably a weakened version of trends that would have been magnified without indexing. Unfortunately, it is impossible to prove whether the relationship between the actual and counterfactual trends is in the hypothesized direction and magnitude.

Each method has important flaws in assessing the effects of indexing: notably, inability to distinguish between indexing effects and other influences on policy. Thus examination of outcome data must be accompanied by an examination of program decisionmaking. By understanding these relationships between outcome data and program context, one can develop a tentative understanding of how and why indexing matters.

The Future of Indexation

A final set of questions concerns the future of indexation. What kinds of reforms are feasible and likely in the future? And what kinds of changes should be made? Should indexing be curtailed or limited to certain types of programs? Should current indexing mechanisms and bases be modified, and, if so, how? This discussion inevitably draws upon the analyses of the political forces influencing indexation policy choices and of the consequences of those choices. For it is only with a firm understanding of those choices and their consequences that one can understand what changes can and should be made.

Solving the Indexation Policy Puzzle

This study attempts to answer these questions by examining the indexation politics and policy of six federal programs. The first three chapters provide a general introduction to the problem of indexing. The next six chapters examine the policymaking process for the old age survivors insurance (OASI) component of social security, food stamps, congressional pay, dairy price supports, the minimum wage, and federal income taxes over the periods of adoption and subsequent modification of indexing. These chapters will also include a discussion of the consequences of indexing for those programs. The last four chapters attempt to draw general lessons from the cases, paralleling the four sets of questions posed in this chapter.

2

Politicians' Objectives

Indexing government programs to compensate for inflation is only one manifestation of a much broader trend toward self-limitation of discretion by politicians. In the federal civil service and in many state governments, patronage appointments have been replaced by civil service mechanisms. In federal grant activity, formula grants now dramatically outnumber discretionary grants in both number and size. More recently, the Gramm-Rudman-Hollings budget-cutting initiative also employed automatic triggers to government action.

Whatever their merits in reducing decisionmakers' workload or in promoting desirable policy outcomes, indexing and other discretion-limiting devices in government seem inconsistent with much of the accepted thinking about how American public policy is made. Policymakers are usually seen as using their activities and votes to claim credit with constituents and clientele groups for actions taken in their interests.[1] But politicians seem willing to sacrifice these credit-claiming opportunities. And once indexing mechanisms are in place, politicians seldom remove them. Why is this so? Is it simply a desire to reduce their decisionmaking load? And how do politicians reconcile these often conflicting objectives?

To answer these questions, it is necessary to develop a more sophisticated picture of politicians' objectives and the forces that influence their behavior. While credit claiming is certainly a major component of policymakers' motivations, it is not the only one.[2] Policymakers are

1. One of the boldest statements of the credit-claiming perspective is Morris P. Fiorina, *Congress: Keystone of the Washington Establishment* (Yale University Press, 1977).
2. David Mayhew argues that legislators can engage in credit claiming only if (1) they can show that they were "prime movers" in the adoption of a measure—for example, a sponsor or member of the legislative committee with jurisdiction over the issue, or (2) the benefits are particularistic, handed out in an ad hoc fashion, with the legislator playing a role in their distribution. He contrasts this with "position taking"—issuing a public judgment on an issue, most notably through roll call votes. I use the term "credit

often placed in situations in which opportunities to claim credit are nonexistent or simply not worth the associated political costs. So politicians must concern themselves with avoiding blame for perceived or real losses that they either imposed or acquiesced in, as well as with claiming credit for benefits they have granted.[3]

Politicians also attempt to generate blame against actual or potential political opponents. They do so for both policy and political reasons. If their opponents are fearful of incurring blame, they may back down and accept a position more to the liking of the blame-generators and their constituents. And even if they do not, identifying a political opponent with an unpopular position may be even more politically profitable than identifying oneself with the popular position.

Policymakers may also have nonelectoral objectives. Most obviously, they may have "good-policy" objectives—that is, they may act because they think an action is worthwhile even if it has no political payoff. They may be guided by power considerations within their respective institutions (their legislative chamber, committee, or caucus, or their agency) or by what they perceive to be the interests of those institutions in conflicts with others (for example, protecting congressional prerogatives against incursions by the president).[4] Politicians may also exchange support on issues of low salience to themselves and their constituents for other legislators' votes on seemingly unrelated issues.

This chapter examines three crucial motivations for politicians' behavior—credit claiming, good policy, and blame avoiding—as potential influences on indexing choices. I first sketch out a theory of policy motivations and then apply this analysis to indexation policymaking. Finally, I discuss how this theory of policy motivations can be tested.

Motivations for Policy Decisions

Most politicians and bureaucrats do not pursue just one objective single-mindedly. They are likely to have both policy and political objectives. Different decisions elicit different pressures and hence differ-

---

claiming" in a broader sense than in Mayhew's book, to include position taking when it is done in the expectation of political gain rather than to avoid poitical losses. See David Mayhew, *Congress: The Electoral Connection* (Yale University Press, 1974), pp. 52–61.

3. For a more complete development of the blame-avoidance concept, see R. Kent Weaver, "The Politics of Blame Avoidance," *Journal of Public Policy*, vol. 6 (October–December 1986), pp. 371–98.

4. See Richard Fenno, *Congressmen in Committees* (Little, Brown, 1973), chap. 1.

ent objectives. The urge to claim credit, for example, is likely to be much stronger where there are location-specific benefits (such as river and harbor projects) than where there are not.[5] Ideally, politicians would like to make choices that are consistent with all of their objectives. But many decisions force policymakers to make trade-offs between objectives—for example, to consider voting for a pork barrel project for its credit-claiming potential even though it conflicts with their good-policy beliefs.

The politician's calculus is a complex one, even if his or her sole objective is to maximize prospects for reelection (or reappointment) and advancement. One might expect politically motivated decisionmakers to attempt to maximize benefits for their constituents while minimizing costs to them—that is, to take actions for which they can maximize credit and minimize blame.[6] But this is not an easy calculation to make. Constituency costs and benefits do not translate directly into gains and losses for officeholders. Constituents are much less likely to notice widely diffused gains or losses, for example, than those that are relatively concentrated in a smaller group. Thus politicians will probably give little weight to the claims of constituents in the former category. Groups that are poorly organized and have few political resources are also likely to have their policy concerns heavily discounted.[7]

Taking these caveats into consideration, one might argue that policymakers will, given a range of policy alternatives, strongly support the one that maximizes net benefits (the surplus of concentrated benefits over concentrated costs) to their constituencies. But even this formulation is still too simplistic. Pursuit of a constituency benefit-maximizing, credit-claiming strategy is rational only if constituents respond symmetrically to gains and losses—for example, if a dollar of income gained by one set of constituents as a result of a policymaker's actions wins as much support as a dollar lost to another group costs.

5. See R. Douglas Arnold, "The Local Roots of Domestic Policy," in Thomas E. Mann and Norman J. Ornstein, eds., *The New Congress* (Washington, D.C.: American Enterprise Institute for Public Policy Research, 1981), pp. 250–87.

6. Constituency costs and benefits will be broadly defined here to include taking issue positions contrary to or consistent with those of constituents as well as making policy changes that affect constituents' economic positions.

7. Even if they are equally concentrated, constituency costs and benefits are rarely weighed equally by politicians. If either costs or benefits fall disproportionately on a group that is unlikely to vote for the officeholder in any case, they will be discounted heavily; the same is true for groups that are unlikely to be shaken from support for the officeholder.

But there is substantial evidence that this is not so. Persons who have suffered losses are more likely to notice the loss, to feel aggrieved and to act on that grievance, than gainers are to give credit for their improved state.[8] As Louis XIV noted with dismay, "Every time I fill an office, I create a hundred malcontents and one ingrate." Voters too have a "negativity bias"—they are more sensitive to what has been done *to* them than to what has been done *for* them.[9] This leads politicians to discount constituency benefits relative to costs and very strongly to resist imposing losses.[10]

The calculation becomes even more complex where politicians have policy as well as political objectives. In general, one would expect that in a conflict between objectives, politicians will attach less importance to both constituency gains (credit claiming) and good-policy concerns than to constituency losses (blame avoiding).

The behavior and the policy choices of politicians are strongly influenced by which objectives they emphasize. A politician who seeks credit from his constituents, for example, will probably seek to exercise leadership on policy issues, while politicians who wish to minimize blame will probably shun leadership. Differences between objectives can also be seen in policy "bidding wars," where leaders of one

8. For evidence from the psychological literature on asymmetry in the perception of gains and losses, see Daniel Kahneman and Amos Tversky, "Choices, Values and Frames," *American Psychologist,* vol. 39 (April 1984), pp. 341–50.

9. For a discussion of why voters are likely to give a higher weight to negative than to positive information, see Richard R. Lau, "Two Explanations for Negativity Effects in Political Behavior," *American Journal of Political Science,* vol. 29 (February 1985), pp. 119–38; and Morris P. Fiorina and Kenneth A. Shepsle, "Negative Voting: An Explanation Based on Principal-Agent Theory," in John Ferejohn and James Kuklinski, eds., *Information and Democratic Processes* (University of Illinois Press, forthcoming). The role of personal economic grievances (loss of a job, loss of personal income through inflation) in promoting punishment-oriented behavior is relatively modest, however. Most voters in the United States do not appear to be "pocketbook voters" in this crude sense. Sears and Lau suggest that an individual's personal economic situation will influence political behavior only when (1) the stakes are direct and sizable and (2) responsibility for the individual's situation is attributed to government. David O. Sears and Richard R. Lau, "Inducing Apparently Self-Interested Political Preferences," *American Journal of Political Science,* vol. 27 (May 1983), pp. 223–52. Politicians, may, however, incur blame for general declines in economic conditions, even if they do not affect the individual directly. This finding is consistent with a negativity bias. See Donald R. Kinder and D. Roderick Kiewiet, "Economic Judgments and Political Behavior: The Role of Personal Grievances and Collective Economic Judgments in Congressional Voting," *American Journal of Political Science,* vol. 23 (August 1979), pp. 495–527.

10. Politicians have strong incentives to minimize potential blame, even if voters' judgments are only partially based on a desire to punish behavior or views of which they disapprove, because (1) politicians cannot be certain which issues might be picked up by future opponents and used against them and (2) only some, not all, voters need to pursue retribution as a voting objective for a politician's office to be in danger.

party promise to take some popular action (for example, raise social security benefits, lower the personal income tax rate, or cut the budget deficit by a certain amount). Leaders of the other party may attempt to "raise the bid" by offering more. This is a classic credit-claiming response. Or they may simply "match the bid" offered by the other party. While this wins them little credit with voters, it at least attempts to avoid blame for having imposed losses relative to their competitors. Congress generally relies on its policy specialists to prevent destabilizing bids from getting on the agenda. When they are unable to exercise that control, as in the income tax debate of 1981 (see chapter 9), the consequences can be disastrous.

To flesh out this argument, it is helpful to consider in some detail the situations in which one or another objective is likely to dominate a politician's actions and the strategies that politicians use to attain these objectives.

Sources of Policymakers' Behavior

Individual politicians vary in the emphasis they give to credit claiming, blame avoiding, and good-policy objectives. But their choices are not unconstrained. It is therefore possible to make some generalizations about the conditions under which one or another of these objectives is likely to dominate policymakers' decisions. Two factors in particular are likely to influence which motivations dominate in a specific choice: (1) the costs and benefits of the alternatives for policymakers and their constituents;[11] and (2) whether voters attribute responsibility to politicians for those outcomes. Both of these factors are open to manipulation by politicians.

Figure 2-1 shows how the distribution of costs and benefits affects politicians' objectives in a very simple decision: a choice between the status quo and a single alternative policy that would have different effects on two segments of a policymaker's constituency. It is assumed that the two segments are of roughly equal size. When costs and benefits are low for both segments, politicians will have the most freedom. They can act according to nonelectoral (for example, good-policy or vote-trading) motivations with little concern over the political repercussions (cell 5). When concentrated benefits of the alternative policy are high for one group of constituents and effects on the other group

---

11. *Constituents* will be used here in a broader sense than simply voters in a legislators' district. It also includes potential campaign contributors and elites in interest groups with links to the legislator's electoral constituents.

FIGURE 2-1. *Cost-Benefit Distributions and Policymakers' Motivations*

		Perceived net effects on constituency *B* of adopting new policy		
		Positive	Neutral	Negative
Perceived net effects on constituency *A* of adopting new policy	Positive	(1) Credit claiming	(2) Credit claiming	(3) Blame avoiding
	Neutral	(4) Credit claiming	(5) Nonelectoral	(6) Credit claiming and blame generating
	Negative	(7) Blame avoiding	(8) Credit claiming and blame generating	(9) Credit claiming and blame generating

are slight, the policymaker can claim credit with the first group for making that choice (cells 2 and 4).[12] Because there are no concentrated constituency losses to be allocated, blame-avoiding motives may simply be irrelevant. If both segments of the politician's constituency gain from the change (cell 1), credit claiming is again likely to be the dominant objective.[13] This type of objective can be seen in the distribution of pork barrel projects such as dams and harbor projects. Such projects are virtually pure political profit, for projects are quite visible and costs are broadly spread.

A politician's motives are similar when costs of a proposed alternative are high for one or both groups of constituents and no constitu-

12. This choice can also be seen as extreme cases of a blame-avoiding situation: the costs of a contrary vote are so overwhelmingly negative that this option is not even considered. But the more parsimonious explanation is obviously to focus directly on credit claiming.

13. Having constituency opinion concentrated overwhelmingly on a single side of an issue is not necessarily beneficial for a policymaker, however. When consensus is so pervasive, there is little credit to be derived from agreement with it—conformity is simply expected. A legislator's attendance at roll call votes is a classic example of this type of blame-generating situation: it provides virtually no credit-claiming opportunities (because voters assume that representatives should be present for all votes), but legislators with poor attendance records have had that fact used against them very effectively.

ents benefit: for example, if a federal facility that provides many jobs in a legislator's district is threatened with closure (cells 6, 8, and 9). Here the decisionmaker will probably attempt to turn the situation into a political plus by loudly opposing adoption of the change and claiming credit with constituents for doing so.[14] The politician may attempt to obtain additional political profits by generating blame against rival policymakers who support a change in policy.

Clearly a policymaker's most difficult choice is shown in cells 3 and 7, where bringing benefits for one part of the constituency requires imposing costs on another segment. This is a classic zero-sum conflict. In this situation, the decisionmaker has two options. He or she can attempt to calculate the strength of the effects and the power of the groups involved and then back the side that promises the higher political returns, claiming credit for having done so. But this credit-claiming response risks offending the losers, who are more likely to remember that loss and punish the politician for it. Unless the losing group is drastically outnumbered by the winners, one would expect policymakers to search for compromises that minimize losses—and therefore blame—before worrying about credit from the winners.[15]

Each of the situations described above is an oversimplification, of course. Often the gains or losses suffered by opposing constituents— or the groups themselves—differ greatly in size, easing a policymaker's concern about incurring blame. But other conflicts may have more than two sides, increasing the difficulty of accommodating all groups without leaving at least some of them unhappy. And in many cases, the policymaker holds strong independent views flowing from good-policy or personal interests. These views may or may not be consistent with constituency interests. When they are, politicians can both claim credit with constituents and achieve their own aims, as shown in cells 1 and 9 of figure 2-2. But when they are incompatible (cells 3 and 7), politicians are very likely to try to minimize blame, either by sacrific-ing their own views or by manipulating the way the issue is considered so that constituents do not realize that the policymaker is acting in

14. Even here a credit-claiming approach is not without risks. If leading the opposi-tion to a measure has little prospect of success, and the policymaker is likely to be blamed for failure in spite of having tried, it might be more fruitful to portray himself as powerless to influence the decision—that is, to pass the buck on responsibility to others.

15. In some situations, all possible alternatives have strong negative consequences for at least some of the policymakers' constituents. Here there is no credit to be ob-tained. Policymakers can only hope to limit their exposure to blame—for example, by passing the buck. This form of blame avoidance is particularly likely to arise when gov-ernment is allocating budgetary cutbacks.

FIGURE 2-2. *Interaction of Policymaker and Constituency Interests*

Effects of proposed change on constituents

		Positive	Neutral	Negative
Effects of proposed change on policymaker's policy or personal interests	Positive	(1) Credit claiming and policy or personal interests	(2) Policy or personal interest	(3) Blame avoiding
	Neutral	(4) Credit claiming	(5) Vote trading or other	(6) Credit claiming and blame generating
	Negative	(7) Blame avoiding	(8) Policy or personal interest	(9) Credit claiming, policy or personal interest, and blame generating

opposition to their views or interests. A classic illustration of this is the effort by legislators to keep their own pay raises off their agenda by providing for an automatic process of increases. When this proved impossible to implement, legislators were forced to vote down pay raises (see chapter 6).

Manipulating Perceptions, Agendas, and Payoffs

Policymakers' motivations are not entirely determined by the distribution of costs and benefits among their constituents. They are also determined by whether constituents connect them with outcomes and by the way choices are structured. Voters often err in attributing credit and blame. On the one hand, they may attribute a linkage where the policymaker's influence was really weak or nonexistent (for example, in creating an upturn in the economy). On the other hand, they may fail to link policymakers to choices they have in fact made or outcomes to which they have contributed.[16]

Politicians are not passive bystanders as voters attribute praise and

16. For a social psychology perspective on this issue, see Kelly G. Shaver, *The Attribution of Blame: Causality, Responsibility and Blameworthiness* (Springer-Verlag, 1985).

blame. They try to influence voters' perceptions of who should be held responsible for policy choices.[17] They often try to claim credit for things that benefit their constituents (for example, receipt of a federal grant) even when they had little to do with obtaining it.

Policymakers have developed an even more complex set of strategies to deflect or diffuse negative perceptions of themselves. They often try to redefine a blame-generating issue or make their own position on it more obscure. Legislators, for example, often provide themselves with a series of votes to soften (or obfuscate) their position on controversial issues. In public statements on such issues, politicians tend to be ambiguous, presumably because they are more concerned about potential blame from those who might oppose any specific position than they are enticed by potential credit from those who agree with the position.[18] Alternatively, the politician may be able to find a scapegoat for their positions or actions: President Reagan, for example, has claimed that austerity measures were required because of profligate spending by past Democratic administrations and Congresses.

On issues that pit a policymaker's views versus those of his or her constituents, the politician may avoid blame by switching sides unobtrusively—"jumping on the bandwagon"—if the risk of incurring blame becomes too high. If his original position has not been made publicly, he may even be able to claim credit for holding the popular position all along. Finally, in situations where there are only losses to be allocated and no way of evading the unpleasant choices, decisionmakers may attempt to diffuse the inevitable blame by agreeing on a consensus solution. Thus no one has to stick his or her neck out:

17. In addition, Richard Fenno has shown that legislators work to develop enough trust on the part of their constituents that they will have leeway to vote their conscience on some issues. Legislators from relatively safe districts—whether as a result of their own leeway-building efforts, absence of party competition, or some other factor—presumably do not need to be as concerned with avoiding blame as those with only a marginal hold on office. Richard Fenno, *Home Style: House Members in their Districts,* (Little, Brown, 1978), chap. 5. Any leeway that is achieved is never complete, however. There is evidence that legislators (specifically U.S. senators) seeking reelection moderate their voting decisions as an election approaches, presumably because they believe that their constituents are more likely to remember and punish recent "deviant" votes than older ones. The pattern is just the opposite among legislators not seeking reelection. Martin Thomas, "Election Proximity and Senatorial Roll Call Voting," *American Journal of Political Science,* vol. 29 (February 1985), pp. 96–111.

18. James E. Campbell, "Ambiguity in the Issue Positions of Presidential Candidates: A Causal Analysis," *American Journal of Political Science,* vol. 27 (May 1983), pp. 284–93. See also Kenneth A. Shepsle, "The Strategy of Ambiguity: Uncertainty and Electoral Competition," *American Political Science Review,* vol. 66 (June 1972), pp. 555–68; and Benjamin I. Page, "The Theory of Political Ambiguity," *American Political Science Review,* vol. 70 (September 1976), pp. 742–52.

everyone provides political cover for everyone else, making it difficult
for a future political opponent to raise the issue. This might be called
a "circle-the-wagons" strategy. When it works best, this approach may
even yield political dividends—for taking the hard, gutsy stand that
everyone else is taking as well (for example, voting to "save" the social
security system by delaying a COLA increase).[19]

Politicians also attempt to manipulate policy agendas in ways that
will maximize political credit and minimize blame toward themselves
while generating blame toward their opponents.[20] They take the lead
in pressing onto the agenda legislation that benefits their own constituents, and they claim credit for doing so. Sponsors of legislation that is
hard to vote against, such as congressional pay freezes and social security benefit increases, use blame-generating strategies: they try to
force the issue onto the agenda in such a way that politicians who
would oppose it on good-policy grounds will support it because of
their fear of electoral retribution. It is not necessary that a majority of
policymakers have strong blame-avoiding motivations for there to be a
substantial effect on public policy: it is enough that blame avoiders
hold the balance of power in decisionmaking. Blame-avoiding politicians may use a variety of tactics to keep the issue off the agenda so
that they do not have to take an unpopular stand. Even if blame-
generating decisions cannot be kept off the agenda completely, policymakers can often delay consideration until after an election. They
can take any needed loss-imposing actions then and hope that losers
will either have recovered from their losses or have forgotten about
them by the time the next election rolls around. If a blame-generating
decision has to be made, policymakers may try to delegate that decision to someone else ("pass the buck").[21]

Policymakers also try to manipulate policy payoffs in ways that fit
their political interests. They often try to package together a number
of projects with strong location-specific benefits in order to appeal to

19. "Circling the wagons" is invariably a risky strategy, however. It will work only if
near-unanimity can be maintained. If some participants in the process see an opportunity to deflect the blame to others and claim credit for resisting the loss-producing
solution, they will be sorely tempted to defect from the consensus. Thus all participants
will be afraid to publicly take the lead in proposing solutions; unless agreements can be
negotiated quietly, with commitments of support made in advance, they are unlikely to
succeed.
20. The idea that structuring political choices can have a major effect on policy
outcomes is the fundamental theorem of social choice theory. See, for example, William
Riker, *The Art of Political Manipulation* (Yale University Press, 1986).
21. See Morris P. Fiorina, "Legislative Choice of Regulatory Forms: Legal Process or
Administrative Process?" *Public Choice*, vol. 39, no. 1 (1982), pp. 33–66.

the credit-claiming instincts of a majority of legislators (pork barreling). Some analysts have even suggested that policymakers skew decisions into areas that offer maximum credit-claiming opportunities.[22] Conversely, policymakers seek to prevent or delay blame-generating losses by committing extra resources to shore up failing policies ("throwing good money after bad").

Even if politicians have strong good-policy objectives, they will find it necessary to use credit-claiming, blame-avoiding, and blame-generating strategies to achieve their policy preferences. Often politicians must choose between a credit-claiming opportunity—voting for a popular program—and what they believe to be a responsible though unpopular policy position. If policymakers are simply credit-claimers, they will sacrifice their policy preferences, jump on the bandwagon, and support the politically popular position. If they limit their discretion to make those choices, however, they may be able to obtain their policy preferences without risking their political future. This logic is used by many proponents of automatic budget-cutting measures and constitutional limits on government expenditures: that is, it is seen as the only way to force legislators to collectively exercise spending restraint, since none of them wish to vote against individual spending programs.[23] These discretion-reducing devices are examples of what might be called a "stop me before I kill again" strategy, because they allow politicians to stop themselves from taking policy actions that they find repugnant, just as a criminal, by turning himself in, can prevent himself from taking actions he knows are wrong but cannot resist.

Politicians manipulate perceptions, agendas, and payoffs not just to benefit themselves politically, but also to mobilize or neutralize others who do not share their objectives. If they can add provisions to their proposals that cater to the credit-claiming interests of other policymakers, they have a much better chance of clearing the many hurdles needed to win adoption. If they can tailor their proposal in such a way as to make it impossible to vote against, their prospects are even better. If, however, their proposal generates substantial blame (for example, a congressional pay increase or a social security benefit cut), it is likely to go through only if policymakers can be protected from having to

22. See Fiorina, *Congress: Keystone of the Washington Establishment*, p. 46; and Bruce Cain, John Ferejohn, and Morris Fiorina, *The Personal Vote: Constituency Service and Electoral Independence* (Harvard University Press, 1987).

23. See, for example, Aaron Wildavsky, *How to Limit Government Spending* (University of California Press, 1980).

take an open stand favoring it. In the battle over the 1981 budget rec-onciliation bill in the House of Representatives, for example, both sides sought to shape the agenda in ways that would limit blame for a vote cast on their side, while maximizing the blame-generating poten-tial of a vote for the opposition. The Democrats sought (and the Rules Committee approved) a rule that would have forced separate votes on five sections of the bill. The result was, as Office of Management and Budget Director David Stockman put it, that "Republicans—and Boll Weevils—were going to be forced to vote against food stamps and Medicaid and Social Security, out loud and one at a time." The admin-istration and House Republicans, on the other hand, sought a single up-or-down vote on the entire package in order to disguise votes to cut individual programs. It thus maximized the prospects of winning blame-motivated support from wavering Democrats who, in Stock-man's words, "weren't even remotely genuine fiscal conservatives . . . [but rather] simply muddle-minded pols who had been scared by the President's popularity in their home districts."[24] A closed rule was adopted in a House floor vote, ensuring passage of the administration-backed package.

Indexation and Politicians' Objectives

The argument about politicians' objectives has thus far been stated in very general terms, beginning with the hypothesis that politicians' motives are complex, not simple. In many decisions, politicians are torn between conflicting motives: for example, between perceptions of what is good policy and desire to claim credit for a popular action or avoid blame for an unpopular action. Which motive dominates de-pends upon context: both the political vulnerability of the individual politician and the opportunities and dangers posed by the specific choice being made. And politicians seek to manipulate this political context.

These complex political interactions are evident in the decisions that politicians make about creating and modifying indexation schemes in government programs. The political pressures and policy arguments that influence indexing decisions vary over time and across policy areas; resource constraints vary as well. It is helpful to begin,

24. David Stockman, *The Triumph of Politics: Why the Reagan Revolution Failed* (Harper and Row, 1986), pp. 218, 207.

however, by examining how each of three objectives—good policy, credit claiming, and blame avoiding—is likely to influence politicians' response to indexing initiatives.

Good-Policy Objectives

Policymakers may have either procedural or substantive good-policy motives for indexing programs. The procedural justification for indexing is to put in place an efficient, low-cost mechanism for making inflation adjustments and to lower the decisionmaking load. If policymakers' primary interest is in alleviating public problems, they may be very willing to limit their own policymaking discretion so long as it produces effective policy. They will presumably be especially willing to do so in programs where program standards (such as social security benefit levels) are written into law and hence would be eroded without regular adjustments.

This good-policy logic can also be used to explain the scope of indexing. Policymakers are especially likely to favor indexing in programs where maintenance of stable individual purchasing power (or tax burden) is an important consideration. Because inflation adjustments were generally being made in these programs anyway on an ad hoc basis, the main effect of indexing may be to lower the costs of decisionmaking and to even out short-term income changes.

If politicians act according to this good-policy rationale, inflation-sensitive revenue and benefit programs should be indexed with equal frequency. Indexing of prices paid in purchase programs, however, should be limited to those programs where automatic price adjustments are least likely to disturb market mechanisms (for example, by leading to an over- or undersupply of the good or service) and are most needed to prevent sharp fluctuations in supply or price.

Nor should budgetary stress necessarily put an end to indexing: it remains an efficient decisionmaking mechanism. Nevertheless, some experimentation and changes at the margins can be expected. If indexing is abolished or cut back for some programs, it is likely to be in those where it is discovered to be inappropriate (for example, because of perverse supply effects) rather than because of political weakness of the program's clientele.

Policymakers may also have substantive good-policy motives for supporting or resisting indexing. For example, they may believe that undesirable increases or decreases are likely to occur in real benefit standards without indexing, or that indexing would indicate that government is not serious about fighting inflation. Executive and legislative budget guardians may see indexing as a means of meeting their policy objective of restraining real spending growth. Obviously, the specific content of these policy concerns determines how substantive good-policy motives affect the scope and timing of indexing. These substantive policy concerns are best observed in specific policy debates.

Credit-claiming Objectives

The credit-claiming perspective suggests that politicians index because of the political rewards it offers. This approach has both strengths and weaknesses in explaining indexation policy choices. Policy specialists in the executive and Congress might endorse indexing during a period of fiscal stress as a mechanism to protect program budgets, but it is doubtful whether they would do so if they thought that surplus resources were available for real increases. Similarly, the onset of persistent inflation might lead clienteles to be increasingly concerned with maintaining their income; they would thus support indexing in order to keep up with inflation over the long term.

Indexing is a double-edged sword, however, for both policy specialists and clienteles. It prevents clienteles' benefits from declining in purchasing power, but it is also likely to keep ad hoc benefit adjustments—including real benefit increases—off the political agenda. In so doing, it also removes future credit-claiming opportunities from the agenda. Some legislative specialists may, like Esau with his inheritance, be willing to give up future credit-claiming opportunities for the big credit of supporting indexing now. In particular, those that have the strongest ties to a single constituency may feel that they have to support indexing when that clientele seeks it. Specialists on multiclientele committees, on the other hand, may have more autonomy from the preferences of any particular clientele, as will those whose clienteles are poorly organized. These legislators will probably want to retain as much discretion, and credit-claiming opportunities, as possible by not adopting indexation. They may, however, be willing to index if they feel that constituents are no longer giving them credit for ad hoc policy changes.

Clientele groups may oppose indexing if they believe that they can do better through ad hoc increases. Group attitudes toward indexing may also have a temporal dimension: if it is linked to a big benefit increase, or occurs immediately after one, indexing can "lock in" high benefit levels, but if it occurs after a period of high inflation and no benefit increases, it is likely to perpetuate low benefit levels. Groups may not be able to obtain indexing even if they favor it, however. Weak groups, which have the least ability to win favorable ad hoc changs, are also least likely to be able to obtain indexing. The strongest, best-organized groups may in fact be relative latecomers in obtaining indexing, waiting until they feel that the onset of budget deficits has eroded their capability to do better through ad hoc increases.

In general, the credit-claiming perspective suggests that whether or not specific programs are indexed will be determined less by the type of program than by the characteristics of its clienteles and specialists. In federal benefit programs and most other areas of government activity, indexing will be directly related to the political strength of clienteles and inversely related to the autonomy of program specialists. But the expectation is just the opposite with respect to payments *to* the federal government: here strong groups should oppose, and be able to defeat, automatic increases in their required payments to the government.

Once in place, indexing is likely to be maintained because powerful groups see it as a way to maintain real benefit levels in a period of high inflation and fiscal stress. However, the credit-claiming aspirations of politicians may lead them to raise the bid—creating persistent pressures to make indexing bases and mechanisms more generous. Politicians may also claim credit by challenging indexing procedures where those mechanisms either impose losses on clienteles or are perceived to do so (for example, with user fees for government services).

Blame-avoiding Objectives

Blame avoidance suggests perhaps the broadest scope of the three objectives for indexing. There are three distinct blame-avoiding reasons why politicians might favor indexing a program. The first is in order to make ad hoc adjustments that offend their constituents without incurring blame for doing so—for example, increases in congressional pay, in fixed-sum taxes and user charges, or in regulated prices that pit one economic interest against another. Hence indexing flows from a "pass-the-buck" strategy, as policymakers cede to an automatic process the responsibility for politically painful choices. Buck passing faces serious constraints, however: if a constituency is powerful enough to inflict political wounds on policymakers for making ad hoc adjustments, it may also be capable of blocking indexing and ensuring that its burden lags behind inflation.

It is relatively easy to understand why politicians would give up discretion over unpopular, blame-generating decisions. But they also give up authority over decisions where inflation adjustments may offer credit-claiming opportunities—for example, benefit levels in income transfer programs. This may be because they have been maneuvered into a position where *not* supporting indexing would be politically costly. Recipients of income transfer programs are especially likely to notice the erosion of the nominal value of their benefit checks through inflation. If they in fact give more weight to these losses than to occasional benefit increases, they will be particularly inclined to press for indexing and to punish politicians who refuse to support it, even if they could have done better through ad hoc increases. Politicians may try to keep indexing proposals off the policy agenda. However, if a politically powerful constituency believes that it would be better off with its program indexed, the indexation proposal reaches the agenda, and decisionmakers have to take a stand for or against it, they will be sorely tempted to shift to a "jump-on-the-bandwagon" strategy and support it.

Indexing in benefit programs may also result in part from a third, "stop me before I kill again" strategy. Here policymakers are assumed to have good-policy objectives (limiting spending) that clash with a credit-claiming opportunity (raising real benefit levels). Voting their policy preferences, however, is likely to generate substantial blame. The position of fiscally conservative Republicans in Congress with respect to social security benefits in the early 1970s is a good example (see chapter 4). As long as beneficiaries seem not to know or care that ad hoc changes might leave them better off, indexing removes the political liability of having to vote against benefit increases and may provide fiscal conservatives with an opportunity to claim credit for stabilizing current benefits.

Blame avoidance also suggests why politicians are unlikely to repeal or cut back indexing provisions in a program once they have been enacted. As noted earlier, repeal of indexing requires legislators to impose rather than simply acquiesce in losses suffered by constituents. This is precisely the situation that blame-avoiding legislators seek to avoid. If indexing mechanisms for some programs are subsequently cut back or eliminated, those cuts will presumably be handled in ways that minimize blame. Cuts will probably be concentrated in programs with a weak political base. But what makes a strong base for resisting cutbacks is somewhat different from what is required for obtaining new benefits from government. Organizational cohesion is very important in lobbying for new benefits. Thus relatively small groups, which tend to be more cohesive, may have an advantage.[25] Because individuals and groups are more sensitive to losses than to gains, they are likely to respond to real or threatened losses even without a group to mobilize them (except where losses are very small). Hence, in allocating cutbacks in indexed programs, those programs with a large but poorly organized clientele may fare better than those with a smaller but better organized clientele.

When visible cutbacks are required in politically popular programs, policymakers will attempt to "circle the wagons" by obtaining massive bipartisan support. In any case, cutbacks will probably be disguised or imposed through automatic mechanisms that distance policymakers from the losses associated with those cuts. Cutbacks in indexing may, for example, be applied only to future recipients, who will suffer a loss in protection that is relative only to others rather than relative to their own situation before the cuts.

Interpreting Policymakers' Objectives

Support for indexing may be compatible with each of the objectives outlined here, and a variety of actors may—under certain conditions—support indexing. But which actors and objectives have in fact led to the current system?

If all politicians shared only a single objective, and all of them pursued that objective consistently, it would be relatively easy to predict which programs will be indexed and which ones will not, as well as which programs will be left untouched once they are indexed. Political life is not so simple, however. Politicians must consider not only whether indexing makes policy sense, but also whether it offers opportunities to claim credit or risks of incurring blame. Politicians are always striving to make their own decisionmaking context more palatable and that of their opponents less so. Thus politicians' attitude to-

25. See Mancur Olson, *The Logic of Collective Action: Public Goods and the Theory of Groups* (Harvard University Press, 1965); and Terry M. Moe, *The Organization of Interests: Incentives and the Internal Dynamics of Political Interest Groups* (University of Chicago Press, 1980).

ward indexing a program may shift over time depending upon the political pressures they confront and how their choices are framed.

One can attempt to understand how politicians' objectives influence indexation policy outcomes in three ways.[26] A first way is to examine the overall distribution of policy outputs. The three policy objectives outlined in the previous section each suggest some distinctive patterns for the scope of indexing and the distribution of any subsequent cutbacks across programs. These patterns are outlined in table 2-1. This data can at best provide indirect evidence regarding policymakers' objectives. Moreover, this evidence is likely to be helpful only if one objective clearly dominates in almost all indexing decisions; otherwise, the data will be too jumbled to provide clear results.

Policymakers' objectives can be examined more directly by studying policymakers' self-understanding of their behavior as displayed in public statements, interviews, and other sources. But this type of evidence is often not available and may be unreliable. On the surface, debate on policy alternatives is usually carried out in terms of which option is the best policy. When legislators jump on the bandwagon, for example, most are unlikely to proclaim that they are voting for a position that they believe to be irresponsible but that they feel they must support for political reasons.

When many policymakers are involved (for example, in congressional roll calls), it may also be helpful to look at patterns of decisions and decisionmaking for individual programs. If indexing decisions are usually taken in "bundled" votes on unrelated programs, for example, it suggests that credit-claiming and vote-trading objectives may be at work. Several other patterns are suggestive of blame avoidance. For example, if legislators oppose indexing consistently when the issue has low salience, but switch to support the other side when it attains a higher profile, they are probably suppressing their own preferences in a situation of policymaker-constituency conflict. Legislators who are electorally vulnerable (for example, senators who are facing reelection within the next two years or legislators from marginal districts) should have a greater propensity to bow to popular pressure than those in safe seats. Similarly, legislators who are subject to cross-

26. For a similar approach to detecting the influence of decisionmakers' objectives on policy outcomes, see James M. Enelow, "Saving Amendments, Killer Amendments, and an Expected Utility Theory of Sophisticated Voting," *Journal of Politics,* vol. 43 (November 1981), pp. 1063–89. On the general question of testing theories of motivation, see Axel Hadenius, "The Verification of Motives," *Scandinavian Political Studies,* vol. 6 (new series), no. 2 (1983), pp. 125–50.

TABLE 2-1. *Politicians' Objectives and Hypothetical Indexing Choices*

Indexing choice	Objectives		
	Good policy	Credit claiming	Blame avoiding
Scope			
Most likely to be indexed	Programs in which statutes with nominal dollar "bases" create serious distortive effects (income transfers, tax brackets); programs in which indexing meets policymakers' substantive policy goals (such as lower spending)	Programs in which well-organized constituencies have strong links to policy specialists (except in user charge programs), especially when there is little prospect of real gains through ad hoc changes	User charges and regulation (as a result of "pass-the-buck" strategy); benefit programs (as a result of "jump-on-the-bandwagon" and "stop me before I kill again" strategies)
Least likely to be indexed	Programs in which authorization and appropriation are reconsidered routinely	Programs where constituencies are poorly organized and legislative specialists have substantial autonomy from clientele	Programs with politically weak clienteles in which politicians can exercise discretion without incurring blame (such as poverty programs)
Modification			
Changes most likely	Programs in which indexing creates distortions (such as perverse supply effects)	Programs in which harmful effects of indexing create credit-claiming opportunities for politicians (such as user charges)	Programs with small clienteles
Changes least likely	Programs in which indexation continues to reduce decisionmaking costs without serious distortive effects	Programs in which modification of indexing offers no credit-claiming opportunities	Programs with large, well-organized clienteles

cutting constituency pressures should take the lead in developing alternatives that obfuscate blame and exclude blame-generating choices from the agenda. Blame-avoiding politicians should match but not raise policy bids that expand demands on the federal budget. Each of these phenomena, when buoyed by more direct evidence of policymakers' motivations, provides indicators of blame-avoiding activity.

Data on voting patterns must also be interpreted with care, however. For example, politicians can respond to blame-generating pressures in several ways, which can lead to very different voting patterns. In some cases, one would expect to see distinctive political behavior by legislators with marginal seats—at least if the issue under discussion is a salient one for their constituents. But if politicians are able to keep blame-generating choices off the agenda, there will be no roll call evidence whatsoever. If pressures to avoid blame result in a "jump-on-the-bandwagon" or "circle-the-wagons" strategy, votes may be nearly unanimous. It is only by examining the maneuvering that preceded those votes that they can be interpreted properly.

Taken individually, each of the three methods for understanding politicians' objectives has shortcomings. But using the three methods together and paying close attention to the context within which indexing decisions were made can increase the reliability of interpretations.

The need to put decisions into context suggests that it is not enough to look just at overall patterns of where indexing is and is not used; a comparison of detailed case studies is also necessary. A discussion of overall patterns is, nevertheless, a good starting point for understanding indexation and the motivations behind it.

3

An Overview
of Indexation

Much can be learned about indexing by simply looking at its overall distribution among federal programs. This chapter surveys where statutory indexing provisions have been employed in federal government activity, and where they have not. It then examines the timing of decisions to index and subsequently modify those decisions. Finally, it compares the three policy objectives outlined in chapter 2 as explanations of these patterns.

The Scope of Indexation

The extent to which the federal government has employed indexing mechanisms across sectors and types of governmental activity is shown in table 3-1. This table shows both the number of programs in each sector that are indexed and an estimate of the relative weight of those programs within each sector. The latter numbers exaggerate the importance of indexing somewhat: these provisions often affect only a small part of a program or its clientele. Indexing the tax base of OASDHI (social security retirement and disability insurance plus medicare hospitalization insurance), for example, affects only high-income individuals, whose income subject to social insurance taxation is increased annually for inflation.

The table nevertheless shows some dramatic contrasts across sectors. Clearly indexing is very common in federal benefit and social service programs. In purchase programs indexing is used fairly extensively, but within limited sectors. In other areas, such as regulation, indexing is hardly used at all. As might be expected, use of indexing is especially heavy in areas where program standards are set in nominal dollar amounts. But the scope of indexing cannot be explained solely in these terms. Within almost every category of federal activity, some programs are indexed while others are not. Table 3-2 provides a listing of some of the most important indexed and nonindexed programs within various categories.

Benefit and Social Service Programs

Programs providing benefits to individuals contain by far the greatest number of indexing mechanisms used by the federal government. They also comprise the bulk of spending on indexed programs. Indexed benefit programs are divided here into three categories: federal retirement programs, social insurance programs, and means-tested benefit and social service programs (see table 3-3).

The first set of programs provides inflation-adjusted retirement, disability, and workers' compensation to former federal employees through the civil service retirement, military retirement, and a variety of smaller programs (such as federal judiciary survivors). Almost all federal programs of this type have indexed benefits. The major exception is compensation for veterans with service-connected disabilities and their survivors.

Social insurance programs provide income support to the nongovernmental sector.[1] The old age survivors insurance (OASI, commonly known as social security) and its companion social security disability insurance (SSDI) program are the core programs of this type. The federal government also operates a few much smaller indexed benefit programs for workers in specific industries—coal miners' disability, railroad retirement, and longshoremen's and harbor workers' compensation. Despite the credit-claiming opportunities presumably afforded by ad hoc benefit increases, indexing of benefit levels in social insurance programs is close to universal. The major exception is unemployment insurance, where benefit and eligibility criteria are set by the states.

The third category of indexed benefit and social service programs provides cash, goods, or services on a means-tested basis. Two large programs, supplemental security income (SSI) for the aged, blind, and disabled who are poor and veterans' pensions, provide inflation-adjusted cash assistance to individuals who are both categorically eligible and meet a means test. The means test for these programs is also

---

1. Civil service employees hired beginning in 1984 are also covered by social security.

TABLE 3-1. *Federal Programs with Indexing Provisions, by Sector*

Sector	Number of programs[a]	Relative weight of indexed programs in sector, fiscal year 1986[b]
Benefit and social service programs	57	87
Federal employee retirement and disability programs	11	80
Social insurance programs	6	92
Means-tested programs[c]	40	79[d]
Cash assistance	3	56[e]
Housing assistance	5	95
Nutrition assistance	6	93
Education and training assistance[f]	15	72[d]
Energy assistance	3	100
Health and mental health assistance[f,g]	5	96[d]
Other social services	3	5[d]

SOURCES: Congressional Budget Office, *Indexing with the Consumer Price Index: Problems and Alternatives* (CBO, 1981); Congressional Research Service, *Indexation of Federal Programs* (Government Printing Office, 1981); *The Budget of the United States Government, Fiscal Year 1988* and *Appendix; Background Material and Data on Programs within the Jurisdiction of the Committee on Ways and Means, 1987 Edition,* Committee Print 100-4, House Committee on Ways and Means, 100 Cong. 1 sess. (GPO, 1987); U.S. Office of Personnel Management, Office of Workforce Information, *Work Years and Personnel Costs: Executive Branch, United States Government, Fiscal Year 1986* (GPO, 1987); and U.S. Department of Defense, *Manpower Requirements Report for FY 1988* (DOD, 1987).
n.a. = Not available.
* Negligible.
a. Includes a small number of programs in which indexing procedure, or the program itself, have since expired or been repealed. These include title XX grant authorizations, medicaid spending targets, the cap on medicare supplementary medical insurance premiums, and the Comprehensive Employment and Training Act program. As a general rule, only the first type of indexation procedure for a program is counted here and in figure 3-1. Thus if eligibility, deductions from income eligibility, and benefit levels for a means-tested program were all indexed in the same or different years, they would in any case be counted only once. In addition, the coal miners' disability programs run by the Departments of Labor and Health and Human Services are counted only once. The old age survivors insurance and disability insurance components of the OASDHI program are counted separately as two benefit programs. Indexation of the OASDHI tax base, which occurred at the same time (1972) as indexation of OASDI benefits, is treated as an additional instance of indexation. Other cases where a program has indexation provisions fitting into more than one of the categories in table 3-1 are also counted separately. Most notably, indexation of medicare part A reimbursement (1983), part B reimbursement ceilings (1972), the part A deductible (1965), and the cap on part B premiums (1972) are treated as four separate instances of indexation, the first two as medical care vendor payments and the second two as user charges. Four nutrition programs (school lunch, school breakfast, the child care food program, and special milk program) are also listed twice, once under means-tested nutrition programs (because income limits for eligibility are indexed), and once under purchase programs (because reimbursement rates to providing institutions are indexed). Section 8 housing assistance is also listed twice, once under means-tested housing assistance (income limits for eligibility) and once under miscellaneous purchase programs (for fair market rents). Veterans' health care is included under both user charges and means-tested health care. Three programs (community health centers, migrant health centers, and home health centers) where indexed income eligibility limits also influence user charges are counted only in means-tested health programs.
b. Generally defined as the budget (or revenues) of all indexed programs in the sector as a percentage of the budgets (or revenues) of all programs in that sector. Where more differentiated program data are available (for example, for indexed and nonindexed sources of revenue for social security and medicare), those sources are used. Programs in which indexing provisions have been repealed are not counted as indexed.
c. Indexing provisions in means-tested programs may include benefit levels, income limits for eligibility, or deductions from income limits for eligibility.
d. Relative weight calculated as a percentage of all outlays in this sector, including programs that are targeted at the poor but not explicitly means-tested.
e. Excludes earned income tax credit, where indexing provisions do not take effect until 1988. Indexed share of means-tested cash programs would be 61 percent if credit were included.
f. Includes programs in which some participants may establish eligibility by a means other than an eligibility limit, such as categorical eligibility through participation in another program (for example, eligibility for medicaid for AFDC recipients), or in which not all participants are required to meet indexed eligibility (Job Training Partnership Act).

TABLE 3-1 *(continued)*

Sector	Number of programs[a]	Relative weight of indexed programs in sector, fiscal year 1986[b]
Purchases of goods and services	**42**	**30**
Commodity price support programs	8	n.a.
Medical vendor payments[g]	2	24[h]
Nutrition programs	7	71[i]
Federal pay programs	11	83[j]
Scholarships and training stipends	5	*
Miscellaneous purchase programs	5	4
Intergovernmental grants[g]	**8**	**5**
User fees and revenue programs	**6**	**79**[k]
Loan and loan guarantee programs[l]	**2**	**n.a.**
Regulatory programs	**4**	*
Total	104[m]	48[n]

g. Medicaid is counted as an indexed program for purposes of means-tested programs because eligibility levels are indexed for some recipients, but not with respect to medical vendor payments or intergovernmental grants, because neither payments to providers or authorization levels are explicitly indexed.

h. Total sectoral spending on medical vendor payments includes the (nonindexed) costs of the Veterans Administration health care system, federal expenditures on the medicaid program, and the costs of the federal employees health program.

i. Food stamps and the Puerto Rico nutrition block grant are excluded from both indexed programs and from totals for purchase programs. The women, infants, and children program is included in totals, but is not counted as indexed.

j. U.S. Postal Service salaries included in total.

k. Percentage excludes supplementary medical insurance premiums, where explicit indexing provisions have been repealed, although implicit indexing (premiums are required to meet a specified share of program costs, which rise with inflation) have been retained. If SMI premiums were included, percentage would be 79 percent. Medicare hospital insurance deductibles are excluded both from revenue totals and from percentages, as are veterans' health care user charges, which had not gone into effect in fiscal year 1986.

l. Excludes commodity price support loans, which are included here under purchase of goods and services. Also excluded are secondary guaranteed loans and lending by government-sponsored enterprises and programs in which interest rate provisions are indexed.

m. Total figure has been adjusted to eliminate cases of double-counting of programs in more than one category. See note a for details.

n. Expenditure programs only. Includes federal pay programs, where indexing provisions are usually ignored in practice. If pay programs are excluded, indexed share of total outlays is 37 percent.

indexed. The aid to families with dependent children (AFDC) program, where the states again set eligibility and benefit levels, does not provide such indexing provisions, however.

In the noncash programs, it is more often income eligibility limits than benefits that are indexed, although there are some cases of benefit indexing, such as food stamps (see chapter 5). Benefits in these programs are rarely indexed, either because individuals' needs for the benefit vary widely (for example, medicaid, mental health, or legal services) or because the cost of providing services varies substantially (for example, federally subsidized public housing).

TABLE 3-2. *Selected Indexed and Nonindexed Federal Programs,*
by Sector

Sector	Indexed programs	Nonindexed programs
Benefit and social service programs		
Federal employee retirement and disability	Civil service retirement Military retirement Federal employee retirement	Veterans' compensation
Social insurance programs	Social security benefits Coal miners' disability	Unemployment insurance benefits
Means-tested programs	Veterans' pensions Food stamp benefits and eligibility Eligibility for most non-cash programs	Aid to families with dependent children benefits
Purchases of goods and services	Most commodity support prices Most federal pay Medicare part B maximum payments to physicians	Medicaid payments to hospitals and physicians
Intergovernmental grants	Maximum allotments to individual states under social services block grant	Medicaid, AFDC, and most other federal grant budgets
User fees and revenue programs	Individual income tax brackets OASDHI wage base Medicare part A deductible	Corporate income tax

The patchwork of indexed and nonindexed federal benefit programs has no uniform political or policy basis, however: veterans' pensions are indexed, for example, while compensation for veterans with service-connected disabilities is not. Indexing has been applied to programs with both strong and weak clienteles.

Program and Agency Budgets

The federal government has used indexing most often where the effects on individuals are both identifiable and measurable—usually a check mailed by or to government. There is no reason why this need be so—why social security recipients, for example, must receive indexed benefits while the operating budgets of the National Weather

TABLE 3-3. *Selected Benefit and Social Service Programs with Indexing Provisions*

Program	Year indexing enacted	Provisions indexed	Index mechanism
Federal retirement programs			
Civil service retirement	1962	Benefits	Change in CPI
Federal employee retirement	1986	Benefits	Change in CPI (minus 1 percent)
Military retirement	1963	Benefits	Change in CPI
Social insurance			
Old age survivors and disability insurance[a]	1972[b]	Benefits	Change in CPI
	1977[c]	Wage histories	Average wages
Coal miners' disability (black lung)	1969	Benefits	Change in GS-2 salary
Railroad retirement[a]	1974[b]	Tier I benefit	Social security benefits
Pension benefit guarantee	1974	Maximum benefit guarantee for terminated pension plan	Social security taxable wage base
Means-tested cash programs			
Supplemental security income	1974[b]	Benefits	Change in social security benefits
Veterans' pensions	1978[c]	Benefits and eligibility	Change in social security benefits
Earned income tax credit	1986	Maximum earning to which credit applies and income levels for phase-down of credit	Change in CPI
Means-tested in-kind benefit programs			
Food stamps[a]	1971	Benefits	Thrifty food plan
Medicaid	1971	Eligibility	Poverty line
	1973	Eligibility	In part to eligibility for supplemental security income
Veterans' health care	1986	Eligibility for free care in Veterans Administration hospitals for veterans without service-connected disabilities	Percentage increase in veterans' pensions

a. Additional provisions of this program are indexed; see Vee Burke, "Inventory of Federally Indexed Programs," in Congressional Research Service, *Indexation of Federal Programs.*
b. Effective in 1975.
c. Effective in 1979.

TABLE 3-4. Selected Purchase Programs with Indexing Provisions

Program	Year indexing enacted	Provisions indexed	Index mechanism
Medical vendor payments			
Medicare supplementary medical insurance (SMI)	1972	Increase in "reasonable charges" by physicians for outpatient services	Medicare Economic Index
Medicare hospital insurance (HI)[a]	1983	Increase in reimbursement to hospitals for diagnosis-related groups (DRGs)	Index of hospital costs, plus 1 percent
Commodity price supports			
Dairy price supports	1949	Price support for milk	Index of farmers' production costs (parity)
Federal pay programs			
White-collar salaries (general schedule)[b]	1970[c]	Salaries	Salaries for similar positions in private sector
Executive, legislative, and judicial pay[b]	1975	Salaries	Average increase in white-collar pay
Military pay	1967	Salaries	Average increase in white-collar pay

a. This provision was enacted for a transitional period only, and never went into effect because of a freeze on DRG reimbursement rates. This provision replaced a statute enacted in 1982 that created an overall cap on increases in hospital rates, also tied to an index of hospital costs.

b. The president has the option of submitting and Congress of approving an alternative pay proposal.

c. Use of job comparability data to set white-collar salaries was introduced in 1962. The process was formalized by statute in 1970.

Service and community mental health agencies are not indexed.[2] To index agency budgets would assume, of course, that the level of services they provide will remain steady over time or that productivity increases can be made. There are foreign precedents for this type of indexing. The Thatcher government in Great Britain, for example, has announced plans to tie the budget of the British Broadcasting Corporation to that country's Retail Price Index—much to the consternation of the company's executives, since the BBC's budget has been growing at a rate faster than inflation.[3] Explicit indexing of agency budgets remains essentially nonexistent in the U.S. government.

Inflation adjustments for programs and agencies have been given an institutionalized role in the budget process, however. The president is required to produce a "current services budget"—a projection of the amounts needed to fund all programs currently authorized—as part of the annual budgetary cycle. The Congressional Budget Office produces similar estimates. These figures are often used by the House and Senate Budget committees as a baseline for adjusting agencies' budget shares. Recent budget battles—notably in defense—have often been waged around adjustments upward or downward from such an inflation-adjusted base.

Purchase of Goods and Services

Even if agency budgets are not indexed, prices paid by government for the purchase of specific goods and services can be. But this system has been limited primarily to three areas: medical care vendor payments, commodity price support programs (some of which are technically loan programs), and federal pay (table 3-4).

Indexing mechanisms in federal purchase of health care services were introduced in response to the failure of earlier pricing mechanisms to contain the rapid growth of medicare expenditures. In its original form, medicare reimbursed both hospitals and physicians for individual services provided on the basis of "customary, prevailing and

2. Capital budgets, which tend to vary more from year to year, are presumably less suited to indexing—for example,the Weather Service might not need a steady stream of expenditures to purchase weather satellites every year. Indexing of capital budgets might nevertheless help to limit political conflict and keep real budget increases off the political agenda in pork barrel programs such as dredging of rivers and harbors by the Army Corps of Engineers. This would also inhibit efforts to cut real expenditures, however.

3. Raymond Snoddy, "BBC Director General Forced to Quit under Political Pressure," *Financial Times,* January 30, 1987, p. 1.

reasonable" rates.[4] These rates were designed to ensure that providers were reimbursed at a rate that was no higher than either that provider's usual charge for that service or than the charges of a specific percentile of charges by all providers (the prevailing rate) in that region.[5] While the prevailing charge "screen" does provide an automatic adjustment process for adjusting the cap on medicare physician fees, it is not a true index, but rather a rolling average of physicians' charges. Increasing concern that this reimbursement system was contributing to medical inflation led Congress to adopt an additional check on physicians' fees for medicare in 1972. Henceforth, an "adjusted prevailing" rate capped charges at the level of the "prevailing rate" in fiscal year 1972, adjusted by changes in the Medicare Economic Index, a composite of physicians' expenses and general earnings levels.[6]

In the case of medicare hospital insurance, reforms enacted in 1983 replaced a fee-for-service reimbursement plan with a prospective payment system. Hospitals are compensated at a flat rate based on one of 467 diagnosis-related groups (DRGs). The DRG reimbursement rates were to be indexed during the phase-in period for the new payment system, after which the secretary of the Department of Health and Human Services was supposed to set increases in conjunction with an advisory panel.

Various components of federal workers' pay are also adjusted by automatic mechanisms. The most important of these is the pay comparability process for general schedule (GS) employees. A survey is held every year to compare federal and private-sector wages in various occupations. Recommendations are then made to the president on pay increases to establish rough comparability of GS pay with that of the private sector. However, the president can and usually has submitted alternative raises to Congress, which then go into effect unless Congress rejects them. Thus what in theory is a highly automatic process for determining federal pay really operates in a much less automatic

4. This reimbursement system was chosen over a fixed-fee schedule to weaken opposition from health care providers. See Theodore R. Marmor, *The Politics of Medicare*, rev. ed. (Aldine, 1973), p. 80.

5. This prevailing charge for physicians' services was originally set at the ninetieth percentile of all charges for that service in the locality. This was lowered to the eighty-third percentile in 1969, and then to the seventy-fifth percentile in 1971. U.S. Congress, Office of Technology Assessment, *Payment for Physician Services: Strategies for Medicare*, OTA-H-294 (Government Printing Office, 1986), p. 223.

6. Benson L. Dutton, Jr., and Peter McMenamin, "The Medicare Economic Index: Its Background and Beginnings," *Health Care Financing Review*, vol. 3 (September 1981), pp. 137–40.

fashion. Congressional, judicial, and top executive pay is also tied in part to the comparability pay process for general schedule workers (see chapter 6).

Intergovernmental Grants

Grants from the federal government to the states and localities cover almost as broad a range of benefits to individuals and purchase of goods and services as do those programs operated directly by the federal government. There are currently about 500 federal grant programs, ranging enormously both in size and in the amount of discretion that recipient governments have in using the money. As might be expected, the relative frequency of indexing across these programs is similar to that for direct federal programs: it is quite common in benefit programs, much more unusual in purchase programs, and very unusual for overall agency budgets. Federal grant programs for benefits and purchases that include indexing provisions are included in those categories in table 3-1; the remainder are shown separately under "intergovernmental grants." Clear explicit indexing of grant program budgets is quite rare. The authorization for title XX social services was indexed in 1980, but deindexed the following year. Indexed targets for medicaid spending were established for a two-year period by the 1981 Omnibus Reconciliation Act, but the program remained an open-ended grant (see below in table 3-6).[7]

User Fee and Revenue Programs

Perhaps the most surprising information revealed in table 3-1 is the small number of programs in the category of user charges and taxes.[8] The sectoral share of indexed programs is nevertheless quite large. Most major tax programs except for the corporate income tax have some indexing provisions (table 3-5). Still, one might expect many of the smaller user charge and excise taxes to be indexed. If politicians are blame avoiders, they should seek to lower the political costs of price increases by indexing "prices" charged to consumers and tax-

7. The Reagan administration had proposed an indexed cap on medicaid expenditures in 1981, but Congress enacted a cut in matching rates instead. States that cut spending levels below the indexed targets received higher grants. See P.L. 97-35, sec. 2161. See also Randall R. Bovbjerg and John Holahan, *Medicaid in the Reagan Era: Federal Policy and State Choices* (Washington, D.C.: Urban Institute, 1982), pp. 7–9.

8. On statutory regulation of user charges, see "The Assessment of Fees by Federal Agencies for Services to Individuals," *Harvard Law Review*, vol. 94 (December 1980), pp. 439–56.

TABLE 3-5. *Selected Revenue and User Charge Programs with Indexing Provisions*

Program	Year indexing enacted	Provision indexed	Index mechanism
Tax programs			
Old age survivors disability and health insurance	1972	Individual income subject to social security tax (wage base)	Average earnings
Individual income tax	1981[a]	Income tax brackets and standard deductions	Change in CPI
User fees			
Medicare hospital insurance	1965	Deductible paid by medicare payment for each spell of illness before medicare insurance begins payment	Average daily rate for in-patient hospital services
Medicare supplementary medical insurance (SMI)	1972	Percentage increase in SMI premiums capped at percentage increase in social security COLA[b]	Social security COLA
Veterans' health care	1986	Cap on user fee for Veterans Administration hospital care	Medicare hospital insurance deductible
Communications	1986	License fees for a variety of services, including commercial broadcast outlets, cellular phone systems, and satellite ground stations	Change in CPI

a. Effective in 1985.

b. This provision was later repealed. However, increases in SMI premiums are still capped at the dollar amount of social security COLAs—that is, when social security recipients have their SMI premiums deducted from their checks, the nominal value of those checks cannot fall when both social security benefits and SMI premiums are adjusted for inflation.

payers. Indexing revenue programs is a perfect opportunity to pass the buck to a formula, but this opportunity has been little used.

Of course, many taxes—those calculated as a percentage of a base amount, such as sales and excise taxes—are implicitly indexed: they rise automatically with nominal increases in prices. Many other opportunities for indexing federal revenues have not been exploited, however. Gasoline taxes are perhaps the foremost example: the combination of skyrocketing oil prices, a fixed per-gallon federal tax, and declining consumption led to a squeeze on federal highway revenues in the late 1970s. While a number of states adopted variable taxes (indexed to the retail price of gasoline), generally with a cap, the federal government did not. Thus the federal gasoline tax dropped from 13 percent of the retail price of gasoline in 1960 to 7 percent in 1976 and 3 percent in 1980.[9]

Not only are there few indexing mechanisms in this category, but the most important one, indexing of personal income tax brackets, is clearly not a case of passing the buck on an unpopular decision. Bracket indexing protects individuals against rising tax burdens due to higher nominal incomes, decreases rather than increases government revenues, and—most important politically—deprives legislators of an opportunity to claim credit by lowering tax rates as nominal income increases (see chapter 9).

Three of the other indexing mechanisms in this category are connected with the social security and medicare systems, and two of those are clearly related to efforts to keep the trust funds in actuarial balance. Indexing the OASDHI tax base (the amount of income subject to OASDHI taxation), for example, was enacted simultaneously with indexation of social security and social security disability benefits, and was intended to pay for benefit indexing.[10] Moreover, it affects only a small percentage of taxpayers, since most employees earn less than the ceiling. Medicare hospitalization insurance deductibles are linked to the cost of the first day's average hospital stay, limiting government's liability for real increases in medicare expenditures. (The deductible is not, it should be noted, a direct payment to government.)

Medicare supplementary medical insurance (SMI) premiums initially had a looser link to actuarial principles. They were intended to

9. See General Accounting Office, *Deteriorating Highways and Lagging Revenues: A Need to Reassess The Federal Highway Program,* CED-81-42 (GAO, 1981), p. 37.

10. This logic does not apply directly to the portion of OASDHI taxes used to pay for medicare part A (hospitalization insurance), but these costs also rise with inflation.

pay half the cost of the program (and thus were implicitly rather than explicitly indexed for inflation), with federal general revenues paying the rest. But the rapid increase in SMI was so unpopular that Congress placed an explicitly indexed lid on premium increases in 1972, limiting their growth to the rate of increase in OASDI benefits. As a result, premiums paid less than one-fourth the cost of SMI by 1982, when the provision was repealed.[11]

In short, explicit indexing of direct payments to the federal government has been enacted primarily when (1) it lowers rather than increases individuals' payments, as in the case of income taxes and SMI premiums, or (2) it has a fairly clear relationship with the actuarial soundness of federal benefits, as with OASDHI taxes.

Federal Credit Programs

Two of the fastest-growing areas of federal activity in the United States are interest payments on the federal debt and extensions of loans and loan guarantees. The federal government's debt service payments tend to rise and fall with inflation. As inflation heats up, the market's expectation of the nominal rate of interest needed to provide a given real rate of return goes up as well; thus the Treasury must offer a higher fixed interest rate to be able to sell the bonds. As inflation cools down, the process works in reverse. Interest rates also incorporate a "risk premium." Because buyers cannot be certain that the nominal interest rate offered will provide a reasonable rate of return in the future, they demand a higher rate than would otherwise be the case.

Although the interest rates on U.S. Treasury bonds tend to rise and fall with inflation, this is not a result of indexing of individual bonds.[12] Instead, the change occurs as the debt is "rolled over"—old securities

11. Premiums are currently set at an amount equal to 25 percent of costs, with an upper limit on increases equal to the dollar amount of the increase in OASDI benefits. See "Legislative Update," *Health Care Financing Review*, vol. 6 (Fall 1984), p. 71.

12. Both the private sector and foreign governments have pioneered debt instruments in which return is directly linked to inflation or current market interest rates. In the private sector, the best-known example is adjustable rate mortgages (ARMs), used primarily to finance purchases of homes. (This is an imperfect case, however, since most ARMs have caps that prevent them from rising above a specified level.) Many governments (for example, Britain, Israel, and Brazil) have issued government securities for which interest rates are directly based on the inflation rate. Promoters of the concept in the United States have argued that it has advantages both for the investor (providing additional inflation protection) and for the seller (limiting the need to provide a risk premium). To date, however, the U.S. Treasury has not issued bonds of this type. See Alicia H. Munnell and Joseph B. Grolnic, "Should the U.S. Government Issue Index Bonds?" *New England Economic Review* (September–October 1986), pp. 3–21.

are paid off and new ones are issued at the current market rate to take their place.

The federal government does use statutory inflation adjustments in many of its own lending and loan guarantee programs. The government pays inflation-linked allowances to lenders under the guaranteed student loan program and provides an inflation-adjusted ceiling on Federal Housing Administration mortgages. In addition to these programs, there are about fifty loan and loan guarantee programs for which interest rates charged to new borrowers fluctuate according to statutory formulas.[13] These latter programs are not counted in table 3-1, but they comprise a major share of federal lending activity.

Regulatory Programs

Another area where explicit indexing has made little headway is in regulatory decisions (table 3-6). Again, there seems to be substantial room for its use. Economic regulation is perhaps the most obvious example: public utilities and (before deregulation) the rail, airline, and trucking industries have made almost continuous requests for across-the-board rate increases. These disputes are very repetitive and time consuming, and they generally have ended with the industries obtaining needed inflation adjustments. Again, indexing appears to have great potential to cut down on workloads and to allow regulators or legislators to avoid making unpopular decisions explicitly by allowing increases to go into effect automatically. Indexing could even be combined with a mechanism allowing regulators or legislators to retain some discretion—for example, by substituting some other increase for the one scheduled to go into effect automatically. This type of mechanism was in fact included in the legislation indexing social security benefits (see chapter 4). But indexing has been used very little in economic regulation in the United States. Two rare examples are a provision in the Staggers Rail Act of 1980, providing an indexed "zone of rail carrier rate flexibility" within which carriers could raise rates without challenge, and temporary indexed limits on natural gas prices provided in the Natural Gas Policy Act of 1978.[14]

In many other regulatory arenas, standards are set by statute in nominal dollar terms and thus eroded by inflation. This sometimes

13. See General Accounting Office, *Catalog of Federal Credit Programs and Their Interest Rate Provisions,* PAD-83-12 (GAO, 1982).

14. The Staggers Act allowed carriers to raise rates by specified percentages each year above the inflation-adjusted figure. See P.L. 96-448, sec. 203.

TABLE 3-6. *Selected Miscellaneous Programs with Indexing Provisions*

Program	Year indexing enacted	Provisions indexed	Index mechanism
Intergovernmental grant programs			
Title XX social services	1980[a]	Program authorization	CPI
Medicaid	1981	Target amount for state medicaid allocation for FY 1983 and FY 1984	Change in medical care expenditures component of CPI
Regulatory programs			
Federal campaign expenditure limits	1974	Expenditures by candidates for federal office[b]	Change in CPI
Natural gas price regulation	1978	Prices for several categories of natural gas, up to 1984	GNP deflator
Railroad rate regulation	1980	Zone of rail carrier rate flexibility within which carriers are allowed to increase rates without challenge	Index of railroad costs

a. Repealed in 1981.
b. This provision originally applied to both congressional and presidential candidates. However, the Supreme Court ruled in *Buckley v. Valleo* that it could only be applied to presidential candidates who choose to accept public financing for their campaigns. (There is no federal financing of House and Senate campaigns.)

leads to results that seem absurd; in 1864, for example, Congress limited attorneys' fees in claims for veterans' benefits to a maximum of ten dollars. Minor variations have been enacted over the years, but the basic ten-dollar limit remains in effect today.[15] Indexing has been extended into a few regulatory programs, such as campaign finance. But even here, the use of indexing has been uneven. Limits on contributions by individuals and political action committees (PACs) in presidential campaigns, for example, are not indexed, while campaign expenditure limits are.

Indexing might also be expected in sectors where the very applicability of regulations is stated in dollar terms. Some regulations apply only to businesses with sales over a certain figure, or to contracts over a certain figure. The Davis-Bacon Act, for example, requires that employees on federally funded construction projects be paid the "prevailing wage" for that type of work in the local community. The minimum threshold for contracts covered by the prevailing wage requirement is $2,000—a figure that has not been changed since 1935.[16] Some criminal offenses are also defined in specific dollar amounts in many jurisdictions. In both cases, inflation tends to widen applicability of the statute beyond the original intent unless ad hoc adjustments are made.

Finally, one might expect to encounter indexing in government regulation of wages, salaries, and benefits in the private sector. Indexing is, after all, quite prevalent when government provides those directly. The minimum wage is perhaps the most obvious candidate, and automatic adjustment of the minimum wage was in fact considered—and rejected—by Congress in the mid-1970s (see chapter 8). A requirement that private-sector pension plans provide inflation adjustments is another possible area for action.[17] (Such a move would almost certainly be opposed by pension fund managers, however, since it would upset the actuarial calculations on which their funds are financed.) However, an indexed cap on contributions and benefits under tax-qualified pension and profit-sharing plans covered by the Employees'

15. *Legislative History of the Ten Dollar Attorney Fee Limitation in Claims for Veterans' Benefits,* Committee Print no. 8, House Committee on Veterans' Affairs, 100 Cong. 1 sess. (GPO, 1987).

16. The Reagan administration proposed raising the Davis-Bacon threshold in its fiscal year 1988 budget. See *The Budget of the United States Government, Fiscal Year 1988* (GPO, 1987), p. 2-39.

17. The Canadian province of Ontario has passed legislation that mandates inflation protection in private-sector pension plans. See Ronald Anderson, "Pension Reforms Have Eased Major Stresses," Toronto *Globe and Mail,* September 4, 1987, p. B5.

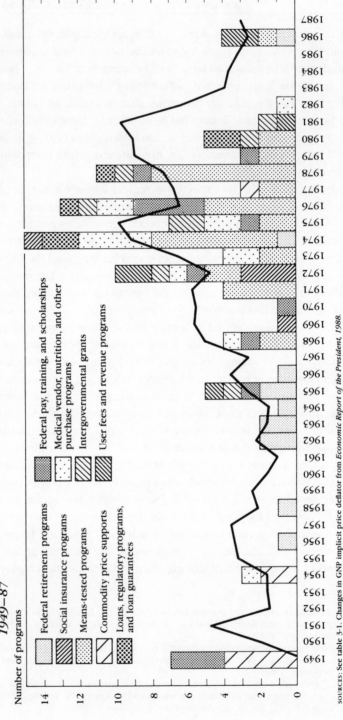

FIGURE 3-1. *Initial Indexing Decisions for Federal Programs, with Annual Changes in GNP Implicit Price Deflator, 1949–87*

Number of programs

Federal retirement programs
Social insurance programs
Means-tested programs
Commodity price supports
Loans, regulatory programs, and loan guarantees

Federal pay, training, and scholarships
Medical vendor, nutrition, and other purchase programs
Intergovernmental grants
User fees and revenue programs

SOURCES: See table 3-1. Changes in GNP implicit price deflator from *Economic Report of the President, 1988.*

Retirement Income Security Act is the only statutory indexing mechanism of this type currently in place.[18]

The Timing of Indexation

Indexing of federal program standards has a fairly long history. An early precursor can be found in an 1861 statute that provided that "wages to be paid to all employees in [navy] yards shall be, as near as may be, the average price paid to employees of the same grade in private shipyards or workshops in or nearest to the same vicinity, to be determined by the commandant of the navy yard."[19] This "prevailing wage" concept was later applied more generally to blue-collar pay programs, for example, in the Davis-Bacon Act of 1931. But explicit federal indexing to well-defined indexes is a post–World War II phenomenon, for the most part. This indexing has occurred in three waves, with each wave dominated by a particular type of federal program. Figure 3-1 shows this temporal distribution of indexing decisions, broken down by program type.

The first wave, in 1949, saw the indexing of a number of commodity price support programs. Most of these programs had been created during World War II, but the 1949 legislation gave them a permanent basis. The second wave, peaking in the mid-1960s, focused primarily on federal retirement and pay programs. Indexing of these programs was largely completed by the time the third wave began in the early 1970s. This third wave, by far the largest, primarily involved other federal benefit programs for individuals, both social insurance and means-tested programs. For the latter, it was generally eligibility levels rather than benefits that were indexed.

The creation of new statutory indexing mechanisms almost ceased by the end of the Carter administration. And the few indexations that have occurred under the Reagan administration were generally consistent with the administration's theme of governmental restraint. Indexing of income tax brackets in 1981, for example, made it more difficult for the effects of the Reagan tax cut of that year to be undermined by "bracket creep." Indexing of medicare reimbursement to hospitals in 1982 and 1983 was intended to curb rising costs of the

18. Vee Burke, "Inventory of Federally Indexed Programs," in Congressional Research Service, *Indexation of Federal Programs* (GPO, 1981), p. 27.

19. Quoted in President's Panel on Federal Compensation, *Staff Report of the President's Panel on Federal Compensation* (GPO, 1976), p. 107.

medicare program. Indexing of benefits under the new federal employees' retirement system (FERS), created for employees hired after 1984, is in a sense not a totally new program: it is a companion to the civil service retirement (CSR) for employees hired earlier. Moreover, the FERS program contains a cap on inflation adjustments that the CSR program does not.[20] And the indexed cap on user fees and indexed eligibility limits for free care for some users of Veterans Administration health care (established in 1986) replaced formerly free provision of services.

Why have indexing decisions occurred in this pattern of peaks and valleys, rather than evenly over time? One obvious explanation is inflation: it might be expected that pressure for indexing would be positively related to high inflation, which lowers the real value of benefits and denies eligibility for means-tested programs to individuals who were previously eligible. The year-to-year changes in the GNP implicit price deflator shown in figure 3-1 indicate that there is a rough correspondence between periods of high inflation and increased indexing activity. In particular, the high inflation of the late 1960s and 1970s was accompanied by a huge jump in the number of programs indexed.

Inflation is not a sufficient explanation, however. First, high inflation cannot explain the clustering of specific types of programs into more limited time periods. The barriers to indexing seem to have broken down at about the same time for similar programs, either as a result of a "demonstration effect" or some other mechanism. Second, there clearly are limits to explicit indexing. Although high inflation continued in the late 1970s, new indexing slowed down. Most of the potential for indexing within the type of programs then indexed had been exhausted. Continued high rates of new indexing would have required a breakthrough into new types of activity, notably overall program budgets, revenue programs, and regulation. With the exception of income tax bracket indexing in 1981, this did not occur.

Expansionary Changes

Just because a policy innovation like indexing is adopted does not mean that the program is set in stone. Program expansion can take place in several ways, including (1) expanding its applicability to new

20. Julie Rovner, "New Federal Retirement Plan Wins Approval from Congress," *Congressional Quarterly Weekly Report*, vol. 44 (May 24, 1986), pp. 1201–03.

TABLE 3-7. *Major Expansionary Changes in Indexing Mechanisms*

Program	Year	Nature of change
Civil service retirement	1969	1 percent "kicker" added to COLA whenever inflation reaches 3 percent level needed to trigger benefit increase
Food stamps	1973	Change from annual to semiannual adjustments in benefits and eligibility standards
Dairy price supports	1977	Change from annual to semiannual adjustments
Supplemental security income	1983	Ad hoc increase in benefit base
Medicare supplementary medical insurance	1983	Six-month delay in SMI premium to match social security COLA freeze
Medicare hospital insurance	1986	Deductible for medicare hospitalization insurance capped
Social security	1986	Repeal of requirement that CPI increase at least 3 percent over last adjustment before COLA goes into effect

persons or things not previously covered, (2) altering the program base that is indexed, and (3) altering the indexing mechanism itself to make it more generous. The first type of change is outside the scope of this study. But if changes in program bases and indexing mechanisms are frequent, it would suggest that indexing does not seriously limit policymakers' discretion or stabilize real program standards.

Table 3-7 provides a sample of major expansionary changes in federal indexing mechanisms enacted in recent years.[21] Changes that restricted indexing in revenue and user charges—and thus were "expansionary" in the sense of increasing the federal deficit—are also listed in this table.[22] In 1986, for example, Congress capped the deductible for medicare hospital insurance, which is indexed to the cost of an average day's hospital stay. Legislators argued that changes in medicare

21. Here and in table 3-8, program changes that did not involve the indexing mechanism (such as elimination of the food stamp purchase requirement) are excluded.
22. The 1972 cap on SMI premiums also fits into this category, but since the mechanism it supplanted was only an implicit rather than an explicit indexation, I count the 1972 cap as an original act of indexing rather than as an expansionary adjustment.

reimbursement of hospitals enacted in 1983 have caused the deductible to rise much more quickly than actual hospital costs, forcing patients to shoulder an unanticipated and unfair share of the burden.[23] Similarly, legislative changes that have limited medicare supplementary medical insurance premiums have been intended largely to keep those fees from rising faster than the social security checks from which most of the elderly have their premium deducted. In short, these changes have been designed to prevent a loss in highly visible nominal income, with its high blame-generating potential.

Expansionary changes in the indexing provisions of benefit programs have been quite rare, especially since 1980. Taken together, the relative paucity of expansionary changes suggests three conclusions. First, indexing has had a restraining influence on ad hoc program expansion once it has gone into effect. There have been few successful efforts to "raise the bid" by making the indexed bases or mechanisms more generous.[24] At the very least, expansionary impulses have been pressed into other forms. Second, expansionary changes have generally been program specific rather than across the board, suggesting that there is little in the way of a common politics of indexing: there are instead the varying politics of many individual programs, with indexing issues surfacing at different times and in different forms for each program. Finally, the continuation of some very limited expansionary changes in the 1980s, despite the budget-cutting fervor in this period, suggests that program-specific policy and political concerns can overcome that fervor.

Indexation and Fiscal Stress

Expansion is not the only possible direction for policy change. What Congress gives, Congress can also take away. And the pattern of indexing in the 1980s has indeed been very different from the previous decade. Whereas the 1970s were marked by the extension of in-

---

23. The reason for the change in the first day's costs as a percentage of total hospital costs is that the new reimbursement system encourages hospitals to discharge patients earlier than in the past. As a result, later hospital stay days, which usually require less intensive care than the first days, have been eliminated. Because the dividend (cost of a hospital stay) has fallen more slowly than the divisor (days in hospital), the expenditure per day has risen dramatically.

24. A series of ad hoc increases in social security benefits was enacted after the program was indexed in 1972, but before the indexing took effect in 1975.

dexing to additional programs and sectors and by expansionary adjustments, the 1980s have been notable for indexing cutbacks. There were some contractionary adjustments in indexing mechanisms before 1981, as table 3-8 shows. (Complementing table 3-7, adjustments to indexed revenue programs that increase constituency user charges or payments to government are shown here as contractionary.) But the most significant of these changes—in military pay (1974), civil service and military retirement (1976), and social security (1977)—reflected a broad perception that the mechanisms in place were seriously flawed and were leading to an unfair and irresponsible overcompensation for inflation.[25] This perception helped to create a blame-reducing cover for cutbacks.

The cutbacks enacted in 1981 and thereafter have a rather different appearance. While a few of the changes (for example, in dairy price supports) have been directed at clearly flawed mechanisms, most have been designed primarily to lower expenditures or raise revenue. They have their roots in the Reagan administration's desire to cut domestic spending and general concern about federal spending. It is the president's popularity rather than flaws in the program that has most often provided political cover.

There are two notable patterns to the Reagan-era indexing cuts, however. First, they rarely involved the sudden and complete abolition of indexing for a program. Instead, the periods between adjustments have been stretched out or indexation formulas have been made less generous. Even in one of the few cases where a clear move away from indexing has taken place—dairy price supports—that shift was gradual, first taking the form of freezes.

Second, not all programs have been cut equally. A few programs' indexing provisions have undergone major changes, while others have been left relatively untouched. In short, just as inflation is not a sufficient explanation of the growth of indexing, so increasing concern by policymakers over spending and deficits (hereafter referred to as fiscal stress) is not sufficient to explain the pattern of cutbacks.

25. On flaws in the military pay adjustment formula in effect from 1967 to 1974, see Martin Binkin, *The Military Pay Muddle* (Brookings, 1975), pp. 62–66. Briefly, the formula added the COLA for all elements of regular military compensation (which includes quarters and subsistence allowances and tax allowances in addition to basic pay) into the basic pay component. This led to overcompensation for many personnel, especially those who received housing and food in kind rather than as a cash allowance, and for personnel at higher ranks, who receive a higher percentage of their regular compensation in the form of basic pay.

TABLE 3-8. *Major Contractionary Changes in Indexing Mechanisms*

Program	Year enacted	Nature of change
Military pay	1974	End to practice of adding COLA for all regular military compensation to basic pay component of compensation
Civil service and military retirement	1976	Elimination of 1 percent "kicker" added to COLA whenever inflation reached 3 percent level needed to trigger benefit increase; increase calculated semiannually instead of annually; elimination of 3 percent minimum trigger
Social security	1977	Wage history adjustment mechanism altered (for those born after 1916 only) to prevent overcompensation for inflation; minimum benefit frozen for new recipients; taxable wage base increased faster than inflation for three years
Food stamps	1980	Change from semiannual to annual adjustments in benefits and eligibility
Food stamps	1981	Establishment of 15-month period between benefit adjustments for 3 years; freeze in most deductions from gross income for 2 years; new indexed cap on gross income
Medicare hospital insurance	1981	Change in base used to calculate deductible paid by patient
Civil service retirement	1981	COLA changed from semiannual to annual basis
Dairy price supports	1981	Cancellation of semiannual inflation adjustment scheduled for April 1981

TABLE 3-8 *(continued)*

Program	Year enacted	Nature of change
Title XX social service	1981	Authorization for grant deindexed and cut
Civil service and military retirement	1982	Establishment of 13-month period between COLA changes for 3-year period; COLAs cut in half for retirees under 62 (if inflation exceeded projected levels, they would receive 100 percent of additional increment)
Food stamps	1982	Further delay in COLA and 1 percent cut from full adjustment for 3 years
Medicare supplementary medical insurance	1982	Medicare supplemental insurance premiums required to equal at least 25 percent of program costs even if premiums grow at faster rate than social security benefits[a]
Social security and related programs[b]	1983	Six-month delay in COLA and permanent shift in adjustment from July to January; future social security COLAs based on lower of increase in wages and prices if trust fund reserves fall below specified levels
Medicare supplementary medical insurance	1984	15-month freeze in customary and prevailing charges for all physicians; freeze in actual charges for "nonparticipating" physicians
Civil service pay	1985	Pay freeze for calendar year 1986
Medical supplementary insurance	1985, 1986	Extensions of physician reimbursement freeze enacted in 1984

a. Originally enacted for a two-year period. Extended by later legislation.
b. Because COLAs for many other programs (such as supplemental security income, black lung disability, veterans' pensions) are linked to that of social security, the COLA delay for that program affected inflation adjustments for many other programs as well.

Gramm-Rudman-Hollings and Beyond

Despite all the attention focused on indexing as a budgetary problem in the 1980s, no comprehensive, across-the-board legislation to limit or repeal COLAs has been enacted. The many budget-cutting initiatives of the first Reagan administration all focused on one program or a series of linked programs. If there was any doubt that indexing is here to stay and that comprehensive attacks on it are bound to fail, these doubts should be put to rest by the budget battles of the second Reagan administration. Efforts by the Senate Budget Committee to impose a wide-ranging spending freeze, including a freeze on COLAs for social security and other social programs, passed the Senate by the narrowest of margins (50–49) in 1985. But when President Reagan refused to endorse the package, it quickly died.

The Gramm-Rudman-Hollings deficit reduction initiative, as enacted by Congress in 1985, excluded many indexed programs from automatic cuts. There is considerable irony here: Gramm-Rudman-Hollings was intended to force the reconsideration of previously unquestioned commitments. In practice, however, it institutionalized a differential status for certain indexed programs, reinforcing preexisting differences in degree of protection from cutbacks. The most obvious exemption from cutbacks was indexing of tax brackets: Gramm-Rudman-Hollings was a creation of fiscal conservatives, and they would not have agreed to any measure that would provide a revenue bonus to government.[26] Thus tax bracket indexing was left unchanged by the act.

The Gramm-Rudman-Hollings initiative also created a four-level hierarchy of protection among indexed expenditure programs.[27] At the top of this hierarchy is social security and several means-tested programs aimed at the poor (most notably, food stamps and medicaid). These programs had their inflation adjustments fully protected from automatic cuts. A second level of programs, primarily medicare, had caps on cutbacks to their inflation adjustments. Cutbacks below full

26. Providing a hidden tax increase by reinstating bracket creep would also have given President Reagan an excuse to veto the measure. A veto on these grounds would have fit the objectives neither of the bill's original sponsors nor of many liberals, who saw Gramm-Rudman-Hollings as a vehicle to increase pressure for defense cuts and a veto of a tax-neutral bill as a way to embarrass the president.

27. For details on House, Senate, and conference provisions for indexed programs, see *Increasing the Statutory Limit on the Public Debt*, H. Rept. 99-433, 99 Cong. 1 sess. (GPO, 1985). See also Harry S. Havens, "Gramm-Rudman-Hollings: Origins and Implementation," *Public Budgeting and Financing*, vol. 6 (Autumn 1986), pp. 4–24.

inflation adjustment were to be limited to 1 percent in the first year and 2 percent in future years.[28] A third set of programs, including federal retirement programs, were subject to sequestration, but only up to the amount of their inflation increase—that is, nominal benefits could not be cut.[29] Finally, some indexed programs were subject to full sequestration—their indexing provisions could be fully overridden and nominal benefits cut.[30]

Even if the new Gramm-Rudman-Hollings enforcement mechanism enacted in 1987 is used, it will have no effect on most of the largest indexed programs. The distribution of cuts is only a default position in any case: the idea is that when faced with across-the-board cuts, Congress and the president would agree on a more selective, "rational" alternative. But the differential protection that Gramm-Rudman-Hollings offers to many program clientele—notably those of indexed programs—makes automatic cutbacks of other programs less unattractive to these groups: clientele of protected programs might do worse under an alternative package. And once any powerful interest (in this case, including social security recipients) is given a strong stake in the default position, the chances of an alternative being adopted decline significantly.

Conclusions

This broad overview of indexing provides some striking evidence about its scope, range, and durability. Conclusions about the reasons behind those patterns, and in particular about the objectives of politicians, must necessarily be more tentative.

Indexing provisions are very common in benefit programs and in certain types of purchase programs. They are used very sparingly in other sectors. Indexing has occurred in three successive waves, dominated in turn by commodity price supports, federal retirement, and social insurance and means-tested benefit programs. The third wave, in the 1970s, was by far the largest both in terms of number and size

28. If required cuts under Gramm-Rudman-Hollings were less than these amounts, medicare cuts were to be limited to the overall percentage cutback.
29. Civil service and military retirement were exempted from future Gramm-Rudman-Hollings cutbacks by the fiscal year 1987 reconciliation bill.
30. The most important examples of indexed programs subject to full sequestration are commodity support programs. But due to the contractual nature of Commodity Credit Corporation transactions, all contracts made before a sequester order were to be fulfilled under their original terms, with the additional savings required to meet the Gramm-Rudman-Hollings targets to be made up in the following fiscal year.

of programs indexed. Although indexing of additional programs virtually stopped in the 1980s, and there have been cutbacks at the margins of some programs, indexing as a procedure has survived intact in almost all of the programs where it was initiated. Even the Gramm-Rudman-Hollings budget reduction initiative left the most important indexing mechanisms untouched.

How can these patterns be explained? Indexation politics in the United States seems to have been driven in large measure by two successive economic developments: the persistent high inflation that began in the late 1960s and rising concern over federal spending and budget deficits in the 1980s. Inflation put indexing on government's agenda, and fiscal stress led to a trimming of commitments to maintain spending levels. But the effects of policy waves were far from uniform across programs. To explain these patterns, one must understand how inflation and fiscal stress were mediated by the policymaking process, and in particular by the objectives of politicians.

The most obvious finding is that none of the three motives—credit claiming, blame avoiding, and good policy—taken individually provides a sufficient explanation of why some programs are indexed and others are not. The scope of indexing is broader than credit-claiming objectives would suggest, but narrower than suggested by either good-policy or blame-avoiding objectives. The simplest form of the good-policy motivation—indexing as a response to decisionmaking overload—clearly does not provide a sufficient explanation of the observed patterns of behavior. Policymakers were not indiscriminate in their choice of programs to index. Certain types of programs were indexed far more than others. The desire to lessen their workload may have influenced policymakers' decisions to index, but it could not have been the only force at work. Agency and program budgets, after all, have not been indexed.

A more sophisticated version of the good-policy argument—indexing as a response to the problem of statutory and regulatory provisions written in nominal dollar amounts—is more helpful in explaining these patterns. The need to adjust these provisions clearly is a persistent problem in an inflationary age, and frequent adjustments may open up raids on the treasury. But this cannot be the whole story either. The need to adjust nominal dollar standards is also a problem in revenue and regulatory programs, but indexing has made little progress in either arena.

The absence of greater indexing of regulation and user charges also suggests a failing in one of the blame-avoidance explanations of why politicians index. Policymakers have not simply indexed in sectors where doing so would allow them to pass the buck, that is, to pass on the effects of inflation without appearing to impose costs on groups or getting caught in group conflicts. In fact, indexing has been used very sparingly in these areas. And when indexing provisions have been employed with user fees, most notably with respect to medicare, they have often been overridden to keep fees from rising as fast as the statute would have provided.

One possible explanation for the concentration of indexing mechanisms in benefit programs for individuals and their relative paucity in other sectors (such as agency and program budgets) is that both credit-claiming and blame-avoiding objectives may be at work. Legislative specialists are reluctant to surrender de jure discretion over expenditure decisions, even if they use informal rules of thumb that have the same de facto impact, because they want to maintain credit-claiming opportunities. But politicians must weigh this reluctance against the possible costs of being perceived as imposing losses on individuals who also happen to be voters. It is not just that politicians want to claim credit for indexing benefits; they may also fear voters' wrath if they do *not* vote to protect benefits. Individual recipients of transfer payments are more likely to notice when the real value of their benefits declines, and their claims for statutory protection against inflation are likely to be perceived by themselves and by others as legitimate. Weather forecasters and mental health agencies and users of their services are less fortunate in this respect, because inflationary erosion of program budgets has less direct and less measurable consequences for individuals. In short, the ability of program clientele to force politicians to "jump on the bandwagon" in support of indexing proposals seems to be a stronger impetus to indexing than "pass-the-buck" incentives.

The fact that the Gramm-Rudman-Hollings initiative, the major effort enacted by Congress to impose widespread cutbacks in indexing, used automatic cutback mechanisms to distance legislators from those cuts suggests that a "pass-the-buck" strategy may be more successful in cutting indexed programs. But the fact that most indexed programs were exempted from automatic cuts suggests that in this situation, too, it is hard to pass the buck. In particular, the inclusion of many means-tested programs in the list of programs fully protected from these automatic cutbacks might be considered surprising: these programs do not, after all, have very strong constituencies. It is important here to remember that voters' and politicians' perceptions, as well as actual constituency losses, are important considerations in the politics of blame. Democrats in Congress portrayed the inclusion of poverty programs as an issue of "fairness." Republicans felt that the "fairness" issue was one that had hurt them politically and did not wish to be seen as "balancing the budget on the backs of the poor." Cutbacks in low-income programs thus had political limits: they could take place so long as they did not cause a broader portion of the electorate to develop a negative image of the sponsoring party.

This broad overview of indexing goes only a short way toward explaining indexing choices. Many of the patterns observed are consistent with more than one set of policymakers' objectives, and the overall pattern is consistent with no single objective acting alone. Moreover, politicians' objectives have merely been imputed rather than observed directly. To make those direct observations, and understand how politicians' objectives interacted to produce current policy, it is necessary to turn to a detailed discussion of specific indexing decisions.

4

Social Security

The old age and survivors insurance program—more commonly known as social security—is by far the largest indexed federal expenditure program in terms of both outlays and the size of clientele. Outlays in fiscal year 1986 totaled $180 billion. Social security is a contributory system, with payments from employers and employees being placed in a trust fund from which benefits are paid to retirees.[1]

The distinguishing political characteristic of social security is its immense popularity. Pledging to restrain social security offers little political reward and the potential for great blame from current and future recipients. Proponents of restraint have attempted to employ a variety of blame-avoiding strategies in developing their proposals, but have had only limited success. It is not surprising, therefore, that real benefits grew during the early 1970s and have been touched relatively lightly by the retrenchment initiatives of the Reagan administration.

What is harder to understand is why indexing was adopted in the first place, since it limits politicians' opportunities to claim credit for benefit increases. This chapter suggests that this resulted from a failure of established mechanisms of agenda control. Congress has long relied on the two chambers' finance committees—notably House Ways and Means—to act as gatekeepers, keeping blame-generating and fiscally irresponsible choices off the congressional agenda. Both the adoption of indexing and the benefit expansions that contributed to a financial crisis in the system resulted in large part from a breakdown of the committees' performance of this role in the early 1970s. The implementation of indexing has made it more difficult to cut social security benefits.

1. There are separate trust funds for social security disability insurance and medicare hospitalization insurance, both of which are financed by social security taxes, and another for medicare supplementary medical insurance, which is financed by premiums and general revenues.

Origins and Development

The social security system was created by the Social Security Act of 1935. Over the next thirty years, it was expanded in a series of incremental steps, adding new benefits (such as disability in the 1950s and health care in the 1960s), increasing cash benefits, and extending the population covered.[2]

Benefits for retired workers and their survivors were (and are currently) based on their wage history. Before indexing, statutory provisions stated retirees' benefits in terms of a percentage of their average monthly wages over the period that they contributed to the social security system, with the lowest earnings years excluded. Without an ad hoc statutory change, retirees' benefits remained fixed over time in nominal terms and hence declined in real terms.

By the late 1960s, a well-developed mechanism had evolved to compensate for the effects of inflation.[3] As Martha Derthick outlines in her comprehensive study of social security policymaking, this mechanism involved a false assumption that workers' earnings would remain level in the future. They did not, of course. Thus contributions rose and actuarial surpluses developed in the trust funds over time after each benefit increase. These surpluses could then be distributed by Congress through new benefit increases. Ad hoc adjustments by Congress went into effect in 1952, 1954, 1959, 1965, 1968, 1970, and 1971. But until 1972, neither workers' wage histories nor their benefits after retirement were explicitly indexed.

These ad hoc benefit increases were very popular, as Senate Finance Committee Chairman Russell Long, Democrat of Louisiana, noted in a congressional hearing:

> Senator Long: . . . it has been my experience since I have been here, that the easiest bill to pass is a simple across-the-board increase of benefits to offset inflation that has occurred since the last social security increase.
>
> It is almost impossible for a Senator to explain why he did not vote for it.

2. Martha Derthick, *Policymaking for Social Security* (Brookings, 1979).

3. Before indexing, the mechanism for benefit increases was a change in the "replacement rates" (the percentage of a retiree's wage replaced by social security benefit) at each level of a worker's historical average monthly wage. In 1952, for example, a worker would receive 55 percent of the first $110 of his average monthly wage. By 1972 this had been increased to 108 percent. *Social Security Bulletin Annual Statistical Supplement, 1984–85*, p. 5.

Mr. Chase [Chamber of Commerce of the U.S.]: It is an awkward position to be in, I am sure.[4]

This system of periodic increases allowed credit claiming by all legislators, but not until actuarial surpluses in the trust funds had been accumulated, which pleased fiscal conservatives.[5] There was no debate over the principle of whether inflation adjustments were desirable or necessary. As Social Security Commissioner Robert Ball noted in 1970, "It is really a settled policy by now that the [social security] benefits will at least be kept up to date with changes in the purchasing power of the dollar. The problem is, though, that this is accomplished with a time lag."[6]

The purchasing power of benefits did in fact increase dramatically in the postwar period, as shown in figure 4-1. The figure also shows a substantial increase in the average monthly benefit in relation to the average weekly wage. The benefit-earnings ratio rose steadily in the postwar period until the mid-1950s, remained relatively stable until the late 1960s, and then began another fairly steady climb that continued into the 1980s.

This aggregate view, however, conflates the benefits of new retirees and past retirees. Congress did allow already retired workers to share in an expanding economy through ad hoc benefit increases. But higher benefit payments were due in large part to the entry of new beneficiaries: because these individuals had a higher wage history, they earned higher benefits. Workers who retired in 1954 and 1959 (admittedly, years in which benefit increases took place), for example, kept up neither with rising wages nor with rising prices in the mid-1960s.[7]

Political Alignments

The increase in inflation of the late 1960s and early 1970s clearly placed indexing of social security on the public agenda. Indexing gained much support from policy experts. For example, a Brookings Institution study issued in 1968 suggested adjusting benefits automat-

4. *Social Security Amendments of 1970,* Hearings before the Senate Committee on Finance, 91 Cong. 2 sess. (Government Printing Office, 1970), pt. 2, p. 817.

5. Derthick, *Policymaking for Social Security,* pp. 48–51, 350–57.

6. *Social Security Amendments of 1970,* Hearings, p. 12.

7. Joseph A. Pechman, Henry J. Aaron, and Michael K. Taussig, *Social Security: Perspectives for Reform* (Brookings, 1968), pp. 99–101.

FIGURE 4-1. *Average Monthly Social Security Benefit for a Retired Worker, 1947–86*

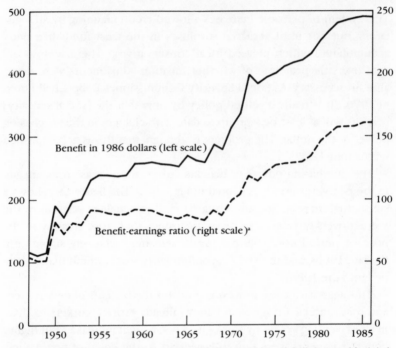

SOURCES: Average monthly benefit for a retired worker from *Social Security Bulletin Annual Statistical Supplement, 1986,* for 1947–84, and *Social Security Bulletin,* vol. 50 (December 1987), p. 47, for 1985–86. Data on implicit price deflator for personal consumption expenditure component of GNP and average gross weekly earnings for production and nonsupervisory workers in private nonagricultural earnings from *Economic Report of the President, 1988* (Government Printing Office, 1988), pp. 252, 299.

a. Ratio of social security monthly benefit to average weekly earnings in private nonagricultural employment.

ically to changes in the CPI.[8] Indeed, the idea of social security indexing had achieved by 1968 one of the major indicators of political platitude: both parties endorsed it in their platforms.

Indexing of social security benefits was not, however, simply a better mousetrap, proposed by program experts and adopted with little controversy. Although there was widespread support for the principle of indexing, there was strong disagreement on its precise form. Other issues, stemming from the sheer size of social security and its clientele and from the program's financing through a payroll tax–trust fund mechanism, intruded on the debate. Specifically, Congress had to

8. Ibid., pp. 96–104, 219–20.

wrestle with (1) the size of the benefit base from which indexing would begin, (2) the precise indexing formula, and (3) how to finance benefit increases.

Organized labor was the most active backer of indexing social security benefits, but its position was impractically expansionist: in 1967, the AFL-CIO called for indexing of social security benefits to wage levels as well as prices, so that beneficiaries would share in the fruits of a growing economy. This was accompanied by a call for a 50 percent benefit increase, with the new expenditures being financed by an increase in the tax base and a "modest" injection of general revenues.[9]

Indexing received its biggest boost in 1969, when President Richard Nixon endorsed linking benefits to the CPI, coupled with a 10 percent benefit increase. The president also proposed indexing the social security tax base (amount of earnings subject to taxation) to help pay for future benefit adjustments.[10] For the president and congressional Republicans, indexing offered a way to depoliticize benefit increases and avoid costly bidding wars that could drive up benefits to unacceptably high levels.

Nixon's proposal had several problems, however. First, it was sent to Congress shortly after his controversial welfare reform (family assistance plan) proposal, creating a huge workload for the congressional committees (House Ways and Means and Senate Finance) with jurisdiction over both pieces of legislation. This was a conscious strategy by the Nixon administration, which sought throughout its first term to tie politically popular social security benefit increases to welfare reform as a way to get the latter through Congress. Second, the Nixon plan did not have the support of organized labor, which felt that it would simply perpetuate unacceptably high levels of poverty among the aged. The AFL-CIO's representative argued that indexing linked to the CPI was acceptable only after a much larger benefit increase and "a clear public policy that benefits will be adjusted upward periodically, in addition to any increases due to the cost of living."[11]

9. See the statement by AFL-CIO President George Meany in *President's Proposals for Revision in the Social Security System,* Hearings before the House Committee on Ways and Means, 90 Cong. 1 sess. (GPO, 1967), pp. 571–601.

10. "Special Message on Social Security, September 25, 1969," *Public Papers of the Presidents: Richard Nixon, 1969* (GPO, 1971), pp. 740–45.

11. See the statement by Andrew J. Biemiller, director of the Legislative Department of the AFL-CIO, in *Social Security and Welfare Proposals,* Hearings before the House Committee on Ways and Means, 91 Cong. 1 sess. (GPO, 1970), pt. 5, pp. 1775–79.

The business community was skeptical about indexing on very different grounds. Indexing the wage base—an invariable companion to benefit indexing—would affect only high-income individuals, because middle-income workers' entire wages were already subject to the tax. It would also steadily increase the payroll tax burden of businesses. In addition, business representatives feared that "if the cost-of-living escalator is incorporated in the social security program, it will inevitably spread to other public programs, private pension plans, and, conceivably, to the entire wage structure.... It is difficult to visualize a more likely means of institutionalizing inflation, barring, of course, a flat mandate that the total wage structure in this country be predicated on a cost-of-living escalator." [12]

Perhaps most important, the proposal suffered from opposition by House Ways and Means Committee Chairman Wilbur Mills. And Mills's role in the process was central. Because social security reforms generally have revenue components, action originates in the House—and thus with Ways and Means. Mills exerted strong control over his committee through his refusal to establish (and thus cede power to) subcommittees and through his close working relationship with the Republican minority. He gained further control over legislation from the Ways and Means Committee's authority over all House Committee assignments (this power was removed in 1974). And the House of Representatives' long-established practice of considering Ways and Means legislation under a closed rule further increased Mills's power by making it extremely unlikely that the committee could be "rolled" on the floor.[13]

Mills's objections to indexing were several. First, he and other conservatives feared that its adoption would signal that the federal government was giving up on efforts to control inflation. Second, increasing benefit levels without linked tax increases (either in tax rates or the tax base) would upset the actuarial soundness of the social security trust funds. Indexing the tax base could provide some of the needed revenues, but automatic escalators in the tax base would mean surrendering congressional (and the Ways and Means Committee's) taxing powers. And Mills was very sensitive both to the institutional preroga-

12. Testimony of Henry H. Chase, representing the Chamber of Commerce of the United States, in *Social Security Amendments of 1970,* Hearings, p. 818. See also statement of William P. McHenry, Jr., in *Social Security and Welfare Proposals,* Hearings, pp. 1617–19.

13. See Derthick, *Policymaking for Social Security,* chap. 2.

TABLE 4.1. *Policymakers' Objectives and Strategies in Indexing Social Security Benefits*

Player	Dominant objective	Strategy
Legislative specialists	Credit claiming, good policy	Keep indexing proposals off the agenda in order to retain discretion over benefit increases
President and congressional Republicans	Blame avoiding, good policy	Index benefits to avoid bidding wars leading to unacceptably high benefit levels
Congressional Democrats	Blame avoiding	Defect to support indexing if forced to take open stand on it
Organized labor and lobbies for the elderly	. . .	Win large benefit increase before indexing
Business interests	. . .	Oppose most benefit increases and indexing

tives of Congress and to the possible political consequences of indexing. As he argued in a 1970 House debate, "This is what it boils down to: Is the Congress going to get any credit for the future adjustments of benefits, or are we going to . . . let the Secretary of Health, Education and Welfare get all that credit and [by indexing the tax base] be accused in the forthcoming election with having voted in 1970 to fix the amount of income subject to taxation at better than $22,000 [by 1993?]"[14]

Mills's opposition gave opponents of indexing a bargaining position that was strong, but not impregnable. Proponents of indexing had several channels available to go around Mills and get the issue onto the agenda—most notably introducing it in the Senate, where there are fewer restrictions on amendments. And once legislators were forced to vote on indexing, it is not clear that their credit-claiming interests would prevail. Protecting social security benefits is an issue that appeals to traditional Democratic constituencies, and many constituents would not understand that an ad hoc adjustment process might lead to higher benefits than indexing. A vote against "protecting benefits from inflation"—which is how electoral opponents would certainly portray it—would be difficult to explain.

The position of the major players in social security politics at the beginning of the 1970s is summarized in table 4-1. The positions of

14. *Congressional Record* (May 21, 1970), p. 16582.

the major governmental actors were to shift dramatically as the indexing debate unfolded, however.

Indexation on the Agenda

Congress failed to act on Nixon's indexing proposal in 1969, with Mills pleading a lack of time. But it did, in a portent of things to come, give overwhelming support to an "emergency" benefit increase of 15 percent, outbidding the president's proposal. Nixon first considered vetoing the plan as excessive, but given its overwhelming support (400–0 in the House), he acquiesced.[15] In 1970 the Ways and Means Committee once again excluded indexing from its social security package and reported the bill under a rule allowing only committee-offered amendments. Usually this was sufficient to protect Ways and Means legislation from unwanted changes. But this time advocates of indexing, led by the ranking minority member of the Ways and Means Committee, offered a "motion to recommit with instructions" after the bill had passed. This rarely successful maneuver requires the sponsoring committee chairman to report the just-passed legislation back immediately with the changes requested in the motion—in this case, indexing provisions.[16] Despite Mills's objections, the motion was adopted by a vote of 233–144.[17] The coalition of support for the measure was an odd one (table 4-2). Indexing enjoyed solid support from Republicans both on and off the Ways and Means Committee. The opposition was led by Ways and Means Democrats and southern Democrats, who followed Mills's lead. But a majority (64–55) of northern, non-Ways and Means Democrats jumped on the Republican bandwagon, voting in favor of the Republican proposal. And it was clearly the most liberal Democrats in this group who furnished the margin of victory for indexing.

Amendments added by the Senate Finance Committee made index-

15. During House consideration of the benefit increase, a number of legislators mentioned that automatic adjustments for the cost of living were a necessary next step in social security policy. See *Congressional Record* (December 15, 1969), pp. 39006–29.

16. Walter J. Oleszek, *Congressional Procedures and the Policy Process*, 2d ed. (CQ Press, 1984), pp. 145–46, 261.

17. Originally the Nixon administration and Ways and Means Republicans had proposed indexing as an alternative to the 5 percent benefit increase in benefits recommended by the Ways and Means Democrats, but they proposed it on the floor as an addition to the committee's proposal. See "Supplemental Republican Views," in *Social Security Amendments of 1970*, H. Rept. 91-1096, 91 Cong. 2 sess. (GPO, 1970), pp. 141–44.

TABLE 4-2. *1970 House Roll Call Vote on Indexation of Social Security, by Party and Ideological Classification*

Party and ideological classification of members[a]	Percentage voting yes	Total number voting[b]
All Republicans	97.0	168
Members of Ways and Means	100.0	9
Nonmembers of Ways and Means	96.9	159
All Democrats	33.5	209
Members of Ways and Means	13.3	15
Southerners	0.0	7
Nonsoutherners	25.0	8
Nonmembers of Ways and Means	35.1	194
Southerners	5.3	75
Nonsoutherners	53.8	119
Very conservative	66.7	3
Conservative	20.0	10
Moderate	23.8	21
Liberal	50.0	40
Very liberal	77.6	45
Total	61.8	377

SOURCES:Roll call data from *Congressional Record* (May 21, 1970), p. 16587, and *Congressional Quarterly Weekly Report*, vol. 28 (May 29, 1970), pp. 1470–71. Data on ADA scores from *Congressional Quarterly Weekly Report*, vol. 29 (April 16, 1971), pp. 866–77.

a. Ideological classification for nonsouthern, non-Ways and Means Democrats is by members' Americans for Democratic Action (ADA) score for the 1970 session. Members with scores of 0–20 are classified as "very conservative," those with scores of 21–40 as "conservative," etc.

b. Total number of representatives in category who voted, including both supporters and opponents.

ing somewhat more palatable to legislators' desire to preserve discretion by stating that benefits would rise automatically only if Congress had not otherwise acted to change benefits within the last year; there was thus a statutory presumption that Congress could and probably would do so on some occasions.[18] However, the Senate did not complete action until so late in the session (in part due to controversy over welfare reform, which was eventually split off from the social security provisions) that Mills refused to go to conference; so no action was taken.

Congressional action early in 1971 mirrored that of late 1969. The administration again asked for a benefit increase (6 percent) coupled with indexing of benefits and the tax base. Mills countered with a bill that outbid the administration (a 10 percent increase) but did not mention indexing. Again, an "emergency" ad hoc increase following

18. See *Social Security Amendments of 1970*, S. Rept. 91-1431, 91 Cong. 2 sess. (GPO, 1970), p. 10.

the Ways and Means plan was adopted—this time attached to an urgently needed increase in the debt limit to make it veto-proof.[19]

It was clear by this time that indexing would be adopted shortly, however; in Senate debate on the debt ceiling bill, Chairman Russell Long of the Finance Committee stated that it would be considered soon in a more comprehensive social security package. The Social Security Commission's outside Advisory Council added its support for indexing in its report, issued two weeks after passage of the debt ceiling–benefit increase bill. The recommendation was not unanimous, however. The council's business representatives argued against indexing on the ground that it would contribute to the institutionalization of inflation.[20]

By 1971 even Mills realized that indexing was simply too popular to be ignored any longer. Thus an indexing provision was included in the committee's report on H.R. 1, the package of welfare reform (President Nixon's revised family assistance plan) and social security changes. Mills's proposals generally followed the Senate plan of the previous session. Automatic adjustments would be made only when inflation exceeded 3 percent. Moreover, the secretary of the Department of Health, Education and Welfare was to give advance notice to Congress when such changes had been triggered, giving Congress the opportunity to enact some alternative increase.[21] Increases in the tax base would also occur automatically at the time of the benefit increase.

Even with Mills's acquiescence, the path to indexing was neither swift nor sure. The Senate Finance Committee fought for more than a year over the welfare reform provisions of H.R. 1 before reaching a tentative agreement in June 1972. Meanwhile, Wilbur Mills, in the midst of a short-lived presidential candidacy, abandoned his usual caution regarding benefit increases, proposing an unprecedented 20 percent increase. Although he made vague references to keeping benefits up with the cost of living, his bill did not contain an indexing mechanism. Mills argued that most of the funds for the benefit increase could be obtained from expected surpluses in the OASI trust fund, if a change were made from an actuarial assumption of level earnings to

19. P.L. 92-5.
20. 1971 Advisory Council on Social Security, *Reports on the Old Age, Survivors, and Disability Insurance and Medicare Programs* (Washington: The Council, 1971), pp. 17–18, 104. The three business representatives were joined in their dissent by the representative of the American Medical Association.
21. *Social Security Amendments of 1971,* H. Rept. 92-231, 92 Cong. 2 sess. (GPO, 1971), pp. 40–41.

one of "dynamic" (that is, rising) earnings.[22] President Nixon suggested a more modest 5 percent increase.[23]

Once again, however, the Senate Finance Committee's failure to agree on welfare reform seemed likely to delay changes in social security. But in June, Senate liberals, with the agreement of Senate Finance Committee Chairman Long, took the most popular elements of the social security package being considered by the committee—a 20 percent benefit increase (effective in September 1972, in time for the election), indexing of benefits beginning in 1975, and a delay in a planned increase in OASDI tax rates—and offered them separately.[24] The wage base and minimum benefit were also indexed. Once again, an urgently needed extension of the debt ceiling was the vehicle used to make the measure veto-proof. Republicans in both the House and Senate proposed amendments to limit the benefit increase to 10 percent. Both efforts were defeated by three-to-one margins. Again Nixon considered a veto, but he was in a politically impossible situation. The benefit boost was very popular, and the timing—just before the national party conventions and four months before the 1972 election—could not have been worse for a veto. Moreover, the huge margins of victory in Congress (302–35 in the House; 82–4 in the Senate) made it clear that his veto would be overridden. And a veto would also create havoc because it would cause the debt ceiling to drop automatically to a level far below the current level of national debt. Thus he quickly signed the measure, praising Congress for adopting indexing while criticizing it for failing to fully fund the 20 percent benefit increase through new revenues.[25]

22. The bill also included an increase in the social security tax rate. Mills cited the recommendations of the 1971 Social Security Advisory Council that OASDI should abandon the level-earnings assumption and move toward "current-cost" financing, abandoning efforts to build large trust fund surpluses. The commission had not specifically backed a large benefit increase, however. On Mills's proposal, see H.R. 13320 (92 Cong. 2 sess.) and *Congressional Record* (February 23, 1972), pp. 5269–72. See also Marjorie Hunter, "Mills Asks 20% Rise in Social Security," *New York Times*, February 24, 1972, p. A19.

23. Robert B. Semple, Jr., "Nixon Asks a Rise in Aid to Elderly," *New York Times*, March 24, 1972, p. 37.

24. The wage base was also increased, but not until January 1973. The Finance Committee had approved only a 10 percent benefit increase in its tentative agreement on H.R. 1 earlier in June, but Senator Long agreed to back the larger increase on the floor, where fifty-nine other senators were already committed to support it. See *Congressional Quarterly Weekly Report*, vol. 30 (June 17, 1972), p. 1495.

25. Nixon promised to make up the spending increase through cuts in other programs. *Weekly Compilation of Presidential Documents*, vol. 8 (July 3, 1972), pp. 1122–23. On the political maneuvering surrounding passage of the act, see *Congressional Quarterly Weekly Report*, vol. 30 (July 1, 1972), pp. 1630–31 and (July 8, 1972),

After three years of wrangling, Congress had finally approved indexing, and by huge margins. But the overwhelming congressional support has a curious aspect: if it was really so popular, why did Congress not put it into effect immediately, rather than after the two-and-one-half-year waiting period enacted in the debt limitation bill? After all, such a delay was not included in most other indexing plans. But the delay had several political advantages for legislators. It allowed them to claim credit for indexing and a 20 percent benefit increase in the short term, while mollifying fiscal conservatives with the knowledge that inflation would erode the value of the benefit substantially by the time indexing went into effect. Thus its consequences for the actuarial soundness of the fund would be much less severe than with immediate indexing. And if inflation were to be extremely high, there might be another bonus: an opportunity for a final ad hoc increase before indexing took effect.

Congress did not give up its discretion over benefit levels entirely in 1972, in any case: automatic benefit increases were to occur only if Congress did not enact an alternative increase. In fact, there were no less than four pieces of social security legislation enacted in the next eighteen months. The first, in October 1972, represented the final defeat of the strategy of linking social security changes to welfare reform. Unable to reach agreement on a welfare reform package, the Senate finally passed a number of social security reforms that had been on the agenda for four years, but had repeatedly been cast aside in efforts to pass benefit increases.[26] It also raised OASDI tax rates (effective after the election) to pay for the increased benefits passed earlier. The second, in April 1973, made technical changes in the system. But in the final two pieces of legislation, Congress once again granted ad hoc benefit increases. In July 1973 Congress voted to increase benefit levels by 5.9 percent, effective the following June.[27] In December, after the Arab oil embargo sent inflation rates skyrocketing, Congress voted a two-step increase for 1974, superseding the measure passed just a

pp. 1701–03; and Marjorie Hunter, "20% Social Security Rise Is Voted by Both Houses; Nixon Approval in Doubt," *New York Times,* July 1, 1972, p. 1.

26. The remaining reforms were generally noncontroversial (for example, raising the benefit for the surviving spouse from 82.5 percent to 100 percent of that of a deceased beneficiary) and passed almost unanimously.

27. The measure originally provided for the increase to begin in April. House and Senate Confereees changed the date to June (with payments mailed in July) so that its effect would not be felt until the new fiscal year. This was done to make the measure more palatable to President Nixon. See Richard L. Madden, "Social Security Increase Is Approved by Congress," *New York Times,* July 1, 1973, p. 1.

few months earlier: 7 percent beginning in March, with a further 4 percent in June.[28]

Retrenchment

By 1976 it had become obvious that the social security benefit increases of the last few years, in combination with a prolonged recession that lowered system revenues, had seriously compromised the long-term viability of the system. The result was a long-range trust fund deficit estimated at a staggering 8 percent of the nation's payroll.[29] There were short-term problems too, with the OASI trust fund expected to run dry by 1979. Part of the problem stemmed from the interaction of the benefit indexing mechanism enacted in 1972 with the method used to calculate workers' initial benefits (by adjusting their wage histories for inflation). This combination inadvertently overcompensated new retirees for inflation, leading to progressively higher replacement rates (the percentage of preretirement earnings replaced by social security payments). Expert opinion quickly united on the need to change the wage history adjustment mechanism.[30] Predictably, there was less agreement on what combination of benefit cuts and tax increases would be needed to solve the broader funding problem. Just as predictably, Congress was reluctant to address these issues during an election year.

The problem was thus left to the new Carter administration to resolve in 1977. The new administration's reform package, which included injection of general revenues and higher payments by employers, was rejected by Congress.[31] But Congress did put together a

28. This represented a compromise between a Republican proposal for a 10 percent increase and a more costly Democratic counterproposal.

29. See the testimony of HEW Secretary David Mathews in *Decoupling the Social Security Benefit Structure*, Hearings before the Subcommittee on Social Security of the House Committee on Ways and Means, 94 Cong. 2 sess. (GPO, 1976), p. 31.

30. *Reports of the Quadrennial Advisory Council on Social Security*, H. Doc. 94-75, 94 Cong. 1 sess. (GPO, 1975). See also Colin D. Campbell, *Over-Indexed Benefits: The Decoupling Proposals for Social Security*, (Washington, D.C.: American Enterprise Institute for Public Policy Research, 1976); and Campbell, ed., *Financing Social Security* (Washington, D.C.: American Enterprise Institute for Public Policy Research, 1979). The faulty mechanism for adjusting wage histories caused replacement rates to be erratic rather than constantly rising; under certain combinations of wage-price change, replacement rates could actually decline.

31. See James W. Singer, "Carter Is Trying to Make Social Security More Secure," *National Journal*, vol. 9 (June 11, 1977), pp. 893–95; and Singer, "Help Is On the Way for the Sagging Social Security System," *National Journal*, vol. 9 (October 1, 1977), pp. 1535–36.

package of changes that increased tax rates and modified the mechanism used to calculate initial benefits in order to prevent overcompensation for future beneficiaries. Current retirees did not have their benefits cut, however, and individuals who became eligible to retire through the end of 1978 were also allowed to use these rules.[32] Policymakers felt that changing the formula retroactively, and thus cutting benefits for individuals who were retired or very close to retirement, was neither fair nor politically viable. But this meant that individuals with very similar wage histories might receive very different benefit levels, simply because some were born before January 1, 1917, and others (the so-called notch babies) afterwards. The legislative effort to avoid blame from the former group by "grandfathering" their benefits thus led to a major horizontal equity problem. This change was relatively noncontroversial at the time; the major lobbies for the elderly supported it as a needed "technical" change.[33] But as individuals on the "wrong" side of the dividing line began to retire, the alleged "notch" became very controversial.

In the search for further savings, the 1977 act also changed some of social security's other indexed provisions: the program's minimum benefit was frozen for new recipients, and the wage base for social security taxes was increased faster for the 1979-82 period than would have been called for by the automatic provisions in current law.[34] Thus in the short term Congress managed to avoid cutting benefits for current recipients (who are most likely to notice the change) and to target loss-imposing provisions at relatively small groups (high-income FICA taxpayers and minimum benefit recipients), but in the long term it created a new disgruntled group (the notch babies).

The 1977 fix soon proved insufficient to solve social security's finan-

32. For a comprehensive overview of the legislative history and final provisions of the 1977 Social Security Amendments, see John Snee and Mary Ross, "Social Security Amendments of 1977: Legislative History and Summary of Provisions," *Social Security Bulletin,* vol. 41 (March 1978), pp. 3–20; and "Congress Clears Social Security Tax Increase," *Congressional Quarterly Almanac,* vol. 33 (1977), pp. 161–72.

33. See testimony by representatives of the National Council of Senior Citizens and the National Retired Teachers Association–American Association of Retired Persons, in *Decoupling the Social Security Benefit Structure,* Hearings, pp. 89–103. On the effects of the decoupling statute, see *Proposal to Deal with the Social Security Notch Problem,* Legislative Analysis 51, 99th Congress (Washington, D.C.: American Enterprise Institute for Public Policy Research, August 1985).

34. Minimum benefit provisions were in fact targeted more narrowly: by increasing and indexing the special minimum benefit for individuals who had worked for many years at low wages, Congress sought to limit the effect of the minimum benefit cuts to former government workers who were receiving a "windfall" second pension based on limited employment in the private sector.

cial problems. By the time the Reagan administration took office in 1981, it was clear that a short-term funding crisis was imminent and that the system faced another huge long-term shortfall. The details of the ensuing political conflict have been discussed extensively elsewhere.[35] What is of concern here is the role played by indexing both in the debate and in its eventual resolution. And what emerges very clearly is how narrow the scope of that debate was: at no time did fundamental changes in the indexing mechanism come close to adoption. President Reagan's May 1981 reform package included a request for a three-month COLA delay, as well as modifications in the formula used to calculate a recipient's initial benefit (this latter provision aimed at vestiges of past overindexing).[36] But the administration sought to limit its identification with these politically volatile proposals from the outset, and it backed away completely when serious opposition developed.[37] As a result, cuts in social security enacted as part of the 1981 reconciliation act affected narrow groups (such as college student survivors and recipients of minimum benefits) rather than those that would have been affected by a broad-based COLA cut. An attempt by David Stockman later in 1981 to win the president's support for a new three-month COLA delay proposal was rebuffed, as Republican leaders warned of its possible political consequences.[38]

Legislation passed at the end of 1981 provided a temporary respite from the system's financial crisis by allowing the OASI trust fund to borrow from the disability and hospital insurance funds until after the 1982 election. And in a classic "pass-the-buck" maneuver, the president proposed a National Commission on Social Security Reform to recommend changes in the system—but not until just after the 1982 election, when the political risks of cutbacks would presumably be lower. Congress accepted, for it also had no interest in facing the issue before the election or in taking firm stands on a rescue package.

It became clear in 1982 that the commission would not be able to reach a consensus, so another committee—the "Gang of Nine"—be-

35. See in particular Paul Light's comprehensive study, *Artful Work: The Politics of Social Security Reform* (Random House, 1985).

36. See *Congressional Quarterly Almanac,* vol. 37 (1981), pp. 118–19; and ibid., chap. 10. The major savings in this package would have come from almost immediate cuts in early retirement benefits.

37. President Reagan's political advisers insisted that the package be announced by Secretary of Health and Human Services Richard Schweiker rather than the president, to distance him from the proposals. See David A. Stockman, *The Triumph of Politics: Why the Reagan Revolution Failed* (Harper and Row, 1986), pp. 181–93.

38. See Light, *Artful Work,* pp. 132–33.

gan operating behind closed doors. It drew five members from the commission, carefully excluding the most inflexible liberals and conservatives. The other four members were from the White House.[39] Their agreement was then ratified by the commission, the president, and House Speaker Thomas P. O'Neill. Congress modified and added to the commission's plan in some areas, but followed its general recommendations.

Throughout this process enormous effort was devoted to deflecting and diffusing blame. Authorship of one of the most blame-generating proposals (taxation of benefits for high-income recipients) was disguised; tax increases were redefined as "tax acceleration" and cuts in inflation adjustments as "permanent delays." After a package was put together, its backers sought to "circle the wagons"—that is, to obtain the advance consent of all the major players so that no one would have to be out in front on the issue as a target for blame.[40] Opponents of the package were challenged to offer a responsible counterproposal or acquiesce. "Fast-track" congressional consideration was intended to win approval before interest groups could mount effective campaigns against the proposal; limits on amendments in the House provided further protection from blame generators. And of course the timing of the debate, immediately after a midterm election, allowed maximum time for the issue to play out before backers of the package would have to answer for their vote. Even so, the package barely survived several challenges in Congress.[41]

Social security COLAs faired reasonably well in the final legislation.[42] There were two forms of COLA cutbacks, only one of which was assured. First, the 1983 COLA was delayed from July to the following January, and adjustments were to be made in January thereafter. Since inflation adjustments are based on changes in prices over the prior year rather than with reference to some base year, this shift did cause a small permanent cut in benefit replacement rates for current retirees.[43] Second, the COLA was to shift from a CPI measure to the

39. On the establishment of this so-called Gang of Nine, see ibid., chap. 15.
40. Ibid., pp. 177–78, 191–92.
41. Ibid., chaps. 16–17.
42. P.L. 98-21.
43. The Congressional Budget Office estimated in 1984 that the benefit delay in OASI and social security disability insurance would save $1.45 billion in fiscal year 1983 and $20 billion over the next five fiscal years. *Background Material and Data on Programs within the Jurisdiction of the Committee on Ways and Means,* Committee Print WMCP 99-2, House Commitee on Ways and Means, 99 Cong. 1 sess. (GPO, 1985), p. 30. See also *Social Security Act Amendments of 1983,* H. Rept. 98-25, 98 Cong. 1 sess. (GPO,

lower of the increase in wages or prices if the OASDI trust fund reserve fell below specified levels.[44] Most of the improvement in the fund's financial status, however, came from other sources, such as increased taxes, a higher retirement age, coverage of government employees, and taxation of benefits for high-income recipients.[45] The provisions with the broadest clientele, COLAs, proved the most difficult to attack.

Efforts to cut social security COLAs since that time have been rejected. Legislation enacted in 1984 required that a COLA be paid in that year even if inflation fell below the statutory trigger (3 percent). In the 1984 election, challenger Walter Mondale sought to portray the Republicans as threats to social security benefits; President Reagan responded by promising that he would never agree to cut COLAs. After the election, the president backtracked slightly, allowing that he might accept such cuts if they were pressed on him by "an overwhelming bipartisan majority in both houses"—a most unlikely proposition.[46] The president's fiscal year 1986 budget proposed a freeze in some entitlements that were not means tested (for example, civil service retirement, railroad retirement, and black lung disability), but not in social security.

Only the leaders of the Senate Budget Committee were willing to face the political heat of a social security COLA freeze head on. They agreed (on a party-line vote) to a one-year freeze as part of their budget resolution. This move was once again strongly opposed by groups lobbying for the elderly.[47] After consultation with the White House, the plan was altered to provide a 2 percent COLA regardless of the inflation rate; no adjustment for the next 2 percent of inflation; and a full COLA for inflation above 4 percent. This measure would be in effect for fiscal years 1986–88. The package fell apart on the Senate

1983), pt. 1, pp. 20, 172–73. The base quarters for calculating the inflation adjustment were also shifted back six months.

44. P.L. 98-21, secs. 111, 112.

45. Since the threshold for taxation of benefits— $25,000 for an individual, zero for an individual living with his or her spouse and filing separately, and $32,000 for a couple filing jointly—was not indexed, an increasing share of the elderly will have their benefits taxed over time.

46. Margaret Shapiro and Spencer Rich, "Wright Says House Opposes Benefits Curb," *Washington Post,* January 11, 1985, p. A1.

47. Some groups, notably the American Association of Retired Persons, were willing to consider a social security COLA freeze as part of a larger package, however. See Pamela Fessler, "Bid to Rein in Social Security Faces Senate Floor Challenge," *Congressional Quarterly Weekly Report,* vol. 43 (March 23, 1985), pp. 530–31. See also Jonathan Rauch, "Congress Weighs Ideas of Cuts in Social Security COLAs That Shield the Poor," *National Journal,* vol. 17 (April 27, 1985), pp. 901–04.

floor, however, with two Republicans up for reelection in 1986 sponsoring a successful amendment to restore full social security COLAs.[48] Majority Leader Robert Dole then put together another package including the original Budget Committee proposal for a one-year social security COLA freeze; this won passage by a single vote, with Vice-President George Bush breaking the tie.[49]

On the House side, there was no chance of a social security freeze emerging as part of the budget package. The Democrats had a majority in that chamber and the Democratic leadership wanted to use social security as a blame-generating issue against the Republicans in 1986. The pivotal position held by Representative Claude Pepper, Democrat of Florida, the leading champion of preserving social security intact and the chairman of the House Rules Committee, was another constraint on a freeze. In the latter capacity, Pepper promised that any budget resolution coming to the floor would include a separate vote on any cuts in social security—a vote that would clearly focus blame on those who supported the cuts and thus almost certainly could not be won.[50]

The conflicting Senate and House budget plans—the former calling for social security COLA cuts and defense growth, the latter calling for full social security COLAs and defense cuts—presumably offered some room for compromise on both issues. But a compromise on social security ultimately proved unworkable, first, because the Democrats were unwilling to give up an issue that they felt could work very well for them in the 1986 elections, and second, because President Reagan, fearful of being perceived as having walked away from his social security commitment, instead walked away from the Senate budget plan.[51] Once again, the social security indexing mechanism emerged intact.

The political sensitivity of social security benefits continued to be

48. The two senators were Alfonse M. D'Amato of New York and Paula Hawkins of Florida. See Elizabeth Wehr, "Republican Budget Package Picked Apart on Senate Floor," *Congressional Quarterly Weekly Report,* vol. 43 (May 4, 1985), pp. 815–18.

49. See Elizabeth Wehr, "Budget Squeaks Through Senate Floor Vote," *Congressional Quarterly Weekly Report,* vol. 43 (May 11, 1985), pp. 871–74; and "Political Fallout from the Social Security Vote," *National Journal,* vol. 17 (August 31, 1985), p. 1932.

50. Fessler, "Bid to Rein in Social Security Faces Senate Floor Challenge," p. 531. See also Jacqueline Calmes, "Social Security Hikes Divide House Democrats," *Congressional Quarterly Weekly Report,* vol. 43 (May 11, 1985), p. 875.

51. See Jonathan Rauch, "Stalemate Threatening Budget Process as Well as Efforts to Cut the Deficit," *National Journal,* vol. 17 (July 6, 1985), pp. 1556–59; and Jacqueline Calmes, "President Fails to Unsnarl Budget Deadlock," *Congressional Quarterly Weekly Report,* vol. 43 (July 13, 1985), pp. 1355–58.

evident in the following years. When Congress considered adoption of the Gramm-Rudman-Hollings deficit reduction plan in 1985, social security COLAs were the only inflation adjustment fully protected from cuts in both the House and Senate versions of the plan. They were of course protected in the final version.

In the following year, Congress finally did away with the requirement that social security COLA adjustments not take place unless prices had risen at least 3 percent since the last inflation adjustment. In practice, the 3 percent trigger had proven to be an irresistible lure for credit claimers. Whenever it appeared that inflation might not reach the 3 percent trigger, politicians rushed to lead the effort to provide a COLA anyway. The 3 percent requirement placed potential opponents of overriding the trigger—notably the president, who could veto any bill containing it—in the impossible position of appearing to support cuts in social security. Hence their politically responsible, blame-avoiding response: jump on the bandwagon and support a one-year override of the COLA trigger. Given this set of incentives, even the administration came to see the 3 percent COLA trigger as a political headache that gave nonspecialists an opportunity for posturing while providing little savings. A permanent elimination of the trigger was passed shortly before the 1986 election.[52]

The political clout of the social security clientele was demonstrated yet again in the budget-cutting negotiations that followed the October 1987 stock market crash. Congressional and executive budget negotiators sought some form of social security COLA cut, but only if an agreement could be reached in advance to protect their parties from blame. A familiar set of obstacles prevented agreement: the elderly lobby mobilized against cuts, President Reagan was reluctant to back away from his promise that social security would not be "on the table," and Representative Pepper threatened to require a separate vote in the House on social security cuts if they were in the package. Thus before the social security proposal could really get on the table in negotiations, it was removed.[53]

Other social security indexing issues remain contentious, however. One of the most troublesome is a result of the 1977 correction of the

52. P.L. 99-509, sec. 9001.
53. See Peter T. Kilborn, "Official Tells How Social Security was Spared," *New York Times,* November 22, 1987, p. 39; and Hobart Rowen, "Cut COLAs? You Want a Fight?" *Washington Post,* December 3, 1987, p. A23. On Pepper's role, see Julie Kosterlitz, "Still Going Strong," *National Journal,* vol. 20 (January 2, 1988), pp. 13–16.

FIGURE 4-2. *Purchasing Power of the Social Security Primary Insurance Amount, 1959–87*[a]

Index, June 1975 = 100

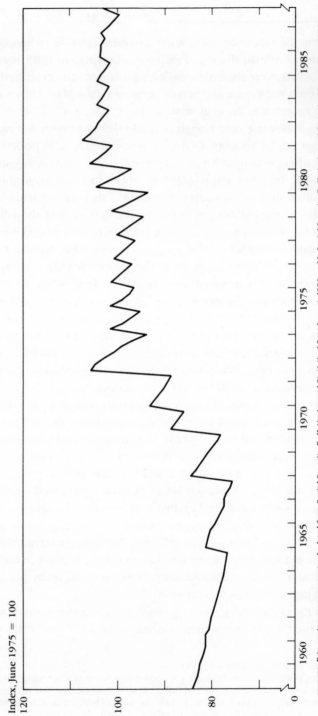

SOURCES: Primary insurance amount calculated from *Social Security Bulletin Annual Statistical Supplement, 1980*, p. 33; *Social Security Bulletin Annual Statistical Supplement, 1986*, p. 32; and *Social Security Bulletin*, vol. 50 (December 1987). p. 2. Implicit price deflator for personal consumption expenditures from U.S. Department of Commerce, Bureau of Economic Analysis, *The National Income and Product Accounts of the United States, 1929–1982* (GPO, 1986), table 7-4; *Survey of Current Business*, various issues, table 7-4; and *Economic Report of the President, 1988* (GPO, 1988), table B-3. Figures for fourth quarter of 1987 are preliminary.

a. Calculated quarterly. See text for discussion.

mechanism used to adjust workers' wage history for inflation. Most of the larger elderly lobbies view the resulting disparity between benefits for workers born before 1917 and those for workers born later (commonly, if mistakenly, referred to as the "notch") as a necessary evil to preserve the financial viability of the social security system. But some of the smaller groups—joined by some veterans' organizations (many of the "1917 generation" are World War II veterans) and even by the advice columnist "Dear Abby"—have championed increased benefits for the latter group. The issue is one with tremendous blame-generating potential, and legislators have sought to keep it off the agenda.[54] As one Ways and Means Committee staffer said, "We get 1,000 letters a week on the notch. Members are counting on Ways and Means to act as the doorkeeper. If it got on the floor, there is no way they could vote against it." As was the case with indexing itself, the "notch generation" awaits a political entrepeneur and a strategy to make use of the issue's blame-generating potential.

Consequences

A summary measure of the effects of this legislative activity, and of the indexing mechanism, on social security benefits is shown in figure 4-2. Once a worker's retirement date is located, moving to the right along the line shows trends, on a quarterly basis, in the purchasing power of that worker's retirement benefit once he or she has retired. The implicit price deflator for the personal consumption expenditure component of gross national product, which avoids the CPI's distorted estimate of housing costs, is used as a deflator. This measure excludes the effects on retirement benefits of both rising real wages of later retirees and the overcompensation caused by the faulty indexing of wage histories for retirees before 1979. The data show that retirees' social security benefits rose substantially in real terms between 1968 and 1975, with the major gain occurring in 1972.

This suggests that the 1972 indexing and benefit increase legislation had three crucial effects on social security policymaking. First, it

54. The leading congressional advocate for the "notch babies" is Representative Edward Roybal, Democrat of California, chairman of the House Select Committee on Aging. That committee has held a series of hearings on the notch under the title *Reductions in Social Security Benefit Levels: The Notch*, pts. 1-8 (GPO, 1984–87). On the problem of the notch, see Timothy Noah, "Notch Babies," *New Republic* (December 1, 1986), pp. 18–21; and the exchange of letters to the editor in *New York Times*, January 25, 1988, p. H22.

created a new set of expectations about the level of benefits—they were now to be set at an unprecedentedly high level. Second, allowing benefits to slip through inflation was no longer permissible. Much of the fiscal damage of the 1972 package could have been undone by simple acquiescence in the erosion of benefits by inflation before indexing went into effect in 1975. That had certainly been the pattern in past years. Instead, however, Congress passed additional ad hoc increases between 1972 and 1975, locking in benefits at a level near that established in 1972. These actions are certainly due in part to the extremely high inflation of that period and to the high level of conflict between the president and Congress. But the fact that Congress had already promised to protect the purchasing power of benefits undoubtedly increased pressures to provide the ad hoc increases. Politicians did not want to be seen by constituents as having broken that promise by acquiescing in a loss in purchasing power.

In the initial postindexing period, the OASI benefit remained fairly steady (although with within-year declines) at the new plateau established in 1974. The defective measurement of housing costs in the CPI pushed the real value of benefits up further in the late 1970s. The 1983 benefit "delay" lowered benefit levels slightly for current recipients. Correction of the CPI in the same year locked them in at this level.

The major benefit gains, however, were made before indexing took effect. Indeed, a third major change resulting from indexing was the virtual disappearance of general benefit changes from the social security policy agenda. Does this mean that OASI beneficiaries would have continued to fare better under a system of ad hoc benefit changes? Certainly some policymakers thought so at the time: it was a belief that indexing was the only viable protection against politically irresistible pressures for real benefit increases that led the Nixon administration and conservative Republicans to support indexing in the first place. However, post-1975 revisions in the program have been almost entirely in the direction of cutbacks. Although the cutbacks were generally minor, the evidence suggests that Republicans' fear of real benefit increases was overstated. A more plausible interpretation is that the earlier benefit expansion reflected a history and expectation of substantial real wage growth. The benefit changes of the early 1970s stretched the political and fiscal limits of the program as far as they could go, and beyond. Pressures to increase benefits slackened when it became clear that these limits had been breached. Indexing ensured that benefits would stay at these limits—or exceed them for short periods.

The postindexing changes in the social security program have been necessitated by the bursting of the program's fiscal limits, specifically the draining of the social security trust funds. Some additional savings might have been possible if there had been no indexing—probably in the form of lengthened lags between COLAs rather than permanent benefit cuts. But the strength of the social security constituency suggests that these changes would probably have been marginal in any case.

Social security benefit politics after 1983 have been characterized by maintenance of the basic indexing mechanism and by the inability of proponents of cuts even to get them on the agenda in most years. This pattern is not surprising when one considers how indexing has shifted bargaining positions and politicians' incentives. The constellation of budget guardians arrayed against real benefit increases and the precarious financial status of the social security system have been sufficient to block serious consideration of such increases. But anyone who proposes changing the indexing mechanism to limit or abolish COLAs is likely to incur enormous blame and unlikely to obtain his or her policy objectives. Thus both the indexing mechanism and the benefit base have survived intact.

Conclusions

Controversies over indexing in the social security program show that politicians are concerned with far more than reducing decision-making costs. Considerations of institutional prerogative and electoral consequence have repeatedly influenced both the timing and the substance of indexing decisions.

But the pluralism of the social security benefit and indexing battles is not the classic "iron triangle" form, with interest groups, congressional committees, and agencies working in concert to shape policy change in their own interests. In the early 1970s debates on the initial indexing of benefits, legislators were responding to what they perceived to be the wishes of a relatively diffuse but immense clientele. Policy specialists in Congress were for the most part reluctant supporters of indexing. But they were unable to control the policymaking agenda, especially after President Nixon gave his support to indexing in 1969. Policy was occasionally made over the objections of program specialists on the floor of the House. And even when this did not occur, the actions of those leaders were strongly influenced by their knowledge that if they did not lead, they would be overwhelmed by immense majorities for extremely popular proposals.

Even today, legislators—in particular the policy specialists—have not forgotten their potential credit-claiming interest in maintaining discretion over benefit increases. As one Ways and Means Committee staffer said in a 1986 interview, "There is widespread resistance to indexation among [committee] members. It takes the program out of their control, and they can't vote for benefit increases. Members react viscerally to this in private, but they would never do so publicly." In short, legislators would like to increase their credit-claiming opportunities, but the blame associated with removing social security indexing now that it is in place makes such a move politically impossible.

The social security case offers two somewhat conflicting lessons about the role of clientele groups in indexation politics. The first is that for well-organized client groups (such as the AFL-CIO), attitudes toward indexing as a procedure are inseparable from their attitude toward the benefit level being indexed. They will not favor indexing for its own sake and will oppose it so long as they believe that they can do better through ad hoc increases or if they believe it will hold them indefinitely at a low benefit level.[55] But the social security case indicates a very different lesson about large, diffuse clienteles. For these groups, perception is likely to be as important as reality. Indexing was seen by many of the elderly as being to their advantage, and that was its politically most salient attribute, regardless of whether it was true.[56] Indeed, indexing did put a stop to the benefit bidding wars that had increasingly characterized social security politics during the Nixon administration. But that is only part of why it was enacted in the first place. It was enacted largely because, as Senator Long had said of ad hoc increases, "it is almost impossible for a Senator [or representative] to explain why he did not vote for it."

It clearly would be a mistake to attempt to explain social security policymaking over the past twenty years in terms of only one of the

---

55. Of course, organized labor and the elderly were able to obtain real benefit increases before social security indexing took effect. Labor's proposal to link the indexing formula to increases in prices as well as wages was rejected, however.

56. On the combination of high public support for and low level of public information about social security, see Light, *Artful Work*, chap. 6.

policy objectives outlined earlier. But it is also clear that blame avoidance played a critical role and contributed to the adoption of social security indexing in four distinct ways. First, although the Nixon administration and conservative Republicans portrayed their support for indexing largely in good-policy terms (protecting benefit levels), their proposal was in large part a blame-avoiding one: to protect themselves and the treasury from Democratic demands for real benefit increases, using indexing to keep that issue off the agenda so they didn't have to vote directly against increases. Second, voting against indexing proved to be sufficiently difficult to explain that many legislators who might have been expected to prefer real benefit increases (and the opportunity to vote for them) instead voted for indexing in 1970—that is, they jumped on the bandwagon. Third, the about-face by leading legislative specialists after the 1970 defeat on the House floor suggests even more clearly a "jump-on-the-bandwagon" effect. Legislative specialists are expected to lead, but they are also expected to listen. If they stray too far from the views of their party's nonspecialists, they lose credibility. And if they lose credibility, they lose power.

Finally, the adoption of indexing in 1972 shows clear evidence of blame-avoiding behavior by President Nixon and conservative Republicans. The social security agenda in that year was set by bidding-war politics. Indexing was hurriedly packaged with the 20 percent benefit increase, based on the desire to make the greatest claim of aid to recipients in the period leading up to the 1972 election. The package did not undergo the usual careful scrutiny given by the Ways and Means Committee. But once Republicans and the president were forced to take a stand on the package, they felt they had to "match the bid" and support it, even though it was no longer consistent with their original policy reasons for supporting indexing.

What made social security indexing impossible for legislators to resist in the early 1970s—the simple appeal of "protecting benefits" to massive numbers of voters—now makes it politically impossible to repeal. Even if an end to indexing did not mean a decline in real benefits—and in today's budgetary climate it almost certainly would mean that—it would inevitably be perceived as such by its clientele. It would, therefore, be another politically impossible vote for a legislator to explain.

Even modest cutbacks in social security COLAs—temporary freezes or caps—have been political hot potatoes, winning passage only when there was virtually unanimous agreement that the existing provisions were distortive (as in 1977), or when an agreement had been worked out in advance through nontraditional mechanisms, so that legislators did not have to get "out in front" of their colleagues in favoring cutbacks (as in 1983). The adoption of contingent cuts in social security COLAs in 1983 also clearly shows the importance of blame-avoiding motives and strategies in indexation policymaking. Legislators and the president did not have to accept blame for immediate cuts because no such cuts were made. And if they are made in the future, the automaticity of the process again provides cover—for the proximate cause of the cuts will be the process rather than its creators.

Clearly, the symbolic power of social security COLAs has interfered with efforts to come to grips both with the system's own financing problems and with the budget deficit in general. In short, the disappearance of opportunities to claim credit for popular actions such as benefit increases has reinforced the dominance of blame-avoiding objectives in social security politics.

5

Food Stamps

The food stamp program, like social security, is a federal benefit program featuring indexed benefits. But in almost every other way, the two programs are very different. The food stamp program is financed from general revenues rather than from social insurance contributions. Its clientele is smaller: 20.9 million recipients in 1984, compared with 32.7 million beneficiaries in social security's old age and survivors insurance program. And eligibility for food stamp benefits is means-tested, unlike social security's contribution test. In fact, food stamps is the largest means-tested federal income transfer program, in both number of clientele and size of federal expenditures.

The means test for food stamps eligibility has several implications. First, a sizable minority of people who are eligible do not participate in the food stamp program, while participation is virtually universal among those eligible for social security.[1] Second, while social security recipients are likely to be perceived by themselves and others as deserving of their transfer payments, there is a strong welfare stigma attached to receiving food stamps. Third, questions of who should be eligible are likely to be much more salient for food stamps, since there is no clear boundary between income levels at which a household is or is not deserving of assistance. Finally, food stamp beneficiaries are drawn exclusively from low-income groups, rather than from the entire income range (indeed, both income limits and benefit levels are

1. Eligibility for social insurance programs is based primarily on past contributions, rather than income level. Thus the eligibility question is likely to be most important in the early years of a social insurance program. At that time, a significant portion of the working population may not meet the contribution test. The eligibility issue declines in salience as a social insurance program matures. The social security system passed that point many years ago. The eligibility issue is now important only for small subpopulations such as civil servants and military retirees (who are receiving benefits from those separate systems, but may wish to work long enough in social security-eligible employment to gain benefits from both systems), high-income retirees, and individuals who continue to work after reaching retirement age.

currently indexed for food stamps). Recipients are, therefore, likely to have relatively few political resources.

Benefits in the two programs also differ. Food stamp benefits are in the form of a scrip (rather than cash) that can be used only for food purchases. They are linked to an objective standard—a nutritionally adequate diet—rather than the loose linkage of benefits to past contributions found in social security.

There are administrative differences as well. The food stamp program is administered federally by the Department of Agriculture and locally by public welfare agencies rather than through a central administrative apparatus such as the Social Security Administration. And funding for the food stamp program requires favorable action by the congressional Appropriations committees, while social security benefits are an entitlement with permanent appropriations authority.[2]

These objective differences between the two programs contribute to an important difference in the way they are perceived. While social security is very popular, the food stamp program has an image problem. The idea of providing nutrition assistance to the needy is widely supported, but the program has been plagued by public perceptions that many recipients are undeserving and that the program is poorly run. These perceptions are especially important politically when (as in the case of food stamps) the recipient clientele has few resources and is poorly organized. In this situation, policymakers will make their decisions on a program primarily on the basis of how these decisions influence public images of them as being fair, compassionate, and fiscally responsible.

The political and administrative differences between food stamps and social security have been reflected in the way the two programs were indexed, the level of the base indexed, and their relative resistance to cutbacks once indexing mechanisms were in place. Legislative specialists attached less political value to preserving discretion over food stamp benefit increases than was the case with social security; in addition, political pressures to protect benefits from erosion by inflation were weaker. There were few political incentives to engage in a bidding war to increase benefit levels immediately before indexing, as there were in the case of social security. As a result, food stamp allotments were pegged at a level that is at best only marginally ade-

2. On the nature of entitlements, see R. Kent Weaver, "Controlling Entitlements," in John Chubb and Paul Peterson, eds., *The New Direction in American Politics* (Brookings, 1985), pp. 307–41.

quate to provide a nutritious diet. After the program was indexed, food stamps clientele—and advocates for them—had weaker resources to generate effective political blame against politicians who supported cutbacks than did social security recipients. However, program advocates did have tremendous technical expertise in the food stamp program. They were able to use this expertise to lessen the long-term effects of the cutbacks.

Political Alignments

The alignment of political forces on the food stamp program is very different from that of social security. Support for the food stamp program by its authorizing committees was ambivalent at best in the early years of the program. Rural legislators, who dominate the two Agriculture committees, were suspicious of food stamps because they believed that the program took up part of the budget Congress and the president were willing to grant to agriculture, even though it provided a limited direct return to farmers.[3] Many of these legislators—who, along with their constituents, tend to be rural conservatives—had a strong suspicion of public assistance programs and their recipients. And many, especially Republicans and southern Democrats, also feared an increasing federal presence in their states. The Agriculture committees also had very conservative leadership under much of the period under consideration here. W. R. Poage, chairman of the House committee from 1967 until his ouster by the Democratic caucus after the 1974 election, and Jesse Helms, chair of the Senate committee from 1981 until 1986, were especially strong opponents of food stamp expansion.[4]

The Agriculture committees have their own problems, however: because they are seen as defenders of special interests, they are susceptible to defeats on the floor. Thus even if most legislative specialists are

3. Reflecting this concern, the 1964 Food Stamp Act stipulated that "amounts expended under the authority of this Act shall not be considered amounts expended for the purpose of carrying out the agricultural price-support program and appropriations for the purposes of this Act shall be considered, for the purpose of budget presentations, to relate to the functions of the Government concerned with welfare" (sec. 16(d)). See also Randall B. Ripley, "Legislative Bargaining and the Food Stamp Act, 1964," in Frederick Cleaveland, ed., *Congress and Urban Problems* (Brookings, 1969), pp. 279–310, especially p. 294.

4. On the House Agriculture Committee, see Alan Ehrenhalt, "House Agriculture: New Faces, New Issues," *Congressional Quarterly Weekly Report*, vol. 33 (February 22, 1975), pp. 379–84.

suspicious of the food stamp program, they have recognized that it provides a valuable logrolling tool to gain urban support for farm bills.[5] Many specialists wish to restrain food stamp expenditures, but not to the point at which food stamps would cease to win support for a logrolling package. It might therefore be expected that specialists would oppose food stamp indexing—after all, without indexing, real benefits and eligibility fall as a result of inflation. But they may support indexing if the substantive package is attractive—that is, if it will lock in benefits at a low level and keep real expansions of benefits and eligibility off government's agenda (as was the case with House Republicans and social security indexing). This is especially true if their proposals have in the past been overridden on the floor of their chamber in favor of more generous provisions. Specialists may also trade indexing for some other concessions.

The antipathy of legislative specialists toward the food stamp program was never unanimous. Some members of the Agriculture committees—for example, Democratic Senator George McGovern, Republican Senator Robert Dole, and Democratic Representative Thomas Foley—took a very strong interest in the program in its early years. But their position was often a lonely one. Foley, for example, described his 1970 efforts to liberalize the food stamp program within the House Agriculture Committee as "a catastrophic failure. . . . The vote was always 25–2."[6] In 1968 the Senate established a Select Committee on Nutrition and Human Needs—composed in part of Agriculture Committee members but chaired by McGovern—to give an independent focus to growing concerns about hunger issues.[7]

Since the mid-1970s, antagonism toward food stamps has declined

---

5. See John Ferejohn, "Logrolling in an Institutional Context: A Case Study of Food Stamps Legislation," Hoover Institution Working Papers in Political Science no. P-85-5 (Stanford, Calif.: Hoover Institution, October 1985).

6. John K. Iglehart, "Hunger Report/Rush-hour Food Stamp Compromise Portends Fresh Quarrel in New Congress," *National Journal*, vol. 3 (January 16, 1971), p. 114. Foley's ally was Representative Allard K. Lowenstein, Democrat of New York. Similarly, conservative Senator Allen J. Ellender, Democrat of Louisiana, noted that in the 1969 debate on food stamp amendments within the Senate Agriculture Committee, "the only opposition was from the Senator from South Dakota [McGovern]." *Congressional Record* (September 24, 1969), p. 26875.

7. The committee contained members from the more liberal Committee on Labor and Public Welfare as well as the Agriculture Committee. The initiative for the select committee came from the Senate labor committee, which had begun to hold hearings on hunger and nutrition issues. The Select Nutrition Committee was abolished at the end of 1977; a Nutrition Subcommittee of the Senate Agriculture Committee was established in that year. The House Agriculture Committee's Domestic Marketing and Consumer Relations Subcommittee added "Nutrition" to its title in 1977 as well.

markedly among members of the Agriculture committees as they have become accustomed to dealing with a new clientele and more aware of the program's potential for maintaining logrolling coalitions. But tensions can resurface, especially when budgetary pressures are severe or program critics like Helms hold powerful positions.

Program advocates inside and outside the specialist committees have attempted to fashion legislation to provide more certain funding for the program and improve benefit levels and participation rates.[8] A variety of nutrition advocacy groups have also pushed for a more generous food stamp program. Although program advocates within the Agriculture committees have often seen their proposals watered down or defeated by the committees, they have appealed to, and on several occasions won, majorities in the full chamber to restore those proposals.[9]

The motivations of congressional program advocates tend to be rather different than those of legislative specialists in the social security case. Leading the fight for an ad hoc increase in food stamp benefits has only modest credit-claiming value. It may also risk incurring blame from specialist leaders. But the political pressures on food stamp advocates are usually fairly weak. Their positions on indexing benefits and eligibility are likely to reflect their good-policy concerns. If they believe that they can win acceptance for a package of benefit and eligibility standards and indexing mechanisms that will help food stamp recipients, they are likely to press for such a package. Program advocates have a difficult challenge, however: such a package is likely to conflict with the priorities of the specialist authorizing committees. In seeking to expand the program, program advocates have had to rely largely on the good-policy and vote-trading instincts of rank-and-file legislators. But many of the latter (conservatives in particular) have severe doubts about the deservingness of some of the program's clientele and are likely to defer to the legislative specialists. The strategy of these participants in the period before indexing was adopted is summarized in table 5-1.

Blame generating and blame avoiding are likely to play a fairly limited role in conflicts over the initial indexing of programs like food stamps. But the program is not without blame-generating potential, especially once indexing is in place. That potential is more complex

8. See Linda E. Demkovich, "The 'Odd Couple' Is Whipping Up a New Dish on Food Stamps," *National Journal*, vol. 9 (March 19, 1977), pp. 428–29.
9. See, for example, Gilbert Steiner, *The State of Welfare* (Brookings, 1971), p. 212.

TABLE 5-1. *Legislators' Objectives and Strategies in Indexing Food Stamp Benefits*

Player	Dominant objective	Strategy
Legislative specialists	Vote trading	Use food stamps to develop logrolling coalitions for commodity price support programs; support indexing only if it locks in benefits and eligibility at low levels
Program advocates	Good policy	Appeal to chamber majorities to liberalize Agriculture Committee proposals; support indexing if linked to benefit and eligibility liberalization
Other legislators	Good policy, vote trading	Support or oppose indexing on basis of general ideological preferences and package of which it is a part; follow cues from legislative specialists or program advocates

than in the social security case, where it almost always works in favor of indexing and against cutbacks. On many eligibility and most administrative issues (including work requirements), food stamp advocates are likely to be on the defensive: it is always possible to find cases of abuse, and policymakers do not wish to be seen as defending welfare cheaters or maladministration. Proponents of cutbacks in these areas can claim they are separating the deserving from the undeserving, a politically popular act. Food stamp program supporters are likely to have a better strategic position with respect to benefit issues, such as cuts in or elimination of COLAs. Cutbacks of this type impose highly visible losses on recipients generally perceived as deserving of assistance, and are politically unpopular.

Origins

The food stamp program, in its current form, is a relatively recent addition to the arsenal of federal benefit programs.[10] In the immediate

___

10. A federal food stamp program of significantly different design operated from 1939 to 1943. Legislative efforts to restore the program began almost immediately, led from the 1950s by Representative Leonor Kretzer Sullivan, Democrat of Missouri. The

post–World War II period, federal expenditures on nutritional assistance consisted primarily of distribution of surplus commodities purchased through federal price support programs. Recipients had a very limited choice of products, and there was no guarantee that the products distributed would be nutritionally balanced. In 1961 the Kennedy administration began a series of food stamp pilot projects; in 1964 regular statutory authority was enacted.[11] Counties could choose whether to participate in the surplus commodities or food stamp program, but could not participate in both.

In the early years of food stamps, state agencies administering the program set eligibility standards, subject to federal approval.[12] Benefit standards and purchase requirements were set by the Department of Agriculture. The food stamp benefit standard followed the "economy food plan," the least expensive of several family food budgets published by the department. Many food stamp advocates have criticized this standard as unrealistically low, citing Agriculture Department studies that only a skilled nutritionist could produce an adequate diet on that budget and that it was never intended for long-term use by families. Indeed, the economy food plan was developed simply by multiplying the low-cost food plan by four-fifths.[13] Benefits originally varied according to household size and region.[14] No allowance was or is made for the special nutritional needs of specific subgroups, such as growing teenagers.

Focusing on the benefit *standard* in isolation is very misleading, however, because individual participants, no matter how poor, were originally required to spend an amount "equivalent to their normal expenditures for food" to purchase stamps with a higher face value.

Democratic party endorsed a food stamp program in its 1956 and 1960 platforms. On the history of the food stamp program, see Steiner, *The State of Welfare*, chap. 6; and *The Food Stamp Program: History, Description, Issues and Options*, Committee Print 99-32, prepared for the Senate Committee on Agriculture, Nutrition and Forestry, 99 Cong. 1 sess. (Government Printing Office, 1985).

11. P.L. 88-525. On the 1964 act, see Ripley, "Legislative Bargaining."

12. The statute required that a state's maximum income limit be "consistent with the income standards used by the State agency in administration of its federally aided public assistance programs" (sec. 5(b)).

13. "Group Seeks to Improve Benefits in Thrift Food Stamp Program," *New York Times*, December 27, 1975, p. 37. See *Nutrition and Human Needs—1972*, Hearings before the Senate Select Committee on Nutrition and Human Needs, 92 Cong. 2 sess. (GPO, 1972),pt. 3B: *Unused Food Assistance Funds: Food Stamps; Administration Witnesses*, pp. 759–78; and Food Research and Action Center, *Food and Nutrition Issues in the Food Stamp Program* (Washington, D.C.: The Center, 1981).

14. A separate benefit schedule was published for ten southern states, reflecting ostensibly lower food costs in that region.

The difference between the purchase price and the value of the stamp allotment constituted the food stamp "bonus," or benefit *level*. Benefit levels were graded by income: poorer families paid a lesser share of their income for their food stamp allotment. The purchase requirement was intended to ensure that recipients really increased their expenditures on food rather than using their increased purchasing power for some other purpose.[15] Changing the purchase requirement offered policymakers a way to raise or lower expenditures (by changing benefit levels) without directly changing the benefit standard.

The purchase requirement also affected expenditures by discouraging many eligible persons from participating in the program. At lower income levels, even a small cash outlay was a major burden. And at the upper levels of income eligibility, the cash outlay was a much larger share of participants' cash income, but it brought a relatively small bonus and carried the stigma of using stamps for most or all food expenditures.

Toward Automatic Adjustments

The food stamp program grew rapidly in its first few years of operation. But because many eligible persons were unable to make the upfront cash outlay to purchase the stamps, participation declined drastically in most areas where food stamps supplanted commodity distribution.[16]

There were other problems as well. State and local control over eligibility standards virtually ensured geographic inequities in coverage. Many communities elected not to participate in either the food stamp or commodity distribution program or did not seek to reach all eligible participants. Moreover, the program provided a fixed authorization ceiling for the program; this funding was subject to further appropriations limits. If expenditures were projected to exceed the funding ceiling, either benefits would have to be cut or emergency legislation would have to be passed to provide additional funding.[17] Finally, the 1964 food stamp legislation made no mention of inflation

---

15. Of course, recipients could sell their food stamps for cash, but stiff criminal penalties were prescribed for doing so. Another reason for imposing the purchase requirement was that supporters believed it would lessen conservative opposition to the program by demonstrating a "self-help" attitude on the part of recipients. See Steiner, *The State of Welfare*, pp. 232–36; and *The Food Stamp Program*, pp. 36–37.

16. On the nonparticipation problem, see Steiner, *The State of Welfare*, pp. 213–32.

17. P.L. 85-525, sec. 16(b).

adjustments in benefits. The problem was not as serious as in the social security program, where benefit standards were written in statutes in nominal dollar amounts. Instead, benefit adjustments—a federal responsibility—were at the discretion of program administrators.

None of these issues were resolved in the second Johnson administration, largely because program advocates and authorizing committees were so far apart in how to address them. Indeed, the logrolling metaphor, which is often used to describe the relationship between food stamps and the commodity support programs, presents an overly benign image of interaction between the two groups in this period. It suggests cooperation between actors who are indifferent to each other's programs; mutual hostage taking between hostile interests would be more accurate, especially in the House. The House Agriculture Committee granted only short-term reauthorizations of the food stamp program, refused administration requests for open funding ceilings, and sought to require the states to share in the cost of benefits.[18] Food stamp advocates used agenda control mechanisms (such as persuading the House Rules Committee to block a bill important to commodity interests) in order to force Agriculture Committee action on the food stamp program.

The Nixon administration proposed a number of initiatives to improve food stamp benefits and coverage. Some of these were imposed administratively—for example, lower purchase requirements and a single higher national benefit standard based on an updating of the economy food plan. As a result of these reforms, monthly program costs rose more than 400 percent in one year, from under $25 million in December 1969 to $130 million in December 1970. Participation rose from 3.6 million to 9.7 million persons in the same period, and the per-person bonus almost doubled.[19] Other Nixon administration proposals, such as an end to the purchase requirement for the poorest families and stiff penalties for states that did not have food stamp or commodity distribution programs operating in all counties, required legislation.[20]

18. On this period, see *The Food Stamp Program*, pp. 23–32. On holding programs hostage, see Ferejohn, "Logrolling in an Institutional Context," p. 26.
19. *The Food Stamp Program*, p. 169. These figures include only the cost of bonus coupons.
20. On the Nixon program, see the testimony of Agriculture Secretary Clifford Hardin in *Nutrition and Human Needs*, Hearings before the Senate Select Committee on Nutrition and Human Needs, 90 Cong. 1 sess. (GPO, 1969), pt. 2: *The Nixon Administration Program*, pp. 2512–20.

The wide differences between the positions of program advocates and authorizing committee majorities took eighteen months to resolve after the Nixon administration program was introduced in Congress. These differences were institutionalized in differences between the House and Senate bills. Senate Nutrition Committee Chairman George McGovern persuaded the full Senate to substitute his committee's proposal for the one reported by the Senate Agriculture Committee. The bill passed by the Senate was much more generous than the administration's proposals. It specified that benefits be set at the level of the Department of Agriculture's low-cost food plan—the second lowest of the department's four food plans. In practice, this meant $134 a month for a family of four at the end of 1970, compared with $106 a month under the economy food plan then used as a benefit standard. The bill also required the Department of Agriculture to update this amount to reflect inflation in food prices at least once a year. In addition, the bill required the agriculture secretary to establish national income eligibility standards (also to be indexed), limited the purchase requirement to 25 percent of annual income, and provided for free stamps to low-income families.[21] It also gave the secretary the authority to operate the food stamp program directly or through nonprofit agencies in areas where local authorities were uncooperative.

The House Agriculture Committee, however, reported a bill far more conservative than the original Senate bill, including a continued ban on free stamps and a work requirement for recipients. Perhaps most important, it required the states to start sharing in the cost of food stamp bonus coupons. Its sponsors felt this would cause the states to be more conscious of costs, but food stamp advocates feared it would cause many states to withdraw from the program altogether. No mention was made of benefit indexing. Efforts to amend the committee bill on the House floor failed.[22]

21. The McGovern substitute specified that the agriculture secretary could set the income eligibility limit for a family of four at no less than $4,000 per year. A four-person family with an income below $60 per month could receive free stamps. The McGovern substitute is printed in *Congressional Record* (September 24, 1969), pp. 26888–90. For the original Senate Agriculture Committee bill, see *Food Stamp Program,* S. Rept. 91-292, 91 Cong. 1 sess. (GPO, 1969). After the House finally passed its legislation on December 16, 1970, the Senate passed the McGovern substitute again to take it to conference. *Congressional Record* (December 17, 1970), p. 42121.

22. A detailed account of the House battle is given in Iglehart, "Rush-hour Food Stamp Compromise," pp. 113–19. The Nixon administration opposed a generally more liberal substitute in the House because its own preferences lay between the House Agri-

The final legislation, predictably, was a compromise between the House and Senate-passed bills, with the House winning most of the battles. The economy food plan remained the basis for benefits, but the Senate provisions on annual indexing were included.[23] The act also included free stamps for very low-income households (under $30 per month for a family of four), a limit on the purchase requirement at 30 percent of family income, a work requirement, and an open-ended authorization for fiscal years 1972 and 1973. The secretary of agriculture was given discretion to set national eligibility requirements, rather than having them set in the statute. In the most significant victory for program advocates, the legislation did not require the states to share the costs of bonus coupons.[24]

It should not be surprising that the House won most of the battles. The program's authorization and funding were due to run out in less than a month, and program advocates wanted to avoid a program shutdown. Moreover, pro–food stamp legislators were in a weak position to influence the House-Senate agreement. Only one of their number (McGovern) was on the conference committee. And the conference debate occurred against a background of explosive program growth after the Nixon administrative changes in the program and a growing public backlash against public assistance in the wake of the administration's welfare reform proposals. These developments made many legislators, and the Nixon administration, leery of further expansion of the food stamp program.

In contrast to the social security indexing debate occurring almost simultaneously, indexing of food stamp benefits was adopted with virtually no debate in either the House or the Senate.[25] Why was indexing given so little attention? And why did legislative specialists and nonspecialists agree to sacrifice discretion? There appear to be at least

---

culture and Senate-passed bills, and it did not wish conferees to be tied to a position more liberal than the administration's.

23. Senate conferees offered to split the difference between the two benefit levels, but this was rejected by House conferees. *Congressional Record* (December 31, 1970), p. 44433.

24. P.L. 91-671. The conference report is published in *Congressional Record* (December 22, 1970), pp. 43325–27. On the conference negotiations, see Iglehart, "Rush-hour Food Stamp Compromise"; and *Congressional Record* (December 31, 1970), pp. 44430–43.

25. The Senate debate is in *Congressional Record* (September 24, 1969), pp. 26848–90, and the House debate in *Congressional Record* (December 16, 1970), pp. 41979–42035.

four reasons. First, the legal requirement for indexing was seen as simply codifying an emerging administrative practice of periodic adjustments.[26] Second, legislators did not perceive themselves to be giving up an important credit-claiming opportunity. They had never specified a specific benefit level by statute in the past, and food stamp recipients were in any case not considered a politically important clientele. Legislative specialists in particular were more concerned with commodity interests. Their major concerns were that program costs be held down and the program come up for reauthorization in 1973 at the same time as commodity programs to facilitate vote trading. They accomplished both of these objectives. The inclusion of indexing in the final bill was a relatively minor House concession to the Senate bill, allowing Senate conferees to show their adherence to the will of the Senate majority. Third, arguments over the base to be indexed did not lead to a deadlock. Program advocates, who wanted benefits at a higher level, accepted indexing without a benefit increase because it was all that they could get. They certainly did not wish to lock in a level of benefits they thought was unacceptably low, but they did want to ensure that benefits did not become even more inadequate over time, until they could fight again for higher benefits.

Fourth, and perhaps most important, there were many other issues that seemed more important at the time than how future adjustments were to be made. The House's work requirement and state cost-sharing requirements and the Senate's free stamps provisions were the most contentious parts of the bill. Indeed, the maximum allotment itself was a figure that was relevant only to the very poorest families. For others, the amount that they had to pay for stamps was at least as important. This figure determined both how many eligible families would participate and the value of the bonus. In the final legislation, the secretary of agriculture retained some discretion in setting the purchase amount.

Although food stamp advocates may have seen the 1970 benefit compromise as simply one skirmish in a long battle to expand the program, its long-term consequences were more important than they anticipated. First, the food stamp benefit standard and indexing mechanism set in 1970 has, with minor variations, remained the policy

26. Joe Richardson, "Indexing in the Food Stamp Program," in *Indexation of Federal Programs,* Committee Print, Senate Committee on the Budget, 97 Cong. 1 sess. (GPO, 1981), p. 256.

baseline since that time. The level of the maximum food stamp allotment—a very lively issue until that time—essentially disappeared
from the policy agenda thereafter. Second, the benefit indexing mechanism in the 1970 act led to an administrative (rather than statutory)
indexing of eligibility limits as well. In regulations implementing the
act, the Agriculture Department linked eligibility to a multiple of the
economy food plan level; thus it rose along with food stamp allotments.[27] Finally, indexing of food stamps established a precedent for
later indexing of other means-tested programs, generally with equally
little debate.

Expansion and Retrenchment

After passage of the 1970 amendments, indexing once again became a matter of only sporadic interest to food stamp policymakers.
In 1973 program advocates responded to huge food price increases by
demanding that food stamp allotments be indexed semiannually rather
than annually. Although the change was opposed by both of the Agriculture committees, it was imposed on them through floor amendments.[28]

During the Ford administration, most of the action on the food
stamp benefit standard took place on the administrative and judicial
fronts. In January 1975, for example, the Ford administration attempted to raise the purchase requirement for almost all food stamp
recipients to the legal limit (30 percent of income).[29] This proposal

27. The department set the income limit for participation at 3.33 times the food
stamp allotment level, which is the level at which a family spending 30 percent of its
income on stamps would see the bonus value of its stamps decline to zero. An exception
to this income limit was made for families that had been eligible under old, higher state
eligibility limits (primarily in the high-cost northeastern states) but would have lost
eligibility under the new uniform income limits. Individuals who would have had to pay
more as a result of the revised purchase requirement were also protected against cuts.
The Agriculture Department originally proposed to cut benefits for these individuals,
but retreated after protest by legislators and governors of affected states and the filing of
a lawsuit by the Food Research and Action Center. See *Nutrition and Human Needs—
1971*, Hearings before the Senate Select Committee on Nutrition and Human Needs, 92
Cong. 1 sess. (GPO, 1971), pt. 3: *Food Stamp Regulations; Congressional Record* (January 27, 1972), pp. 1473–78; and *Rodway v. U.S. Department of Agriculture*, 482 F.2d
722, 725 (D.C. Cir. 1973).
28. P.L. 93-86, sec. 3(m). See "Omnibus Farm Bill: New Target Price System Voted,"
Congressional Quarterly Almanac, vol. 29 (1973), especially pp. 306–09.
29. Individuals receiving free stamps—about 5 percent of recipients—would have
continued to do so under the administration plan. The average food stamp household

would have eroded the food stamp bonus for many recipients. It was the easiest way for the administration to cut expenditures since it did not require a statutory change in the benefit allotment. Ford's timing was terrible, however: the administration's plan was the first legislative issue considered after the 1974 "Watergate" election. Thus the Ford initiative afforded the huge new Democratic majorities in Congress and the new, pro–food stamps chairman of the House Agriculture Committee (Tom Foley, who owed his chairmanship to that Democratic majority) an opportunity both to seize the policy initiative and to castigate the administration as insensitive to the needy. The administration's proposal was overwhelmingly rejected by Congress.[30]

Later in 1975, food stamp advocates won a court declaration that the Agriculture Department's economy food plan did not meet the statutory requirement that the allotment provide "the cost of a nutritionally adequate diet." But the adjustments made by the department to form the newly rechristened "thrifty food plan" were relatively minor.[31] In 1977 Congress changed the statute to make the thrifty food plan the statutory base for benefits, effectively ending challenges to the benefit standard.[32]

The lack of movement toward a higher benefit standard in the 1970s reflects in part the relatively low priority it was given by nutrition advocates. Expenditures on the food stamp program were growing very rapidly under the current benefit standard, making legislators reluctant to increase it further. Program advocates felt that it was more important to increase participation (especially among the very poor) by providing free stamps to all recipients than it was to improve the thrifty food plan. As a nutrition advocate who joined the Carter admin-

had been paying 23 percent of its net income (that is, adjusted for deductions for expenses such as medical care), or 18 percent of its total cash income, for food stamps. See *Suspension of Food Stamp Regulations,* H. Rept. 94-2, 94 Cong. 1 sess. (GPO, 1975), pp. 2–7.

30. P.L. 94-4. The bill rejecting the president's plan passed by margins of 374–38 in the House and 76–8 in the Senate. Realizing that a veto would be futile, President Ford allowed the bill to become law without his signature. See "Congress Blocks Rise in Cost of Food Stamps," *Congressional Quarterly Weekly Report,* vol. 33 (February 8, 1975), pp. 305–08. The Ford administration proposed an even more sweeping set of administrative changes early in 1976, but implementation of the plan was blocked by a court injunction. (*The Food Stamp Program,* p. 69.)

31. "Group Seeks to Improve Benefits in Thrift Food Program," *New York Times,* December 27, 1975, p. 37.

32. P.L. 95-113. The act also changed the standard from "the cost of a nutritionally adequate diet" to "an opportunity to obtain a more nutritious diet." This destroyed the opportunity to challenge the plan based on the claim that Congress had intended that the thrifty food plan furnish an adequate diet.

istration put it, "Our major priority was ending the purchase requirement. We couldn't do both of them at the same time from a budgetary or a political viewpoint."[33]

Comprehensive food stamp reform enacted as part of the farm bill reauthorization reflected many of these priorities. The purchase requirement was abolished. Instead of paying for an allotment of greater value, recipients would henceforth simply receive the difference between the two (the bonus) in food stamps. This was expected to lead to an increase in participation, and it did: participation jumped from an average of 17.1 million in fiscal year 1977 to an average of 21.1 million in fiscal 1980.[34]

Other changes imposed by the 1977 food stamp reform act were more restrictive, however. The "benefit reduction" (equivalent to the old purchase requirement) used to calculate the food stamp bonus was raised to a flat 30 percent: thus the benefit level for many recipients declined. A new, lower income eligibility limit, linked to the poverty line as defined by the Office of Management and Budget (and thus, like the old system, indexed) was adopted at the same time.[35] And in what was potentially the greatest threat to the benefit standard, the new legislation stated that the nutritional objectives of the food stamp program would in the future be "subject to the availability of funds appropriated."[36] Thus food stamps were no longer formally an entitlement. This package was passed with relative ease; program advocates accepted eligibility and administrative restrictions as a way of deflecting criticisms that they felt were undermining congressional and popular support for the program; most of these proposals would have been difficult to defeat in any case.[37]

Food stamp expenditures continued to grow in succeeding years, and so did pressures to cut the program. Restrictive legislation was adopted in both 1979 and 1980. In the latter year, adjustments in the

33. Interview with Robert Greenstein, March 23, 1988. On development of the 1977 food stamp act, see Mary Link, "Food Stamp Program Faces Major Overhaul," *Congressional Quarterly Weekly Report*, vol. 34 (February 21, 1976), pp. 444–53.

34. *The Food Stamp Program*, p. 171.

35. A new indexed standard deduction system for exclusions from gross income was also established at this time. This deduction replaced most itemized deductions for the purpose of determining eligibility and benefit levels. Itemized deductions were retained for both dependent care and high shelter costs. The effect of the new system for most recipients was to increase their countable income. On the 1977 changes, see Richardson, "Indexing in the Food Stamp Program," pp. 257–62.

36. P.L. 95-113.

37. See "Congress Overhauls Food Stamp Program," *Congressional Quarterly Almanac*, vol. 33 (1977), p. 459.

thrifty food plan were shifted back to an annual from a semiannual basis. This change was made under pressure from the Budget committees to eliminate more frequent inflation adjustments in all programs.[38] In addition, the Agriculture Department was permitted to use a less up-to-date version of the poverty standard in setting eligibility. As a result of these changes, both eligibility and benefits lagged further behind inflation.

The major cuts in food stamps, however, came in the first Reagan administration. Not only was the new president very critical of the program, but food stamp supporters lost ground in the specialist committees as well: Tom Foley left the chairmanship of the House Agriculture Committee, and chairmanship of the Senate Agriculture Committee fell to Jesse Helms, one of the program's harshest critics.

The budget that President Reagan sent to Congress in 1981 proposed to reduce expected fiscal year 1982 food stamp expenditures by about 15 percent. Heavier cuts were proposed the following year. Senator Helms proposed even deeper cuts than the administration in both years.[39] Although the administration's proposals did not attack the thrifty food plan or the poverty income standard for eligibility directly, actual eligibility and benefit levels would have been severely affected by the administration's proposals. In 1981, for example, the administration proposed deducting the value of free school lunches from a household's food stamp allotment. The administration also proposed adding a new gross income cap for food stamp eligibility at 130 percent of the poverty line in addition to the old net income (that is, after deductions) cap of 100 percent of the poverty line. Administration proposals in 1982 included counting government energy assistance as income when determining benefits, an end to the earnings deduction that was supposed to provide a work incentive for recipients, and an increase in the rate at which a family's food stamp benefits are reduced as its income rises. Taken together, these proposals would have had a devastating effect on benefits and eligibility at all income levels.

38. *Congressional Record* (May 8, 1980), p. 10428. See also Richardson, "Indexing in the Food Stamp Program," pp. 259–61.
39. The administration's budget revisions submitted to Congress in February 1981 projected reductions of about $1.8 billion from a current services baseline for fiscal year 1982 of $12.5 billion. However, the Congressional Budget Office estimated that the cuts would save closer to $1.5 billion. The Helms proposals included a gross income eligibility limit of 115 percent of the poverty line, compared with the administration's proposal of 130 percent. See Steven V. Roberts, "Committees Settling on Reagan Cuts in Food Stamps," *New York Times*, May 7, 1981, p. B10.

Nutrition advocates were in a weak position to lower substantially the Reagan administration's expenditure reduction targets, especially since the Helms proposals made the administration's cuts seem mild by comparison. Indeed the 1981 reconciliation bill, reflecting relentless pressure from Helms, cut $200 million more from the food stamp program than the administration had originally requested. But for several reasons, program supporters were in a much better position to influence the form that those cuts took. First, nutrition advocacy groups had substantial expertise in the program: for example, Robert Greenstein, one of the key activists in the "hunger lobby," had been head of the Food and Nutrition Service under President Carter. Second, they had good working relationships with some powerful legislators, notably Senator Dole, chairman of both the Senate Agriculture Committee's Nutrition Subcommittee and the Senate Finance Committee. Third, the budget-cutting debate revolved around reaching specific short-term expenditure reduction targets set by the Reagan administration. If program advocates could meet those targets in ways that would minimize long-term cuts in the program, their alternatives were likely to attract support in the committees and on the floor.

A final advantage for nutrition advocates concerned the way that the bases are set in the two major indexed standards in the food stamp program. The poverty income guideline used to determine food stamp eligibility and the thrifty food plan used as the food stamp benefit standard are both calculated with respect to a base period set a number of years ago. Thus even if the COLA in one of these standards is delayed or cut temporarily, the standard remains intact and reverts to its original level when the cut expires. At that time, nutrition advocates need only prevent renewal of the cut. The base for inflation adjustments in social security benefits, in contrast, is simply the previous year's benefit level: the base changes every year. If a social security COLA is delayed or cut, the next year's base is lowered too, and the benefit drop is permanent unless it is legislatively reversed.

Working with Dole and Senator Patrick Leahy on the Senate Agriculture Committee, nutrition advocates developed a series of alternatives to repeated initiatives from the administration and Senator Helms to cut food stamp spending. These alternatives relied heavily on temporary trims in the thrifty food plan that would disappear in three years unless they were reenacted. Many of these initiatives were adopted in lieu of permanent cuts proposed by the administration and Helms. The

1981 reconciliation bill, for example, provided that for the next three years, the thrifty food plan was to be adjusted only every fifteen months. The farm bill passed later in 1981 delayed the first two adjustments even further, and the 1982 reconciliation bill required that for the following three fiscal years the benefit standard would be set at only 99 percent of the thrifty food plan's value, after which it would revert to 100 percent.[40] This method of reducing expenditures fit the blame-avoiding instincts of legislators, since it did not require them to directly cut the nominal value of recipients' benefits.

Temporary delays could not provide all the savings needed to meet the administration's expenditure reduction targets, however. Program advocates also had to set priorities. They chose, as they had in the 1970s, to focus on the needs of the poorest and those most at risk.[41] They gave very high priority to defeating the administration's proposal to deduct the value of free school lunches from a household's food stamp allotment. Defeating a Helms proposal to reinstitute a purchase requirement for food stamps was another high priority. Food stamp supporters won both of these battles. The administration's proposal to add a gross income cap at 130 percent of the poverty line, on the other hand, was viewed as less objectionable by many elements of the hunger lobby since it affected primarily households that were better able to provide for themselves and whose food stamp benefits were relatively low. This proposal was accepted by Congress. Congress also froze income deductions until October 1983 and reduced the earned income deduction.[42] Again, however, the basic principle of indexing and the major standards used to index were left intact.

In reducing food stamp expenditures, Congress attempted to make choices that minimized blame. When Senator David Boren proposed an amendment to exclude households with an elderly or disabled

40. The 1982 proposal originated with the Agriculture Department, which wanted to ensure that expenditure reductions actually occurred. But it was viewed by many of the nutrition groups as the best that they could get in terms of minimizing the long-term effects of cuts.

41. On the strategy and priorities of food stamp program supporters, see Steven V. Roberts, "Antihunger Lobbyists Start their Rounds," New York Times, March 11, 1981, p. B5; Roberts, "Food Stamp Backers Drafting Strategy," New York Times, March 29, 1981, p. A30; Roberts, "Congressional Battle on Food Stamps Is Joined and Already Is Half Over," New York Times, April 8, 1981, p. A25; and Roberts, "House Panel Trims Food Stamp Program Budget," New York Times, April 29, 1981, p. A24.

42. The earned income deduction had been set at 20 percent of such income. This was reduced to 18 percent in 1981. The 1985 farm bill restored the 20 percent level. P.L. 97-35, sec. 106; and P.L. 99-198, sec. 1511.

member from the new gross income eligibility limit, for example, it passed the Senate on a voice vote. Few senators wished to be seen as voting openly against the politically powerful senior citizens.[43] On the other hand, constituencies that could not generate politically effective blame suffered as a result. One blame-minimizing cutback enacted by Congress was the conversion of the food stamp program in Puerto Rico into a block grant in 1981. This allowed the authorizing committees to attack the benefit standard directly, since benefits would now be linked to a budgetary cap rather than to the thrifty food plan (a separate, lower thrifty plan allotment schedule had been used in Puerto Rico). Because Puerto Rico has no voting members in Congress, and the nutritional needs of its residents are not highly visible on the mainland, the only constraint on adoption of this plan was the concern of nonspecialists for the politically defenseless. In the policy-making climate of 1981, this was not a major limitation.

A Reagan administration proposal that could have had much more dramatic consequences for food stamp indexing went nowhere, however. The administration's 1982 call for a "New Federalism" would have transferred food stamps, aid to families with dependent children, and a number of smaller programs to the states, along with some revenues to pay for them; in exchange, the federal government would have taken over complete financing of medicaid. Food stamp advocates charged that this could lead to the gutting of food stamps; certainly the state experience in indexing AFDC benefits—virtually none of them do so—did not bode well for the fate of indexed food stamp benefits in a defederalized program. But the administration omitted food stamps from the list of programs to be transferred in its revised proposal, which was never submitted to Congress in any case.

By 1983 the Reagan administration's efforts to cut food stamp spending were no longer able to command congressional majorities. Most of the changes that have taken place since then have been expansionist. In 1984 Congress responded to increasing reports of hunger and malnutrition by restoring the full value of the thrifty food plan eleven months earlier than provided by existing legislation. The 1985 farm bill rejected most of the administration's initiatives. Income deductions were liberalized, the assets limit on eligibility was raised but not indexed, and the earned income deduction was restored to its

43. See *Congressional Record* (June 10, 1981), pp. 11967–71.

1981 level. Moreover, the food stamp program was one of the first programs to be excluded from automatic cutbacks under the Gramm-Rudman-Hollings deficit reduction act.

Consequences

The food stamp benefit standard has been quite stable since it was indexed to the thrifty food plan. There have been COLA delays and reductions under the Reagan administration, but both the base itself and the principle of indexing have proven to be quite resilient.

A comparison of changes in food stamp benefits with those in other federally funded programs for the poor shows very clearly the importance of being indexed. Figure 5-1 shows changes in benefit standards for food stamps, supplemental security income, and the social security minimum benefit in constant dollars over the period from 1975 to 1987. All three of these benefit standards are indexed. Also shown are trends in the nonindexed AFDC maximum payment in three categories of states: the ten states with the highest benefit level at the beginning of the period, the ten median states, and the ten states with the lowest benefit level in 1975.

The figure shows that the indexed means-tested programs have not been untouched. The food stamp program, in addition to the COLA delays and reductions shown here, has endured more targeted cutbacks. The OASI minimum benefit has been eliminated for most new recipients, but indexing was retained for earlier retirees.[44] The real value of the supplemental security income benefit standard actually rose slightly in this period due to overcompensation for inflation in the CPI and an ad hoc benefit increase in 1983. In general, however, benefit indexing appears to have inhibited changes in real benefits in either an upward or a downward direction. The amount of change in indexed program standards has certainly been very modest in comparison with those in the unindexed AFDC program. The AFDC benefit trend was similar in each category of states: a substantial decline from 1975

44. For retirees who reached age 62 before 1979, the minimum benefit level is fully indexed, reaching a level of $204.50 in 1987. (It is, however, subject to reduction if claimed before age 65.) Legislation enacted in 1977 froze the initial minimum benefit for all retirees who reached age 62 after 1978 at the level existing at the beginning of 1979 ($122). However, this initial benefit is adjusted for inflation after a recipient reaches age 65. For almost all retirees who reach age 62 after 1981, the minimum benefit was eliminated entirely, although a special minimum benefit remained in effect for retirees who worked for many years at low earnings levels.

FIGURE 5-1. *Changes in Selected Federal Benefit Standards, 1975–87*

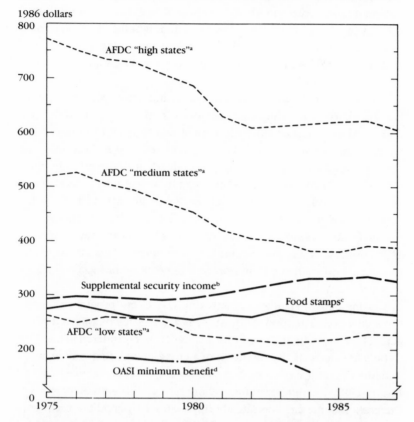

1986 dollars

SOURCES: AFDC payment levels for 1975–77 from U.S. Department of Health, Education and Welfare, Social and Rehabilitation Service (later Social Security Administration), *Aid to Families with Dependent Children,* various issues; for 1978–80, U.S. Department of Health, Education and Welfare (later Department of Health and Human Services), Social Security Administration, *AFDC Standards for Basic Needs,* various issues; for 1981, U.S. Department of Health and Human Services, *Quarterly Public Assistance Statistics,* April–June 1981, tables 18, 20; for 1982, unpublished Department of Health and Human Services data; and for 1983–87, House Committee on Ways and Means, *Background Material and Data on Programs Within the Jurisdiction of the Committee on Ways and Means,* various issues. Supplemental security income and OASI minimum benefit data from U.S. Department of Health and Human Services, Social Security Administration, *Social Security Bulletin Annual Statistical Supplement, 1986,* pp. 35, 45. Data for food stamp allotments for 1975–85 from *The Food Stamp Program: Description, Issues and Options,* Senate Print 99-32, Senate Committee on Agriculture, Nutrition and Forestry, 99 Cong. 1 sess. (Government Printing Office, 1985), pp. 164–65, and for later years from unpublished Department of Agriculture data. Data for implicit price deflator for personal consumption expenditure component of GNP from U.S. Department of Commerce, Bureau of Economic Analysis, *The National Income and Product Accounts of the United States, 1929–82* (GPO, 1986), table 7-4, and *Survey of Current Business,* table 7-4, various issues. Data for at-home food component of the CPI from *Economic Report of the President, 1988,* p. 314.

a. Maximum payment amount for a family of four. Unweighted averages for payment levels in ten states within category. Data are for July through 1982 and for January thereafter. Where payment levels differ within a state, payment levels are for highest in that state, except for New York, where they are for New York City, and Michigan, where they are for Detroit. Data are adjusted by the implicit price deflator for the personal consumption expenditure component of GNP for the appropriate quarter of the year.

b. The benefit for an individual with no countable income who is living in his or her own household. Rate is average monthly benefit for calendar year, weighted by number of months during calendar year that each rate was in effect. Data are adjusted by the annual figure for the implicit price deflator for the personal consumption expenditure component of GNP.

c. The maximum bonus value for a family of four, weighted by number of months during calendar year that each rate was in effect. Data are adjusted by the annual figure for the at-home food component of the CPI.

d. The amount payable at the time of retirement to an individual retiring at age 65 during year. Amounts for 1982–84 are based on transitional guarantee computation from 1978 primary insurance amount table. Data are adjusted by the annual figure for the implicit price deflator for the personal consumption expenditure component of GNP.

through the early 1980s, with a leveling off thereafter. This divergence between food stamp and AFDC benefit standards has occurred despite the fact that the two programs have a common political liability: many adult recipients in both of these programs (and unlike those in social security and SSI) are considered able-bodied, and thus are expected to be in the work force.

The shift in bargaining that indexing brings about almost certainly explains part of the difference between food stamp and AFDC outcomes. AFDC program supporters must win support from state legislators to secure any nominal benefit increases—even those less than the rate of inflation. Food stamp program advocates need only block cutbacks to keep benefit standards steady in real terms. Food stamp program advocates are in a much better position than their AFDC counterparts at the state level to use blame-generating strategies to defend benefit standards. It is always easiest to accuse your opponents of callousness when they support cuts in current benefits: in AFDC, this occurs only when cuts in *nominal* benefits are proposed—a fairly unusual event.

Cutting benefit standards is only one way to cut program expenditures, however. The food stamp story is a bit more complicated when actual benefit levels and eligibility standards are considered in addition to benefit standards. The addition of a gross income limit and changes in deductions allowed some cuts in both eligibility and actual benefits. But by 1981 the number of food stamp households with incomes over the gross income cap was already tiny—about 1 percent of recipients by some estimates. And most of the benefit losses were recouped by 1985.[45] This suggests that indexing did play an important role by preserving the real value of program standards so that they could be restored when the political fortunes of program advocates improved.

Finally, it should be noted that indexing food stamps also changed the nutrition policy agenda. Nutrition advocates realized that winning a food stamp benefit base more generous than the thrifty food plan would be extremely difficult, and they could not make other nutrition improvements at the same time. They concentrated much of their efforts in the 1970s on incremental changes in food stamps and on expanding other nutrition programs aimed at more specific clienteles and needs—for example, the special supplementary feeding program

45. U.S. Department of Agriculture, Food and Nutrition Service, *The Effects of Legislative Changes in 1981 and 1982 on the Food Stamp Program* (Washington, D.C.: Urban Institute for the Department of Agriculture, 1985), vol. 1, chaps. 2, 3.

for women, infants and children (WIC). Because benefits in these programs are not deducted from food stamp allotments, some recipients attained real benefit increases. Food stamp program critics, including the Reagan administration, have tried to change food stamp legislation to make such deductions. This is a blame-minimizing technique to cut nutrition expenditures without having to cut food stamp benefit standards explicitly. But supporters of nutrition programs have to date been successful in beating back these efforts.

Conclusions

Food stamps were the first means-tested income transfer program to be indexed. Indeed, food stamp allotments were indexed even before benefits in the contributory social security program, but for very different reasons. Food stamps were indexed because program advocates (in this case a distinct group from legislative specialists) thought that it would be good policy to protect benefits from erosion; legislative specialists and nonspecialists acquiesced because they saw few political benefits in maintaining discretion.

Changes in indexing bases and mechanisms are only a small part of the food stamp policy change that has occurred since 1971. A complete account would give much more attention to efforts to control fraud and abuse, limitations on eligibility, tightening of the nonindexed assets test, changes in entitlement status, and the stiffening of work requirements (at least in theory). But it is significant that serious consideration was never given to scrapping indexing of either the benefit standard or eligibility standards, despite enormous pressures for cutbacks from the Office of Management and Budget in the Reagan years and an often half-hearted "defense" of the program by the Senate Agriculture Committee. There certainly was trimming and delay of automatic adjustments, but outright elimination of indexing never made it to the agenda. Nor did Congress use its appropriations authority to force a cut in food stamp benefit levels, as it could have done after 1977; instead it repeatedly bailed the program out when funds ran short. Food stamps were also exempted from Gramm-Rudman-Hollings cutbacks.

Why has the scope of conflict over food stamps been so circumscribed, given the strong position of the program's critics and the relative political weakness of its clientele? One part of the answer is that advocates of significant expansion and contraction in the program have lacked room to maneuver in recent years. More generous bases for food stamps are unlikely to be adopted because that would serve the interests of neither budget guardians nor legislative specialists who are concerned with commodity interests. Moreover, the United States is not a society whose citizens have ever believed that "coddling" the poor is a good idea.

The potential for drastic cutbacks is limited as well. Legislative specialists know that if they propose major cuts in food stamps, their bill may be defeated on the floor, or urban legislators may retaliate on commodity issues. And some legislative specialists have developed close ties with nutrition advocates, drawing on the advocates' expertise to propose alternatives that were politically attractive and maintained the structure of the program. This powerful alliance has not been able to control the policy agenda in the Reagan era, but it has been able to compensate substantially for the political weakness of the program's clientele.

In making cuts, critics of the program have had the most success in areas where a defense of existing policies may generate blame (for example, stamps for strikers or college students). They have generally seen direct assaults on the base and indexing mechanism used for the food stamp benefit standard as an unprofitable strategy, and such efforts have had little success. Even the eligibility standard has generally been attacked indirectly—for example, by adding a gross income test to a net income test and by tightening deductions. These policy changes offer substantial savings, but limited visibility.

Part of the reason for the relative sturdiness of both the income and benefit standards lies with the indexes themselves. Both the thrifty food plan (and its predecessor) and the OMB poverty line are widely perceived not as artificial constructs but as objective minimums for an acceptable existence. This attribute makes them easier for program advocates to defend and harder for program critics to attack. Neither legislators nor the administration wish to be seen as having done away with nutritionally adequate diets for the truly needy. If policymakers support abandonment of these criteria, or clear violation of them, future opponents may criticize them as lacking compassion or a sense of fairness. Moreover, these program bases are more objective than those for social security in one important sense: they are calculated from a long-standing base, rather than one that changes annually.

The less visible the losses, the less likely they are to lead to blame, and the more likely are program critics to win approval for them. Thus stretching out the period between benefit adjustments, which imposes a real income loss but not a more visible nominal one, is more likely to win approval than a short-term cut in nominal benefits or abandonment of the benefit standard. Similarly, legislators have been unwilling to permit funding shortfalls to lead to a cut in benefits at the end of the fiscal year, because such a cut would be so visible; it would also reflect poorly on them for setting up a program and then refusing to fund it.

6

Congressional Pay

Decisions on congressional pay are different in several ways from the indexed programs examined in previous chapters. Most obviously, congressional pay is a payment for a service rather than a transfer payment. And an annual process of adjusting congressional pay for inflation coexists with a statutory process to reconsider the pay base every four years. But congressional pay also differs in the pressures that are brought to bear on policymakers, especially those relating to blame. In social security, for example, there were substantial credit-claiming opportunities until the onset of budgetary stress. Blame-avoiding pressures on policymakers were almost exclusively in favor of instituting and maintaining indexing. These pressures were of the "jump-on-the-bandwagon" and "stop me before I kill again" types. There was little public opposition to benefit increases that at least kept up with inflation. Policy specialists saw potential credit-claiming opportunities in maintaining discretion over benefits, however, and they attempted to control agendas to achieve that end. Once indexing was adopted for social security, the question of whether automatic adjustments should be continued almost disappeared from the policy agenda because the political costs of raising that issue were seen as too high.

None of these statements holds true for congressional pay increases, largely because the pressures to avoid blame are very different. Pay hikes for Congress are very unpopular; support for them may earn a legislator credit with his or her colleagues,[1] but it is unlikely to do so with voters. Making the pay adjustment process more automatic stems from a desire to pass the buck on salary increases so that legislators do not have to vote in favor of them. But voters are also suspicious of

---

1. There is some evidence that votes against pay increases prompt retribution, or at least threats of it, when legislators seek projects for their districts and more favorable committee assignments. See Ward Sinclair, "Last Hurrahs and Closed Cases," *Washington Post*, December 17, 1982, p. A6.

efforts by legislators to insulate themselves from the effects of inflation. Challengers to congressional incumbents provide a built-in opposition to either ad hoc or automatic congressional pay hikes. As Senator Robert Dole put it, "The difficulty with pay raises in the Senate is that one-third of its senators are millionaires, one-third are statesmen and the other third are cowards."[2] Because there is political mileage to be gained from challenging pay increases, enactment of an automatic pay adjustment process has not been sufficient to keep the pay issue off the legislative agenda or to keep pay increases from being overturned.

The congressional pay process might seem at the outset to be both an anomalous and an inconsequential case of indexing. But in fact it is neither. Congressional pay, although an extreme case, can reveal much about the political dynamics of programs in which Congress is motivated to index by buck-passing considerations. And congressional pay has important consequences for government because pay for federal judges and senior executives is linked—essentially indexed—to legislators' pay. Thus if legislators are afraid to maintain their own real pay in the face of inflation, they may also limit the ability of the other two branches to attract and retain quality personnel in leadership positions.

The Political Dynamics of Pay

There is perhaps no single issue where the personal and policy interests of legislators come into more direct conflict with their political interests than that of congressional pay. On the one hand, legislators are pushed by the high cost of maintaining two homes and commuting to and from their constituencies. Most of them could earn higher salaries by leaving public service, and they may wish to assure that people of the highest caliber do not leave Congress for economic reasons. On the other hand, they are aware that raising their own pay has virtually no supportive constituency among voters: senators and representatives still make more than four times what the average American worker does. The congressional pay issue shares an important political attribute with compiling a good record of attending roll call votes: it is a simple (or simplistic) indicator to voters of whether their representative seems to be pursuing constituents' interests or the legislator's

2. Quoted in "Senate Kills Administration's Executive Pay Plan," *Congressional Quarterly Weekly Report,* vol. 32 (March 9, 1974), p. 637.

personal interests. As Senator Alan Simpson noted, "I have not heard from a single constituent who thinks our pay should be raised, but I have heard from a very vigorous—and vocal—crew who think rather strongly and clearly that it should not."[3]

It is not surprising, therefore, that legislators' voting records on congressional salary increases have become a favorite theme of "negative" media campaigns by challengers. Liberal Democrats are the most likely targets of such campaigns, but they are not the only ones. In his 1986 reelection campaign, Senator Jeremiah Denton, Republican of Alabama, one of the most conservative members of the Senate, was plagued by television advertisements by his Democratic challenger showing dollars being transferred from a pile labeled "social security" to one labeled "Denton's pay raise" (Denton had, according to the ads, voted both to cut social security and to raise congressional pay).[4] Denton lost a very close race.

The substantial risk of blame posed by a vote in favor of congressional pay increases gives legislators a strong incentive to develop a pay adjustment process that does not force them to take a public stand in favor of increases or that minimizes the political costs of such a stand. There are several ways to do this.

One option is to pass the buck for making the decision to someone else, removing it from Congress's own agenda. A related option is to make the process fully automatic, with adjustments based on some index (such as the CPI) or changes in some other program (such as civil service pay).[5]

A third option is to "bundle" congressional pay hikes with other salary increases (such as those of the judiciary and senior officials in the executive branch) so that the congressional component is a less visible share of the whole. This obfuscates the issue and, if equal percentage increases are given in all parts of the package, also helps to redefine it as one of pay equity. An extension of this strategy is to develop a statutory or informal linkage between congressional salaries and those in other branches. Because federal judges and senior government officials often have very high-paying career options in the

3. *Congressional Record,* daily edition (January 29, 1987), p. S1365.

4. Sidney Blumenthal, "Senator Denton's Margin Being Driven Down," *Washington Post,* October 30, 1986, p. A6.

5. For the many legislators who support congressional pay increases on grounds of good policy as well as personal interest, keeping the issue off the agenda can also be seen as an example of the "stop me before I kill again" strategy: it allows them to attain policy preferences that conflict with political needs.

private sector, the need to maintain pay comparability with nongovernmental employees provides an additional argument for pay increases. This argument may be less credible when made for legislators alone, because they are commonly seen as deriving substantial "psychic income" from holding office.[6]

A fourth option is to increase congressional incomes through channels other than that of direct pay increases—for example, by providing perquisites or by weakening limits on outside income such as honoraria. Allowing legislators to earn additional outside income cannot furnish a complete solution to the congressional pay dilemma, however. Between legislative duties in Washington and the need to return to the home district to mend political fences, being a representative or senator is more than a full-time job. In addition, many legislators do not like to take honoraria from interest groups and corporations, who are most able to afford them. Taking honoraria, like taking political contributions from political action committees (PACs), conveys the image that the legislator may have been "bought."[7] Finally, earning honoraria is an option members do not share equally. Most senators have an opportunity to make substantial amounts of money through speaking fees. But only about 20 percent of House members (generally members of the leadership, committee chairmen, and members of the tax-writing Ways and Means Committee) have similar opportunities, because representatives are less well known and have less individual power.[8]

A final option is to manipulate the schedule for considering pay increases. To minimize political costs, pay votes should be scheduled as far ahead of the next election as possible. Lame-duck sessions—those held after an election but before the new Congress takes office—are an especially propitious time to consider pay increases. Members

---

6. See, for example, *The Report of the Commission on Executive, Legislative and Judicial Salaries* (Government Printing Office, December 1976). (Hereafter Peterson Commission Report.)

7. See Burt Solomon, "Bite-Sized Favors," *National Journal*, vol. 18 (October 11, 1986), pp. 2418–22.

8. In 1985 sixty-five senators retained more than $20,000 in speaking fees. Only ninety-four House members earned that much, up from seventy-two in the previous year (the number retaining that amount was slightly lower because some legislators give most or all of their earnings to charity). See Janet Hook, "House Reverses Itself on Outside Income Lid," *Congressional Quarterly Weekly Report*, vol. 44 (April 26, 1986), pp. 914–15; Hook, "Leaders, Finance Members Top Honoraria List," *Congressional Quarterly Weekly Report*, vol. 44 (May 24, 1986), pp. 1169–70; and Hook, "Ways and Means Members Top Honoraria List," *Congressional Quarterly Weekly Report*, vol. 44 (May 31, 1986), p. 1239.

who are retiring or have been defeated for reelection have no need to avoid blame by voting against a pay increase; they can vote their good-policy interests.[9]

In recent years, legislators have tried each of these options, singly and in combination, knowing that once the congressional pay issue gets on the agenda and they are forced to take a stand, many of their number will have to jump on the bandwagon and oppose salary increases, even those that just keep up with inflation. Additional techniques, such as "surprise attacks"—introducing votes to increase congressional compensation without warning or explanation to potential foes—have also been used to bolster the chances of making these options work.

These efforts to keep legislative pay increases off the agenda or limit their visibility have enjoyed only limited success, however. To understand why this is so, it is important to recognize that what is in the collective interests of legislators is not necessarily in all of their individual interests. Opposing congressional pay increases provides an irresistible lure for many legislators. Many conservatives and populists, in particular, are motivated by genuine ideological and policy concerns, such as a belief that legislators should not be increasing their own pay in a period of huge deficits. The pay issue is also a perfect opportunity for these legislators to claim credit for taking (and perhaps leading the fight for) a politically popular position, while casting blame on others. (This is not to say that moderate and liberal legislators will necessarily favor higher congressional pay, only that they have weaker ideological reasons to oppose it on principle.) Moreover, decentralization of power in Congress has limited the ability of the in-

9. Some nonreturning legislators may also be able to vote their personal interests by supporting congressional pay increases. These members may benefit not only by having higher pay in their last year or term in office, but also by receiving higher long-term pension benefits. Congressional pensions are based on the legislator's three highest consecutive years of congressional salary. The pension is 2.5 percent of that average salary for each year of congressional service, with a cap of 80 percent of their final congressional salary (annual cost-of-living adjustments are made once former members begin drawing the pension). Thus raising their final year's salary increases their pension benefit. In practice, however, this personal interest is limited to members who know early in their final term or session (as a result of either voluntary retirement or defeat in a primary) that they will not be returning. Members serving in lame-duck sessions could in theory vote themselves retroactive pay increases that would raise both their current salary and their future pension benefits. But salary votes scheduled for lame-duck sessions are generally not retroactive, and thus have little if any direct effect on these retirees. A vote for a pay increase may also ingratiate retiring members who plan to stay in Washington as lobbyists with their soon-to-be-former colleagues.

TABLE 6-1. *Legislators' Objectives and Strategies in Indexing Congressional Pay*

Player	Dominant objective	Strategy
Congressional conservatives	Good policy, blame generating, credit claiming	Force pay issue onto the agenda, using threat of blame to compel colleagues to vote against pay increases; try to make pay adjustment process less automatic
Lame-duck legislators	Good policy	Vote for pay increases
All other legislators	Blame avoiding	Allow pay increases to take effect without open votes by passing the buck to an automatic adjustment process; defect to oppose increases if an open vote takes place

stitution's central leaders and its specialists (the authorizing committees) to control and limit congressional agendas, magnifying the opportunities for these political entrepeneurs to create "bandwagon effects." The position of each of these players is outlined in table 6-1.

Conflict between these forces has assured that the pay issue and procedures to deal with it have had a recurrent place on the congressional agenda.

Adjusting Congressional Pay

Voting to raise their own salaries has always been a politically painful and awkward process for legislators. Indeed, several of the Founding Fathers suggested at the Constitutional Convention that in order to avoid the "seeming impropriety" of senators and representatives voting on their own pay, salaries should be set in terms of the average price of a specific number of bushels of wheat or some other commodity.[10] This proposal represented a crude form of indexing (one which,

10. Louis Fisher, "History of Pay Adjustments for Members of Congress," in Arnold R. Weber and Robert W. Hartman, eds., *The Rewards of Public Service: Compensating Top Federal Officials* (Brookings, 1980), pp. 26–27, 51.

given the decline in the relative price of wheat over the past 200 years, would have left legislators very underpaid indeed today). In the absence of automatic pay adjustment mechanisms, salary increases have been subject to open and frequent congressional debates.

The first major step toward a more automatic process of changing pay was enacted in 1967. The Postal Revenue and Salary Act of that year required establishment of a commission every four years to give the president recommendations about pay increases for Congress, the judiciary, and executive schedule employees (the cabinet and higher-level executive branch employees).[11] The president could then modify those proposals before sending them to Congress in his budget message. The president's proposal was to go into effect automatically unless Congress enacted an alternative pay package or one house of Congress voted to disapprove all or part of the president's plan. While this mechanism did not represent formal indexing, it did give proponents of pay increases a strategic advantage: all they had to do for the pay hike to go into effect was prevent adoption of a resolution of disapproval.

The first quadrennial commission's report was issued just after the 1968 election. After being trimmed by the president, the pay hike proposal managed to survive in Congress—in part because the House Rules Committee did not allow any resolutions of disapproval to reach the House floor.

The 1969 salary increases also introduced an explicit linkage between executive, legislative, and congressional pay. Congressional salaries were set equal to those of circuit court judges and executive level II (deputy secretary) officials. This linkage strategy had some dangerous implications, however. If Congress was unwilling to increase its own pay, it was likely to constrain executive and judicial salaries as well, making it difficult to attract and hold the best individuals to these posts. The linkage can also affect the pay of higher civil servants, because civil service pay is capped by statute at that of the lowest level of the executive schedule (which includes cabinet secretaries down to bureau chiefs). If executive schedule salaries do not increase, more

11. P.L. 90-206, December 16, 1967. On development of this statute, see Roger H. Davidson, "The Politics of Executive, Legislative, and Judicial Compensation," in Weber and Hartman, eds., *The Rewards of Public Service,* pp. 76–78. Three members of the quadrennial commision, including its chairman, are appointed by the president, and two each by the chief justice of the Supreme Court, Speaker of the House of Representatives, and president of the Senate.

and more civil servants at the top of the salary schedule will eventually bump up against the ceiling. This in turn creates problems of morale and retention.

Another shortcoming of the quadrennial commission approach quickly became apparent. The four-year lag between commission recommendations would, in a period of rapid inflation, lead to a substantial real income loss over that period. Huge percentage raises would thus be required to restore real earnings. But big percentage increases are bad for public relations, making legislators reluctant to approve the commissions' reports.[12] Moreover, because President Nixon delayed appointing the second quadrennial commission, pay recommendations were considered by Congress early in the election year of 1974 rather than (as in 1969) the January after an election. The commission's report also coincided with the Watergate scandal, which undermined public confidence in government, making legislators even more timid about taking actions that appeared to be self-serving. It was overwhelmingly rejected by the Senate.[13]

To deal with this problem of long time lags between adjustments, Congress narrowly adopted a formal indexing linkage in the Executive Salary Cost-of-Living Adjustment Act of 1975.[14] At this time Congress had not had a pay increase since 1969. The act tied congressional pay increases to the average increase in general schedule (civil service) employee pay under the annual "comparability" pay process. The quadrennial commission procedure was retained for more substantial adjustments in congressional, executive, and judicial pay every four years. As with the quadrennial commission recommendations, annual cost-of-living pay increases would occur automatically if Congress did not vote to reject them. And there was no requirement that Congress vote on these annual increases at all. But opponents of pay raises retained an opportunity to block cost-of-living increases: money for congressional pay still had to be appropriated, and the annual legislative branch appropriations bill gave opponents a chance to force a separate roll call vote on rejecting any increases. The timing of congressional consideration of appropriations bills—usually in the

12. The second quadrennial commission proposed that commissions be appointed every two years rather than every four, but this proposal was rejected by Congress.
13. Davidson, "The Politics of Executive, Legislative, and Judicial Compensation," pp. 78–79.
14. P.L. 94-82.

late summer or early fall—gave another advantage to pay raise opponents, especially during election years.

Annual cost-of-living pay increases for Congress have political problems of their own, moreover: why should legislators receive automatic pay protection when most American workers do not? This was a question that opponents of the process asked repeatedly, and it was a politically difficult question to answer. As was the case with the quadrennial process, legislators felt compelled to reject their second pay increase under the new cost-of-living procedure (in September 1976, one month before an election) after accepting the first. This was a relatively painless vote in financial terms, for a quadrennial report was due in just a few months, and that process presumably offered an opportunity for a much more substantial pay increase.[15] But the 1976 vote proved to be a trendsetter: Congress rejected all but one cost-of-living increase through 1981. The one exception, effective for fiscal year 1980, was accepted only after a titanic congressional battle in 1979. And even that increase was cut substantially below what legislators were entitled to by statute.[16]

The quadrennial pay process was faring little better. In 1977 Congress approved a major pay increase recommended by the third quadrennial commission, but only through the use of very strong agenda control tactics in both chambers to avoid a direct roll call vote on the issue.[17] In recompense for the pay hike, each house of Congress

15. The 1976 legislation turning down the fiscal year 1977 cost-of-living pay increase specifically allowed pay increases pursuant to the forthcoming quadrennial pay process (P.L. 94-440, title II). Because Congress in 1976 simply prevented appropriations from being used for a pay increase rather than rescinding the higher rate, the legal pay limit remained at the higher level. As a result, the next year's cost-of-living pay increase would be calculated from that higher level. On this period, see Davidson, "The Politics of Executive, Legislative, and Judicial Compensation," pp. 80–82; "Pay Raise Cut from Legislative Funds Bill," *Congressional Quarterly Almanac*, vol. 32 (1976), pp. 805–13; and the Peterson Commission Report.

16. Under rules for the cost-of-living increase, legislators were entitled to take a 12.9 percent increase, representing 7 percent for the current year plus 5.5 percent for the pay hike they had turned down in 1978 and interest on the latter. They ended up taking only the 5.5 percent increase. This pay raise passed the House by a vote of only 208–203. It survived in the Senate by only one vote—43–42—and only because one senator switched his vote. See Marjorie Hunter, "House Rejects $4,025 Pay Increase After Approving It Off the Record," *New York Times*, September 20, 1979, p. 1; Hunter, "House Votes Bill Giving Congress a Raise of 5.5%," *New York Times*, September 26, 1979, p. 1; Hunter, "Compromise Is Voted on a Key Money Bill; Senate Accepts Raise," *New York Times*, October 13, 1979, p. 1; and Brigette Rouson, "Abortion, Pay Truce Frees Funding Bill," *Congressional Quarterly Weekly Report*, vol. 37 (October 13, 1979), p. 2260.

17. The Senate did vote to table an amendment that would have killed the pay raise. Senator James Allen, Democrat of Alabama, tried to attach this amendment to an unre-

adopted new ethics codes limiting members' outside earned income to 15 percent of their congressional salary.[18] The quadrennial commission had urged such limits as the "price" for a salary increase. As Roger Davidson has argued, the new ethics codes "reinforced the concept of the full-time legislator. By curtailing outside income and shutting off methods of 'cashing out' office accounts for personal use, the codes also make it more difficult for legislators to raise their allowances in lieu of pay. More than ever, legislators will depend on the pay adjustment process for their livelihood."[19]

In addition to the ethics code, Congress also adopted a new procedure that would make it substantially harder to accept quadrennial pay increases in the future. Henceforth, both houses of Congress would have to hold separate roll call votes on each of the president's pay recommendations for legislators, executive schedule employees (including cabinet members), and judges. An affirmative vote by each house was required for the pay increase to go into effect. No vote was required for annual cost-of-living increases, however.[20]

The new procedure for quadrennial pay increases altered significantly the relative bargaining positions of proponents and opponents of those increases. First, pay increases were guaranteed a place on the agenda. No longer could an increase be adopted simply by preventing a floor vote on the issue. The requirement that a majority of both houses had to go on the record as backing the increase was much stiffer than the old rule, when neither house had to. And members of Congress could no longer argue that it was necessary to increase their

lated bill. Opponents of the quadrennial pay increase did eventually force legislators to take a direct vote on rolling back the pay increase, but not until after it had already gone into effect. "Congress Votes Controversial Pay Raise," *Congressional Quarterly Almanac,* vol. 33 (1977), pp. 751–53.

18. These limits were not to go into effect until 1979. In addition to the limits on outside earnings contained in the new ethics codes, legislators were subject to a statutory ceiling for all government employees of $25,000 in honoraria income.

19. Davidson, "The Politics of Executive, Legislative, and Judicial Compensation," pp. 84–85.

20. Late in 1977, the House Democratic leadership tried to win passage of a bill that would have prevented opponents of pay increases from getting a second vote on quadrennial pay increases once Congress had voted to accept them and would have made challenges to annual cost-of-living pay increases through amendments to appropriations bills much more difficult. In exchange, all pay increases would be deferred to the Congress after the one that had voted for, or acquiesced in, those increases. However, since the bill was brought up under an unusual rule to prevent amendments, conservative Republicans were able to kill it through a procedural maneuver. See *Congressional Record* (November 1, 1977), pp. 36309–15.

own pay in order to increase that of judges and government executives. However it could—and did—continue to reject pay increases for the other branches when it rejected its own.

Real pay fell again following the 1977 pay increase, as Congress rejected cost-of-living pay increases. Legislators sought new ways to increase their income and make the pay adjustment process more automatic. In 1979, only two months after ethics codes limitations on outside income took effect, senators voted to delay the application of those rules to themselves for four years. A statutory limit on honoraria income for all government employees remained in effect, but that limit was repealed in 1981.[21] Later in 1981, House members raised the limits on their outside income from 15 to 30 percent of their congressional salary—but only by taking their opponents off guard and avoiding a direct roll call vote.[22]

Legislators also substantially increased their tax breaks in 1981. Under previous tax law, senators and representatives were limited to a $3,000 deduction for business expenses incurred as a result of living in Washington, far less than their counterparts in the private sector could claim. Removing this cap provided the equivalent of a $9,000–$21,000 annual pay increase for most legislators, depending on their individual financial and living situations.[23] After substantial public outcry, especially by the "citizen's lobby," Common Cause, Congress reinstituted the cap on congressional tax deductions in 1982.

Policy toward direct pay increases had the same inconsistent quality. In 1981 legislators rejected a $10,100 pay hike recommended by President Carter (the quadrennial commission had recommended a

21. The statutory limit of $2,000 for a single honorarium remained in effect. Senators repealed their ethics code limit on outside earned income in 1982 (before its delayed effective date) when they turned down a pay increase accepted by the House.

22. House members had earlier rejected lifting the outside earnings ceiling to 40 percent of their congressional salaries for a two-year period. The roll call vote was 147–271. See Irwin B. Arieff, "House Turns Back Effort to Loosen Its Restrictions on Outside Earned Income," *Congressional Quarterly Weekly Report*, vol. 39 (October 31, 1981), p. 2126; Arieff, "Congress Votes Itself New Income Tax Break, Doubles House Outside Income Limit," *Congressional Quarterly Weekly Report*, vol. 39 (December 19, 1981), p. 2480; and Jonathan Neumann and Ted Gupp, "How Congress Gave Itself Tax, Pay Benefits," *Washington Post*, February 21, 1982, p. A1.

23. P.L. 97-51, sec. 139. In two Senate votes, the removal of the tax deductions passed by the narrow margins of 50–48 and 48–44. *Congressional Record* (September 24, 1981), pp. 21897–901, 21911–13; and (September 30, 1981), p. 22581. See also Irwin B. Arieff, "New Tax Rules Set Deduction Members Voted Themselves," *Congressional Quarterly Weekly Report*, vol. 40 (January 23, 1982), p. 125; and Arieff, "Members Feel Safe in Taking '81 Tax Break; '82 in Doubt," *Congressional Quarterly Weekly Report*, vol. 40 (April 10, 1982), p. 790.

$24,300 increase). The next year, Senate Majority Leader Ted Stevens managed to insert into the conference report on the 1982 reconciliation bill a provision that would have required the appointment of a special quadrennial commission that fall to recommend a new round of pay increases for the government's top officials. The report of the commission would have been issued right after the fall elections— when Congress probably would not be in session to veto its recommendations before they could go into effect. The strategy was a shrewd one: the controversial proposal was buried in a huge package at the last minute so that most members would not even know that it was there; the only vote was on the whole package, so members did not have to take a separate stand in favor of a pay raise; and the strong likelihood of a postelection recess made the commission's recommendations almost veto-proof. The strategy did not work, however. When a group of House members learned of the proposal, they organized their colleagues to reject the conference report, arguing that just the appearance of voting for a possible pay raise less than three months before an election was political suicide. The conference report was rejected, and the Stevens proposal was excised.[24]

Proponents of higher congressional pay had more luck in making annual cost-of-living increases more automatic. In 1981 Congress provided a permanent appropriation for congressional salaries. In the past, opponents of pay increases had repeatedly used votes on legislative branch appropriations bills as an additional opportunity to roll back annual cost-of-living pay increases. With a permanent appropriation, opponents could still try to get such resolutions approved, but they now lacked an easy vehicle for their resolutions.[25] And if proponents of a pay increase could stall such a vote (especially in the House of

24. The motion to reject the conference report carrying the Stevens proposal initially carried by a vote of 209–191. But when it became clear that the report had been rejected, a number of House members jumped on the bandwagon, switching their votes to avoid potential charges that they had supported higher pay for themselves. The final vote was 266–145. With the Stevens proposal excised, the bill passed the next day by a vote of 243–176. See Helen Dewar, "Pay Raise Scare Leads House to Balk on Cuts," *Washington Post*, August 18, 1982, p. A1; and Diane Granat, "After a Brief Panic Over Pay, Congress Clears Bill Cutting Expenditures by $13.3 Billion," *Congressional Quarterly Weekly Report*, vol. 40 (August 21, 1982), pp. 2047–48.

25. Even before 1981, Congress had begun folding legislative appropriations into general continuing resolutions, where they were less visible. The last separate legislative branch appropriations act was passed in 1978. Burying congressional pay increases in continuing resolutions did not reduce attacks on them, however. See Alan Murray, "Congress Tucks Its Funding Into Stopgap Spending Bill; May Seek Pay Raise Later," *Congressional Quarterly Weekly Report*, vol. 40 (October 9, 1982), p. 2624.

Representatives, where rules on amending activity were more strict), the increases would go into effect automatically. Sponsors of the change felt that members would be less likely to reverse a pay raise once it had gone into effect.[26]

Even with this additional procedural protection, legislators initially proved cautious. In the election year of 1982, Congress initially voted not to accept its cost-of-living pay increase for 1983. In a lame-duck session after the election, senators reiterated their rejection of a pay hike but extended their exemption from outside earnings limits. The House accepted a 15 percent salary increase—substantially below what members were entitled to under comparability rules. The pay increase won in the House by the narrowest possible margin: a tie vote, with the Speaker voting, to reject a disapproving amendment. Lame-duck members, who did not need to fear their constituents' wrath, provided the margin of victory for the pay raise, voting against the amendment by a 24–47 margin.[27] Senate pay was raised to the level of that in the House six months later in exchange for a limit on senators' outside income.[28] In both 1983 and 1984 Congress acquiesced in cost-of-living pay increases for the following years. During 1984 Congress even approved a modest (0.5 percent) midyear pay raise for federal workers—and themselves.[29]

Action in the second Reagan administration has taken place on both the pay and honoraria fronts. In 1985 Senator Jesse Helms, Republican of North Carolina, introduced an amendment to the fiscal year 1986 first budget resolution that would have mandated a 10 percent cut in

26. P.L. 97-51, sec. 130(c). See also *Congressional Record* (September 30, 1981), p. 22580. The statute included language providing that when Congress took these automatic pay increases it would lose the right to claim all previous cost-of-living increases that it had previously turned down. However, the comptroller general ruled in 1982 that automatic acceptance of the increases would require accepting previously rejected increases—which made Congress even less likely to accept them. See Andy Plattner, "House, Senate Again at Odds Over Limits on Pay Increases," *Congressional Quarterly Weekly Report*, vol. 40 (December 18, 1982), pp. 3049–50.

27. Returning Republicans opposed a pay raise by a vote of 100–38, while lame-duck Republicans supported it by 21–27. Plattner, "House, Senate Again at Odds," p. 3050.

28. The honoraria limit—30 percent of a member's salary—was equal to that in the House ethics code. However, this limit was a statutory one. P.L. 98-63, sec. 908(b), (d).

29. The Senate voted 66–19 in early 1984 to rescind the first pay raise for that year, but the motion was killed because the House Post Office and Civil Service Committee did not act on it. The 1984 midyear pay raise was retroactive to January. P.L. 98-270, sec. 202(a). The 1984 pay raises of $2,800 were largely offset by a requirement that they, and other federal workers, pay social security taxes for the first time. This cost members who had no other income subject to the social security tax just over $2,500. "Congressional Pay Raises," *Congressional Quarterly Almanac*, vol. 39 (1983), pp. 577–78.

TABLE 6-2. *Senate Vote on Helms 1985 Congressional Pay Cut Proposal, by Party and Year of Reelection*

Year of reelection	Republican		Democratic	
	Percent supporting	Total number voting	Percent supporting	Total number voting
1986	78	18	56	9
1988	50	14	42	19
1990	65	17	20	15
Retirees[a]	33	3	0	3
Total	63	52	35	46

SOURCE: *Congressional Quarterly Almanac*, vol. 41 (1985), p. 13-S.
a. Thomas F. Eagleton, Democrat of Missouri; Barry Goldwater, Republican of Arizona; Gary Hart, Democrat of Colorado; Paul Laxalt, Republican of Nevada; Russell B. Long, Democrat of Louisiana; and Charles McC. Mathias, Jr., Republican of Maryland.

congressional salaries. It fell only one vote short of passage, achieving a 49–49 tie vote. The vote breakdown followed familiar lines. Both party (reflecting ideology) and vulnerability to blame-generating pressures influenced legislators' choices. Republicans supported the measure more than Democrats. Within each party, senators up for reelection in the next election were more likely to vote in favor than those up in later years. Senators planning or seriously considering retirement at the next election showed the lowest support levels of all (table 6-2).

Although the Helms initiative failed, the civil service pay freeze proposed by Reagan and approved by Congress for 1986 meant that congressional pay was frozen as well. Once again, however, Congress attempted to avoid a real earnings decline. Late in 1985 Congress raised the legal limit for congressional honoraria from 30 percent to 40 percent of salary as part of omnibus appropriations legislation. This gave legislators the potential to earn an additional $7,510 at that year's salary rate. Its effect was limited to the Senate, however, because House members remained bound by a rule limiting their income from honoraria to 30 percent of salary.[30] Four months later, Representative John Murtha, Democrat of Pennsylvania, with the apparent acquiescence of House leaders of both parties, slipped a rules change through the House to lift that chamber's outside earnings ceiling.[31] After Mur-

30. P.L. 99-190, sec. 137. See also "$368.2 Billion Omnibus Spending Bill Cleared," *Congressional Quarterly Almanac*, vol. 41 (1985), pp. 360–67.
31. The Murtha resolution might have had a very broad effect, because the House rule limited all types of outside earned income (for example, from law practice), while the statutory ceiling applied only to honoraria. See Edward Walsh, "House Acts Fast, Decisively—to Hike Income," *Washington Post*, April 23, 1986, p. A21.

tha assured his colleagues that his proposal was noncontroversial, it was approved by unanimous consent, with few members actually on the House floor at the time, and fewer still knowing what had been done.[32] But once it became clear what had happened, the subterfuge unraveled. Junior members, who have fewer outside speaking opportunities, were particularly upset. They believed, as one House Democrat put it, that the higher earnings limit "would have helped only 20 percent of House members and given everyone else nothing but a black eye."[33] Democratic rank-and-file members demanded an opportunity to reverse the rules change, and it was done the following day.[34]

New Process, New Outcomes?

The revision of the annual cost-of-living pay increase process in 1981 made it easier for Congress to accept small increases in nominal pay, but those increases were still far from certain. And the new process did nothing to make up for pay slippage over the many years Congress had not accepted increases. The greatest opportunity for reversing erosion of congressional pay came as a result of the Supreme Court's *Chadha* decision, which outlawed the legislative veto. This forced Congress to revise its previous procedure (a one-house veto) for disallowing pay increases proposed by the president in response to the quadrennial commissions' reports.[35] Blocking the president's pay proposal now requires a joint resolution passed by Congress and signed by the president within one month after the president submits his pay recommendation. This new procedure was adopted by Congress late in 1985.[36] It creates much higher barriers for a disallowance resolution: not only must the House and Senate agree, but the president must disavow his own proposal, all within a very tight time frame.

The first experience with the new pay disallowance procedure raised congressional gamesmanship to a new high. When the president's quadrennial commission issued its report in December 1986, it

32. *Congressional Record,* daily edition (April 22, 1986), p. H2051.
33. Representative David Obey, Democrat of Wisconsin, quoted in Hook, "House Reverses Itself on Outside Income Lid," p. 914.
34. See ibid.; and Edward Walsh, "Another Day, Another Rules Change," *Washington Post,* April 24, 1986, p. A21.
35. See Elder Witt, "High Court to Clarify Sweep of Its Legislative Veto Ruling," *Congressional Quarterly Weekly Report,* vol. 44 (December 6, 1986), pp. 3025–30; and 1984–85 Commission on Executive, Legislative and Judicial Salaries [Brady Commission], *The Quiet Crisis* (Washington, D.C.: The Commission, 1985), p. 8.
36. P.L. 99-190, sec. 135.

called for a salary increase of 80 percent, from $75,100 in 1986 to $135,000 in 1987. The commission proposed linking higher pay to a limitation on honoraria, as had been done in 1977.[37]

Even many congressional proponents of a pay hike were fearful that such a huge percentage increase would be politically impossible to accept.[38] The president's budget message cut the pay recommendation to $89,500 (a 19.2 percent increase), citing the need to cut the federal deficit.[39] This proposal, too, generated intense criticism inside and outside Congress.

Despite the fact that there were now Democratic majorities in both houses of Congress, conservative Republicans in Congress sought to force the issue onto the agenda. In the House, the pay hike was referred to a task force of the Committee on Post Office and Civil Service. Committee chairman William Ford, Democrat of Michigan, made it clear that he supported a pay increase and did not plan to have the committee report before the deadline. This made it very unlikely that a resolution to disallow the pay raise could reach the House floor.

Attention thus focused on the Senate, where conservative Republicans believed that they could use the easier agenda access in their chamber to force their colleagues to reject the congressional pay raise. This would then put overwhelming pressure on the House to do the same. They were joined in this campaign by populist consumer advocate Ralph Nader, showing that congressional pay politics does make strange bedfellows.

Senate Majority Leader Robert Byrd, Democrat of West Virginia, considered combining the pay raise with a limit on honoraria to make it more palatable, but then abandoned that idea and agreed to allow a separate vote on disallowing the pay increase before the February 3 deadline.[40] The major challenge for Senate opponents of the congres-

37. Commission on Executive, Legislative and Judicial Salaries [Ferguson Commission], *Quality Leadership: Our Government's Most Precious Asset* (Washington, D.C.: The Commission, 1986). The 1984 commission did not make specific salary recommendations, concentrating instead on designing a new process for quadrennial salary increases to replace the one overturned by the *Chadha* decision. The 1986 commission was a one-time innovation to make recommendations under this new process. Commissions will revert to presidential election years (reporting just after the election) in 1988.

38. Janet Hook, "Pay Boost Recommendation Jangles Nerves on Capitol Hill," *Congressional Quarterly Weekly Report*, vol. 44 (December 20, 1986), pp. 3121–24.

39. Under the automatic comparability mechanisms already in place, congressional pay would have risen to $77,400 in 1987 without congressional action. Judith Havemann, "Pay Raise Proposal Sharply Reduced," *Washington Post*, January 6, 1987, pp. A1, A9.

40. Linda Greenhouse, "Byrd Hints at Earnings Curb," *New York Times*, January 13, 1987, p. A17. Whether a limit on honoraria would have provided sufficient political

sional pay hike was to find a legislative vehicle to which they could attach their resolution of disapproval—something that both houses of Congress badly wanted to clear within the thirty-day time limit. The House provided them with a perfect vehicle on January 27, 1987 (a week before the deadline), in the form of an emergency aid package for the homeless. The symbolism could not have been more perfect for opponents of the increase, contrasting help for the poorest of America's citizens with salary increases for the relatively well-off.

The Senate took up a resolution of disapproval on January 29. The outcome was never in doubt. Because it was widely acknowledged that the House was to serve as the buffer against a disallowance resolution, Senators had little incentive to vote against it. By voting for the resolution, they could turn a blame-generating situation into a credit-claiming opportunity. After rejecting several amendments, the Senate approved it by the overwhelming vote of 88–6. It was then attached to the homeless aid bill and sent back to the House. But meanwhile the House had adjourned for a long weekend, leaving it only one day to approve the resolution before the pay raise would go into effect automatically. Senator Helms argued in the Senate debate that both the prospect of a pay raise without congressional affirmation and the House's adjournment to facilitate that outcome were "copouts." And he charged, in a classic of blame-generating rhetoric, that "if a copout occurs, it will lie like a dead cat on the doorstep of the House of Representatives—who left town on Thursday afternoon to return sometime Tuesday."[41]

The pressure then shifted to the House. The Democratic leadership first considered giving up on a pay raise, but then decided to adjourn early on Tuesday without giving opponents of the pay raise an opportunity to vote on it.[42] The next day—after the deadline—the disallowance resolution was passed intact by a voice vote. In an attempt to build a strong legislative history against possible court challenges, Chairman Ford argued in his floor speech that "the disapproval lan-

"cover" to allow senators to vote for a salary increase is very doubtful. In Senate debate on the disallowance resolution, Senator Lowell Weicker, Republican of Connecticut, proposed an amendment that would lift congressional salaries considerably higher than the president's proposal—to $120,000 rather than $89,500—while banning acceptance of honoraria. It was defeated by a vote of 93–2. *Congressional Record,* daily edition (January 29, 1987), pp. S1351–59.

41. *Congressional Record,* daily edition (January 29, 1987), p. S1357.

42. Tom Kenworthy, "Wright Pledges House Vote On Blocking Salary Increase," *Washington Post,* January 31, 1987, p. A1; and Linda Greenhouse, "House Acts to Get Raise and Ease Political Harm," *New York Times,* February 4, 1987, p. A13.

guage of the Senate amendment, if agreed to by the House today, will have absolutely no effect. . . . Since the House did not act by that [February 3] deadline, what we do is meaningless."[43] The president, in signing the measure, agreed.[44] Congress received the salary increase for 1987.

Whether the "backdoor" congressional pay raise of 1987 can be considered a harbinger of things to come remains doubtful, however. Legislative efforts to roll back that pay increase and a court challenge to the delayed vote of disapproval in the House both failed.[45] But Congress agreed, as part of the budget summit following the October 1987 stock market crash, to freeze for 1988 the pay of all federal employees making more than $72,000 a year, including themselves. (Lower-salaried employees received a 2 percent pay hike.)[46] Legislation that would once again make it easier to block a quadrennial pay increase was introduced in Congress even before the January 1987 vote, and opponents of pay increases will have many opportunities to force their colleagues to support it.[47]

The prospects for restoring congressional salaries to 1969 levels remain very slight in a period of high budget deficits. To do so would require a drastically changed pay adjustment process. Some prominent members of Congress have backed a constitutional amendment that would entrust congressional pay to an outside commission, whose decision would be final.[48] House Ways and Means Committee Chairman Dan Rostenkowski, Democrat of Illinois, has, somewhat facetiously, proposed an even more unusual approach, in which senators and representatives could choose their own salary at any level between that

43. *Congressional Record,* daily edition (February 4, 1987), p. H543.
44. "President Lets Stand Pay Raise," *Washington Post,* February 13, 1987, p. A3.
45. See "Court Dismisses Challenge to Congress' Pay Raise," *Congressional Quarterly Weekly Report,* vol. 45 (July 4, 1987), pp. 1477–78.
46. Judith Havemann, "President Signs 2% Pay Raise," *Washington Post,* January 1, 1988, p. A1.
47. Senator Charles Grassley, Republican of Iowa, introduced S. 309, which would require both the House and the Senate to vote on the president's recommended pay raise within thirty days of its introduction. The salary increase could not go into effect without an affirmative vote by both chambers. See *Congressional Record,* daily edition (January 29, 1987), p. S1350. Grassley's proposal was approved by the Senate, 84–4, as an amendment to a bill raising the federal debt ceiling, but the provision was dropped in conference with the House. See Janet Hook, "Senate Panel OKs $1.8 Billion to Operate Legislative Branch," *Congressional Quarterly Weekly Report,* vol. 45 (September 19, 1987), p. 2237. The current pay increase procedure has also been challenged in a lawsuit by Senator Gordon Humphrey, Republican of New Hampshire, and the National Taxpayers Union. See *Congressional Record,* daily edition (January 29, 1987), pp. S1354–56.
48. Although hearings were held on the proposal, it never reached the floor of either chamber. See Brady Commission, *The Quiet Crisis,* p. 6.

TABLE 6-3. *Quadrennial Commission Recommendations and Salary Outcomes*
Salaries in dollars

Year	Prior year salary	Quadrennial commission recommendation		President's recommendation		Enacted by Congress	
		New salary	Percent increase	New salary	Percent increase	New salary	Percent increase
1969	30,000	50,000	67	42,500	42	42,500	42
1974	42,500	53,125	25	45,700	8	42,500	0
1977	44,600	57,500	29	57,500	29	57,500	29
1980	60,663	85,000	40	70,853	17	60,663	0
1986	75,100	135,000	80	89,500	19	89,500	19

SOURCES: *Congressional Quarterly Almanac*, vol. 25 (1969), pp. 229, 280; vol. 30 (1974), p. 664; vol. 33 (1977), pp. 751–52; *Congressional Quarterly Weekly Report*, vol. 38 (December 20, 1980), p. 3679; vol. 39 (January 10, 1981), p. 117; and *Washington Post*, January 6, 1987, p. A9.

scheduled before the 1987 quadrennial commission recommendation ($77,400) and that recommended by the commission ($135,000). Thus the "apparently small band of us who feel we are worth more, maybe a lot more ... and are willing to take that case to our constituents" could do so, charging whatever they felt the political market could bear.[49] Such a procedure would, of course, create a big salary division between those with safe seats and those from marginal districts. There has been no movement in Congress to jump on Rostenkowski's bandwagon.

The Consequences of Congressional Timidity

Clearly Congress's resort to automatic or quasi-automatic procedures to prevent the erosion of its salaries by inflation has had only limited success. Recommendations by the quadrennial commissions—which are clearly a buck-passing mechanism, although not an explicit indexing procedure—have been enacted without alteration only once, in 1977. The commission's recommendations have been reduced by the president each of the other four times, and only two of those four times were the president's recommendations accepted by Congress, including the 1986–87 round where Congress rejected the pay raise in a way that allowed it to take effect (table 6-3).

The rather dismal record of the quadrennial commission process is not surprising, considering the difficulty of the political task. Even before Congress acts on quadrennial commission pay recommendations, those recommendations have been subject to enormous political gamesmanship. The commissions, which do not have to worry about incurring voters' wrath and are dominated by business executives and lawyers who are themselves highly paid, tend to recommend large pay boosts. By coming in high, they allow the president to cut their requests (thus displaying his frugality) while still proposing a substantial pay boost. The president, in addition to wishing to appear fiscally responsible, is also subject to strong pressures from the executive and judiciary to recommend pay increases that are meaningful and can pass. This is no mean feat: the figure must be high enough that legislators will think the financial gain is sufficient to risk voting for it, but not so high that the risk becomes overwhelming. In 1986, for example, President Reagan received signals from some legislators that the quadrennial commission's $135,000 figure for congressional pay could

49. *Congressional Record,* daily edition (February 4, 1987), p. H545.

never pass Congress. But when he slashed that recommendation by $45,500, others complained that the remaining pay increase was not big enough to stick their necks out for. It may be that in the present political climate, no recommendation can simultaneously meet both criteria—a high-enough financial incentive and a low-enough political disincentive. This is especially true when opponents of a pay increase can force proponents to take a stand in favor of that increase several times in order to make it stick.

Pay hikes under the annual cost-of-living pay mechanism, which indexes congressional pay hikes to those for the civil service, generate much smaller percentage increases. But they have also been rejected about half the time. Most of the success has come since 1981, when it has been easier for legislators to avoid separate votes on congressional pay raises.

The consequences of all these machinations are displayed in figure 6-1, which shows congressional salaries both in current dollars and in constant 1960 dollars. Clearly the enactment of automatic pay procedures since the late 1960s has neither stabilized the base of real pay nor led to consensus on an adjustment mechanism. Congressional pay has undergone substantial nominal increases during 1960-87, but after rising in real terms as a result of increases in 1965 and 1969, legislators' salaries have since failed to keep pace with price trends. Pay hikes have occurred more frequently since the cost-of-living procedure was introduced in 1975 (six between 1975 and 1985, compared with only two between 1965 and 1975), but inflation has also been higher and more persistent in the later period.

The first years of the ostensibly automatic cost-of-living pay adjustment process after 1975 saw additional slippage in the purchasing power of congressional pay. Real pay fell by about 40 percent between 1969 and 1982, but has risen somewhat since that time. The elimination in 1981 of the requirement that Congress annually appropriate funds for legislative salaries seems to have provided at least temporary additional political cover for inflation adjustments. But the cost-of-living pay process can at best only halt the erosion of congressional pay at its current level. It cannot reverse that erosion unless major real increases are made in civil service pay. And that is simply not likely for the immediate future. Real pay increases and adequate salary differentials can only be addressed through the quadrennial commission or an ad hoc process. But the large percentage increases recommended by the commissions have proven to be politically unacceptable, and the

FIGURE 6-1. *Congressional Pay in Current and 1960 Constant Dollars, 1960–87*

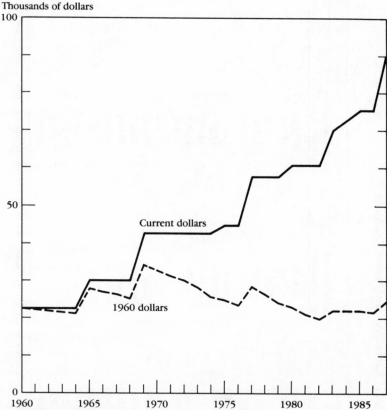

Thousands of dollars

SOURCE: *Current Salary Schedules of Federal officers and Employees Together with a History of Salary and Retirement Annuity Adjustments,* Committee Print 100-7, House Committee on Post Office and Civil Service, 100 Cong. 2 sess. (Government Printing Office, 1988).

idea of Congress voting a substantial increase in its own salary without external prompting (and thus blame limitation) by the commissions borders on the preposterous.

If congressional fears of raising their own salaries affected only the income of legislators, it might not be a source of major concern. After all, most senators and representatives do run for reelection even if they believe that their incomes are too low.[50] But legislators have linked

50. A study of members who voluntarily retired from the House of Representatives in 1978 found that while low pay was a common complaint, it was not a major cause of the increase in voluntary retirement that occurred in the House in the 1970s. See John R. Hibbing, "Voluntary Retirement from the U.S. House: The Costs of Congressional Service," *Legislative Studies Quarterly,* vol. 7 (February 1982), pp. 57–74.

TABLE 6-4. *Linkages between Congressional, Executive, and Judicial Salaries*
Dollars

Year	District court judges	Circuit court judges	Senators and representatives	Deputy secretaries (executive level II)	Cabinet members (executive level I)
1968	30,000	33,000	30,000	30,000	35,000
1969	40,000	42,500	42,500	42,500	60,000
1970	40,000	42,500	42,500	42,500	60,000
1971	40,000	42,500	42,500	42,500	60,000
1972	40,000	42,500	42,500	42,500	60,000
1973	40,000	42,500	42,500	42,500	60,000
1974	40,000	42,500	42,500	42,500	60,000
1975	42,000	44,600	44,600	44,600	63,000
1976	44,000	46,800	44,600	44,600	63,000
1977	54,500	57,500	57,500	57,500	66,000
1978	54,500	57,500	57,500	57,500	66,000
1979	61,500	65,000	60,663	60,663	69,630
1980	57,100	70,900	60,663	60,663	69,630
1981	70,300	74,300	60,663	60,663	69,630
1982	73,100	77,300	60,663[a]	69,800	80,100
1983	73,100	77,300	69,800[b]	69,800	80,100
1984	76,000	80,400	72,600	72,600	83,300
1985	78,700	83,200	75,100	75,100	86,200
1986	78,700	83,200	75,100	75,100	86,200
1987	89,500	95,000	89,500	89,500	99,500

SOURCE: *Current Salary Schedules of Federal Officers and Employees Together with a History of Salary and Retirement Annuity Adjustments*, Committee Print 100-7, House Committee on Post Office and Civil Service, 100 Cong. 2 sess. (Government Printing Office, 1988).
a. House members' salary raised to annual rate of $69,800 on December 18.
b. Annual rates; this rate did not become effective for senators until July.

their own pay to salaries in the judiciary (circuit court judges) and the executive branch (executive level II, or deputy secretaries). Pay for judges and top executives is essentially indexed to what Congress is willing to pay itself (table 6-4). The reasons for and consequences of this linkage were succinctly stated by the 1986 quadrennial commission:

> Congressional pay has been linked to that of top level executive officials and the senior ranks of the judiciary in the hope of seeing congressional salaries rise with them.
> In fact, the reverse has been the case. Pay linkage has not overcome congressional reluctance to vote a pay raise for top officials, including themselves. In simple terms Congress has been unwilling to take the abuse for voting itself a salary increase. Instead, it has arbitrarily suppressed *all* top-level executive and judicial salaries in hopes that the pressure would eventually build to such a degree that like the "rising tide that lifts all boats" it could no longer responsibly hold back other branches and affected salaries would increase.[51]

The linkage between congressional and circuit court judge salaries was broken in the late 1970s because of judicial salary increases resulting from a lawsuit by federal district court judges. The judges charged that a congressional pay rollback of judicial salaries, included in a general rollback with executive and legislative salaries, was unconstitutional—and they won the suit.[52] The 1986 quadrennial commission recommendations would have restored that link if they had been adopted; the president's 1987 recommendations created a new linkage of congressional pay with salaries for district court judges. And the link between legislative and executive level II salaries has remained intact.

The failure of Congress either to vote for real pay increases or to find an automatic process to achieve that result, when combined with congressional determination to maintain the linkage between salaries

51. Ferguson Commission, *Quality Leadership*, p. 19.
52. The Supreme Court ruled that because the rollbacks in two years had occurred after those increases took effect, they violated the Constitution's "compensation" clause, which provides that "judges, both of the supreme and inferior courts, shall ... receive for their services, a compensation, which shall not be diminished during their continuance in office" (article III, sec. 1). Rollbacks for two other years were enacted before the beginning of the fiscal year. They were therefore considered to be freezes rather than diminutions of judicial salaries, and they were allowed to stand. *U.S. v. Will*, 499 U.S. 200.

in the three branches, has led to huge salary differentials between top executive branch officials and federal judges and their counterparts in the private sector. According to the 1986 quadrennial commission, officials at executive level II needed a 90 percent salary boost to achieve pay comparability with private-sector executives with similar reponsibilities; federal judges receive only one-half to one-third the salary of fifty-year-old partners in law firms.[53] Federal judges have been so upset at their decline in real salary that they have broken with their usual reluctance to take public stands by lobbying for pay increases.[54] Others have "voted with their feet," resigning from the bench in unprecedented numbers to take higher-paying positions in the private sector.[55] The current pay process has, moreover, created serious salary compression—that is, reduced pay differentials—within the executive schedule. It has also caused a serious "capping out" problem for officials at the top rungs of the civil service, who cannot earn more than executives at the lowest level of the executive schedule. As a result, the federal government has had serious problems attracting and retaining high-caliber officials.[56]

An obvious solution to the executive and judicial salary problems is to uncouple them from congressional pay. But legislators are very reluctant to surrender linkage for reasons both of prestige and self-interest—that is, the recognition that treating congressional pay raises separately would doom them to defeat. And proponents of breaking the linkage have been unable to devise a strategy to force their col-

53. Cited in *Congressional Record,* daily edition (January 29, 1987), p. S1347.

54. See Linda Greenhouse, "That Sticky Salary Wicket," *New York Times,* January 15, 1987, p. B6; Edward Walsh and Judith Havemann, "House Leaders Face Pay Raise Quandary as Deadline Looms," *Washington Post,* February 3, 1987, p. A4; and Administrative Office of the United States Courts, "Federal Judicial Compensation: A Pressing Need for Increase: A Report to the Commission on Executive, Legislative, and Judicial Salaries," August 31, 1984.

55. Ferguson Commission, *Quality Leadership,* pp. 14–16.

56. The average civil service (general schedule) employee has lost only 5.7 percent of his or her salary's purchasing power (as measured by the CPI) since 1969, compared with 39 percent for executive level II employees. But the problem is much more severe at upper GS ranks because of the salary cap. See ibid., pp. 24–31. A study done for the House Post Office and Civil Service Committee found that both cash and total compensation (including retirement and fringe benefits) at the top levels of the general schedule lag seriously behind that for equivalent positions in the private sector. Total compensation for private-sector equivalents of GS-15s was almost 24 percent higher than individuals at that civil service rank. See *Study of Total Compensation in the Federal, State and Private Sectors,* Committee Print 98-16, House Committee on Post Office and Civil Service, 98 Cong. 2 sess. (GPO, 1984), p. 110. See also *Government Brain Drain,* Hearing before the Subcommittee on Civil Service, Post Office and General Services of the Senate Committee on Governmental Affairs, 97 Cong. 1 sess. (GPO, 1982).

leagues to do so. They are no more likely to give up the linkage voluntarily than a drowning sailor is to give up the life preserver that keeps
him afloat. A vote against separating congressional pay has little blame-
generating potential in itself. And this strategy also splits conservative
ranks, for many in this group would like to disallow pay increases for
all federal officials. In 1987, for example, Senator Pete Wilson, Republican of California, proposed an amendment to the January pay disallowance resolution that would have allowed the president's executive and judicial salary recommendations to take effect while barring
those for Congress. It lost badly—27–66—with similar margins
among Democrats (15–39) and Republicans (12–27). Some of the
most conservative Republicans voted in favor of the Wilson amendment, but many others were opposed. The disunity of conservatives
on this issue makes decoupling unlikely in the near future.

Conclusions

Efforts to increase the automaticity of the congressional pay process
were motivated in large part by legislators' desire to pass the buck on
that blame-generating issue. But for automatic pay adjustments to be
sustained, there must be substantial agreement among policymakers
that neither the program base being indexed nor the procedure to
adjust it should be challenged. It is not necessary that they believe the
base and the adjustment mechanism to be desirable, only that they
feel that the economic or political costs of mounting a challenge to
them are not worth the effort. But neither the base nor the mechanism
for adjusting congressional pay gained this minimal level of agreement,
because there were strong political incentives to challenge them: fighting against a pay hike allows a legislator both to claim credit for one's
actions and to generate blame toward others.

Policy specialists and party leaders attempted to control the
congressional agenda to keep the pay issue from arising, but they did
not succeed. Indeed, on a number of occasions, pay freeze resolutions
were initiated by Democratic proponents of pay hikes because they
knew that such resolutions would pass anyway and they did not want
Republicans to get credit for them. The parliamentary contortions
during repeated pay battles were spectacular and would be amusing if
they did not have such serious consequences for staffing the nation's
top administrative and judicial posts. On the few occasions that forces
favoring higher pay did prevail in roll call votes, it was usually by the

narrowest of margins, presumably because Democratic leaders did not wish to force any more of their troops than necessary to adopt blame-inducing positions.

Several of the lessons of the congressional pay case are applicable to the much broader category of cases of indexing (and potential indexing) motivated by a pass-the-buck strategy. First, the case suggests why there are relatively few indexing mechanisms in sectors where politicians have strong buck-passing incentives to index. Indexing has the advantage of allowing politicians to escape blame for unpopular actions in the future. But precisely because indexing makes it easier to impose costs, the initial indexing decision is likely to provoke adamant opposition from groups who believe that an ad hoc adjustment process will allow them to do better than an automatic one. An ad hoc process presumably makes it easier to block changes from the status quo or even consideration of change. Politicians rarely attempt to institute inflation adjustment mechanisms in sectors where there are strong incentives to pass the buck—for example, in regulations and in setting user charges—because they are unwilling to incur the blame from affected groups in the short term that is required to avoid blame in the long term.

The congressional pay case also shows that the specific index used can make a difference. The more politically popular the index, the safer the inflation adjustment. Thus a program like veterans' pensions, where COLAs are linked to those in social security, is in a much better situation than executive and judicial salaries, with their linkage to congressional pay. Congressional pay, in turn, has suffered through its linkage to civil service pay increases, since presidents have abandoned real efforts to maintain comparability with the private sector in their recommendations for cost-of-living pay raises.

A final general lesson of the congressional pay case is that even after an automatic adjustment mechanism is adopted, it is difficult to pass the buck on politically costly decisions. The critical issue is agenda limitation. Indexing has succeeded in limiting the agenda on social security benefit changes because the outcomes it has wrought are broadly popular—unlike congressional pay hikes. Automatic processes have made it easier, but not easy, to get pay hikes because Congress has limited ability to keep blame-generating choices off the congressional agenda when some participants can profit from getting them on. Once the challenges get on the agenda, proponents of pay increases have great incentives to avoid blame and claim credit by opposing those raises. Efforts to increase the automaticity of the congressional pay process have repeatedly been eroded over time. Time offers the opponents of pay increases more opportunities to get their proposals—both for rejecting specific increases and for changing the adjustment mechanisms—on the congressional agenda. And once legislators are forced to take a stand on those proposals, they are usually approved, often with great outward gusto if inward reluctance. In short, politicians' decisions to reject automatic inflation adjustments reflect once again their unwillingness to incur short-term blame.

7

Dairy Price Supports

Dairy price supports are, along with price supports for other agricultural commodities, one of the oldest cases of indexing in federal programs. Like social security and food stamps, dairy price supports help to maintain a specific standard of living for a particular client group. But dairy price supports have an additional objective: to stabilize the supply of milk, by smoothing out fluctuations in prices paid to farmers.

There are some additional differences between dairy price supports and the indexed programs considered thus far. The first difference is in the cohesiveness of the dairy program's clientele and the complexity of its political linkages to other programs. Given their relatively limited geographic base, dairy interests have had to rely largely on logrolling with other agricultural interests to win approval of and later to defend indexing of price supports.

The dairy price support program is also unusual in the degree of flexibility it has given to the secretary of agriculture in administering indexing: while the parity price was for many years adjusted annually (and for a time, semiannually), the secretary has generally had some discretion, within a range set by Congress, on what percentage of parity will serve as the support price. As a result, the connection between conflicts over indexing as a procedure and specific benefit levels has been particularly noticeable.

Indexing of dairy price supports also differs from the other programs considered thus far by having a major effect on production decisions in specific markets. Automatic increases in price supports have contributed to enormous problems of dairy overproduction. The apparent relationship between indexed price supports and huge oversupply, in turn, has made legislators less reluctant to cut real support levels.

Alice Keck Whitfield is coauthor of this chapter.

146

Finally, dairy price supports differ in the extent to which program supporters can generate blame to ward off challenges to the program's indexing procedures. In the social security case, the reluctance of all major participants to be portrayed as being against social security has kept modifications of that program's indexing procedures off the agenda except at times of severe crisis. In the congressional pay case, the combination of weak agenda control and the blame-generating potential of salary hikes has kept the issue on the agenda, despite the efforts of the program's clientele—legislators—to keep it off. The case of dairy price supports is a bit more like that of food stamps—there is limited blame-generating potential for both support and opposition. Except in the few states with large dairy industries, it is difficult for dairy interests to generate blame toward legislators who oppose the industry. They have, therefore, had to rely on logrolling to build political support. This left them in a vulnerable position in the early 1980s, as fiscal constraints forced legislators to concentrate on defending the programs most important to their own constituents. As with congressional pay, the fact that an automatic adjustment mechanism was in place was not enough to prevent contractionary changes in the program. Although the dairy price support program has been retained, Reagan administration initiatives have essentially dismantled its indexing mechanisms.

Origins

Today's federal dairy program began with legislation passed in the early years of the century. In 1922 Congress passed the Capper-Volstead Act, which allowed dairy farmers to form local milk-marketing associations without the threat of being charged with antitrust violations. This legislation was intended to help farmers, who were perceived as weak in the face of sophisticated corporate interests of suppliers and milk dealers. With Capper-Volstead protection, milk prices and dairy farm incomes increased until the Great Depression, when demand stagnated, prices fell, and farm foreclosures increased. The federal government stepped in again with the 1933 and 1938 Agricultural Adjustment Acts. In order to increase farmers' purchasing power and to "protect the consumers' interest," the Department of Agriculture was allowed to set minimum prices for milk in specific market areas. The final step from cartelization of the industry to outright subsidy was made during World War II. The government purchased surplus milk at a guaranteed price to promote milk production. The price was set at 90 percent of "parity"—a complex index of the purchasing power per hundredweight of milk during 1910–14. Parity is based primarily on the prices all farmers received for their goods and the prices they paid for goods and services.[1]

The 1949 Agriculture Act instituted a permanent federal commitment to dairy price supports. The rationale for the program shifted for peacetime: price supports were justified as stabilizing incomes for farmers and prices and supply to consumers—each, admittedly, at higher levels than would otherwise be the case. The act gave the secretary of agriculture responsibility for setting price supports between 75 percent and 90 percent of parity.[2] In theory, this allows the secretary to respond to changing market conditions. In practice, the secretary has usually set the price at the minimum allowed by Congress. Although the secretary's range of discretion over the support price was altered from time to time, the program established in 1949 remained basically unchanged for the next thirty-two years.

Political Alignments

The dairy industry faces two important constraints in defending its program. First, it is concentrated regionally. While all states have some dairy production, five states produce 50 percent of the country's milk, and ten states produce two-thirds of it.[3] Over half of all dairy production comes from forty-four congressional districts.[4] Second, the number of commercial dairy farms has declined dramatically, from 600,000 in 1959 to 200,000 in 1978, as herd size per farm has gone up and both farm workers and cows have become more productive.[5]

1. The 1910–14 period was chosen because it represented a prosperous period in the history of American agriculture. On the development of the parity concept, see Wesley McCune, *The Farm Bloc* (Garden City, N.Y.: Doubleday, Doran and Co., 1943), chap. 2.

2. On the wartime provisions and development of the 1949 act, see *Congressional Quarterly Almanac*, vol. 5 (1949), pp. 131–46. See also John D. Donahue, "The Political Economy of Milk," *Atlantic Monthly* (October 1983), pp. 59–68; and Congressional Quarterly, *Farm Policy: The Politics of Soil, Surpluses, and Subsidies* (Washington, D.C.: CQ, 1984).

3. U.S. Department of Agriculture, Economic Research Service, *Dairy: Background for 1985 Farm Legislation*, Agriculture Information Bulletin 474, September 1984, p. 2.

4. Elizabeth Wehr, "Dairy Lobbyist: Counting Cows and Votes," *Congressional Quarterly Weekly Report*, vol. 41 (August 27, 1983), p. 1717.

5. The Department of Agriculture reported in 1984 that milk production per labor hour had more than doubled in the last decade, while production per cow increased 85 percent between 1959 and 1983. USDA, *Dairy: Background for 1985 Farm Legislation*, pp. 2, 4.

The dairy industry has attempted to counteract its declining political base in two ways: (1) by a high level of lobbying and campaign finance activity, and (2) by developing logrolling coalitions with other commodity support programs. The industry is unusually well organized for coordinated action. Most farmers sell their milk to cooperatives, which in turn sell it to manufacturers or process it themselves. Cooperatives controlled a staggering 79 percent of the farm milk supply in 1980, with the twenty largest alone controlling 52 percent and the eight largest, 36 percent.[6] Thus the dairy industry has a perfect mechanism to organize and dun its clientele for political action, avoiding the "free rider" problem.[7] The industry has been very active in forming political action committees to support congressional candidates. In 1984 the largest of its political action committees, the Associated Milk Producers, contributed more than $1 million to congressional candidates—the eleventh highest total of any group.[8] The total for all dairy industry PACs in 1982 was about $1.8 million.[9]

Equally important is the mechanism through which the dairy program is reauthorized. Legislation is considered first by the two chambers' Agriculture committees, which have traditionally been dominated by rural members—although more by southerners than representatives from dairy states. The dominance of producer interests is particularly heavy in the House, where subcommittees of the Agriculture Committee are organized around particular commodities—for

6. Ibid., app., table 6. The figures for manufactured dairy products are generally smaller. Cooperatives had an 87 percent share of the milk powder market in 1980, but only 64 percent of butter, 47 percent of cheese, 22 percent of cottage cheese, and 10 percent of ice cream.
7. On this problem in interest groups, see Mancur Olson, *The Logic of Collective Action: Public Goods and the Theory of Groups* (Harvard University Press, 1965); and Terry M. Moe, *The Organization of Interests: Incentives and the Internal Dynamics of Political Interest Groups* (University of Chicago Press, 1980).
8. Stephen Pressman, "Incumbents Relied More on PAC Gifts in 1984," *Congressional Quarterly Weekly Report*, vol. 43 (June 8, 1985), p. 1117.
9. Donahue, "The Political Economy of Milk," p. 62. In a study of the relationship between dairy industry campaign contributions in 1974 and 1976 and House consideration of a price support measure in 1975, W. P. Welch has argued that because dairy industry campaign contributions were biased toward incumbents and members of the Agriculture Committee, their effect on House roll call votes was relatively modest: most recipients would probably have supported positions favored by the industry in any case as a result of constituency interests or ideological or party commitments. See W. P. Welch, "Campaign Contributions and Legislative Voting: Milk Money and Dairy Price Supports," *Western Political Quarterly*, vol. 35 (December 1982), pp. 478–95. Welch did not, however, consider the extent to which dairy industry contributions may, by influencing Agriculture Committee members and helping to maintain a coalition of interests among agriculture-minded legislators, help to set the dairy policy agenda for consideration by the full houses of Congress.

example, the Livestock, Dairy and Poultry Subcommittee. Not surprisingly, this subcommittee has heavy dairy state representation. Dairy legislation has generally been considered as part of a four-year omnibus agricultural bill that combines not only the interests of a number of commodities—for example, wheat, cotton, tobacco, corn—but also programs that will gain the votes of urban and suburban legislators—for example, the food stamp, child nutrition, and food for peace programs. Vote trading also occurs between rural and urban legislators on issues such as the minimum wage.[10] Producer groups are intimately involved in the negotiation of these packages. Having the producer groups reach an agreement among themselves clearly fits the blame-generating interests of legislators. As a long-time dairy industry lobbyist put it, "What Congress likes is for you to come up there with a package to which there is absolute, complete, and total agreement. Then they don't have to make a decision."[11]

Dairy farmers' role in the agricultural coalition is often uneasy, however, for dairy farmers are also major consumers of feedgrains and alternative suppliers of beef. Thus their interests in a variety of pricing and production issues may put them at odds with other farm producers.[12]

The dairy industry has preferred an indexed support program to reliance on ad hoc increases for several reasons. First, with a relatively weak political base of its own, the industry's reliance on ad hoc adjustments would require a major expenditure of resources in an uncertain political environment, and it might lead to tensions within the agricultural coalition. It is, in short, both costly and risky. Second, the parity index used in setting dairy support prices is very favorable to the dairy industry. It is a general index of farm prices and costs rather than specific to dairy farmers, but dairy industry productivity has in recent years risen faster than that of farmers generally. Thus the parity mechanism has tended to overcompensate dairy farmers for inflation. Finally, reliance on an indexed parity base did not preclude increases in the percentage of parity supported. While the range of 75 percent to 90 percent remained set in permanent legislation, omnibus agriculture

10. See, for example, John G. Peters, "The 1981 Farm Bill," in Don F. Hadwiger and Ross B. Talbot, eds., *Food Policy and Farm Programs,* Proceedings of the Academy of Political Science, vol. 34, no. 3 (1982), pp. 157–73.

11. Interview with Patrick Healy, former lobbyist for the National Milk Producers Federation, November 25, 1986.

12. See, for example, Ward Sinclair, "Unlikely Herd Seeks to Trample Dairy Bill," *Washington Post,* November 5, 1983, p. A3.

TABLE 7-1. *Policymakers' Objectives and Strategies in Indexing Dairy Price Supports*

Player	Dominant objective	Strategy
Policy specialists and dairy state legislators	Credit claiming	Build logrolling coalitions to protect dairy support program; keep challenges to indexing structure off agenda; work for higher support levels within parity structure
Legislators from other agricultural areas	Vote trading	Build logrolling coalitions to provide legislative majorities for commodity programs aiding their districts
All other legislators	Vote trading	Vote for commodity support programs so long as they do not conflict with own district's interests
Executive non-specialists and specialists	Good policy, blame avoiding, credit claiming	Resist pressures for higher support levels; defect when necessary to maintain political support

bills provided a vehicle to set a support floor above the 75 percent level on a temporary basis. Moreover, the industry could lobby the secretary of agriculture to use his discretion to set a higher support price than the legal minimum, although these efforts were usually resisted strongly. The motivations and strategies of the major participants in dairy price support policymaking are summarized in table 7-1.

Logrolling among commodity interests served the dairy industry well for many years. It also prevented challenges to the agricultural support coalition from being considered, let alone being adopted. But this arrangement depended on some conditions that were gradually eroding in the 1970s and 1980s. Most important, it assumed a high degree of autonomy for legislative policy specialists. In particular, they needed to control the agenda to ensure that agriculture programs were considered together to facilitate logrolling.

A second condition that facilitated logrolling was an expanding "pie" of funding available for programs. As budgetary stress increased, however, the White House and executive and legislative budget guardians became much more active in attempting to devise sectoral policies that had previously been left to specialists. They also put much more pressure on executive specialists in the Agriculture Department to pursue administration policies rather than the priorities of the dairy industry. They sought to recast the dairy support issue for legislative nonspecialists as a blame-generating one—that is, a vote for higher support prices was fiscally irresponsible and a vote against the president. In addition, defenders of other agriculture programs became preoccupied with defending their own interests. While they realized that if the various support programs did not hang together they would hang separately, increased budgetary strictures inevitably set off competitive pressures within the agricultural coalition. These pressures could not be resolved easily or amicably.

A third condition facilitating logrolling in the postwar period was that those who supported the dairy program through vote trades believed that it "worked." For supporters of other agriculture programs this meant that the dairy program did not upset existing funding relationships by taking up an expanding share of the presumably limited funding available for all commodity support programs. To other legislators, "working" meant that the program did not create obvious, unplanned funding growth or clearly fail to achieve its objectives—a long-term balance between supply and demand.

For most of the postwar period, the principle of indexing itself had gone largely unquestioned; the debate centered on the support price (percentage of parity). In the 1980s, with dairy price support purchases and expenditures exploding, the indexing procedure itself became a central issue. Dairy interests were forced into a more defensive posture. Knowing that they could never gain through ad hoc increases what indexing provided automatically, dairy farmers sought to defend the parity principle. Executive branch officials sought to break with this principle as part of a package of changes to cut runaway expenditures for price supports.

In short, when the conditions facilitating vote trading began to erode, the logrolling game became much more complex, involving both more actors and more complex motivations. These revised relationships are summarized in table 7-2.

While the agricultural coalition was not shattered, it was seriously

TABLE 7-2. *Policymakers' Objectives and Strategies in Maintaining Dairy Price Support Indexation*

Player	Dominant objective	Strategy
Policy specialists and dairy state legislators	Credit claiming	Maintain logrolling coalitions to protect dairy support program; keep challenges to indexing structure off agenda
Budget guardians and executive non-specialists and specialists	Good policy	Disrupt logrolling coalitions in agriculture by bringing up programs one by one; seek to generate blame toward program supporters by portraying them as fiscally irresponsible; press for increased administrative discretion in setting price support level
Legislators from other agricultural areas	Vote trading	Support logrolling coalitions so long as other programs do not take resources from programs crucial to legislator's district
All other legislators	Blame avoiding, vote trading	Vote for commodity support programs so long as they do not conflict with own district's interests or generate blame

weakened. This development made it much harder for dairy interests and their legislative allies to defend the dairy price support program from attacks by the Reagan administration.

The Ford and Carter Years

A brief discussion of dairy support politics in the 1970s serves both to highlight differences from the following decade and to show some of the origins of those differences. In the early 1970s, the dairy industry was still on the offensive. Debate focused on establishing a support level above the 75 percent minimum. The 1973 farm bill established 80 percent of parity as the minimum support level. This expired in March 1975, and Congress tried for two years to set the level at 85 percent of parity. President Ford vetoed these bills. During the 1976 campaign, Jimmy Carter upset dairy farmers by stating that he felt the minimum of 80 percent of parity was probably sufficient. He later backed an 85 percent support rate. Shortly after taking office, the Carter administration increased the support to equal 83 percent of parity.[13]

Soon after the increase, the administration submitted its omnibus farm bill, with no changes in the basic dairy program. The administration wanted to keep the flexibility of the 75–90 percent range, and debate on the farm bill focused on other programs. In general, Carter sought to keep down support payments to all farm producers. The House and Senate bills each provided for a minimum dairy price support level of 80 percent. The support prices for other programs were also higher than the administration's program, and Carter threatened to veto the bill. But the conference committee bill, which provided for 80 percent parity through March 1979, was passed and the president signed it. As an additional bonus to the industry, inflation adjustments were to be made on a semiannual (rather than the previous annual) basis.[14]

When the 1977 legislation expired in March 1979, Agriculture Secretary Bob Bergland had the option to set the support level as low as 75 percent of parity. Consumer groups wanted the administration to allow support to fall that low; they claimed sustaining the 80 percent level would be inflationary. A lower support level would mean not only lower milk and cheese prices but also smaller federal government expenditures for milk purchases— $251 million in fiscal year 1980 rather than a projected $568 million.[15] Milk producers, represented by organizations such as the National Milk Producers Federation, argued that a minimum support level of 80 percent was necessary to ensure a stable supply of milk. They claimed that insufficient support would

13. Mary Link, "Administration Farm Program Draws Fire," *Congressional Quarterly Weekly Report*, vol. 35 (March 26, 1977), p. 537.
14. P.L. 95-113, sec. 203. The secretary was also given discretion to make quarterly adjustments in dairy price supports.
15. Maxwell Glen, "Congress Won't Pull the Props From Under Dairy Price Supports," *National Journal*, vol. 11 (August 4, 1979), p. 1292.

cause dairy farmers to sell their herds to beef processors, reducing milk production and ultimately causing higher prices.[16]

Although the administration was worried about stimulating over-production, it decided to continue the 80 percent support level. However, Bergland also proposed a plan enabling the secretary of agriculture to reduce support below 80 percent of parity in years when Commodity Credit Corporation purchases exceeded 3.5 billion pounds of butter and cheese or 350 million pounds of nonfat dry milk during a twelve-month period.[17] This was not included in the 1979 legislation, ostensibly because legislators felt there was not enough time for a thorough review of the proposal. The bill that was passed maintained the 80 percent parity minimum support level and extended authority for semiannual adjustments.

The 1979 legislative process did, however, foreshadow the policy debates to follow in 1981 and beyond. In particular, Bergland's idea of reductions in price supports based on a purchase trigger was one of the first devices picked up by the Reagan administration in its effort to reduce dairy spending. Although the proposal failed in 1979, it showed that policy nonspecialists in the executive branch were willing to cut the dairy support base in an effort to decrease federal expenditures. But Carter, unlike his predecessor, was unwilling to veto legislation to enforce his will.

Retrenchment under Reagan

As a result of the increased support levels approved in 1977 and 1979, dairy production grew. But demand remained relatively stagnant, in part due to the higher support price. Thus the percentage of production absorbed by federal purchase increased dramatically, from less than 3 percent for most of the 1970s to more than 10 percent by 1981–82.[18] In 1980 the annual cost to the government of buying and storing dairy products topped $1 billion. This cost was projected to rise to $3.2 billion by the middle of the decade.[19] Dairy price supports,

16. This argument was supported by a CBO report that showed that the 80 percent level would provide greater stability than a 75 percent level. Congressional Budget Office, *Consequences of Dairy Price Support Policy* (CBO, March 1979), pp. 27–37.

17. Glen, "Congress Won't Pull the Props," p. 1294.

18. See Emerson M. Babb, "Dairy," in Gordon C. Rausser and Kenneth R. Farrell, eds., *Alternative Agricultural and Food Policies and the 1985 Farm Bill* (Berkeley: University of California, Giannini Foundation of Agricultural Economics, 1985), p. 263.

19. Elizabeth Wehr, "Major Farm Programs Likely to Escape Drastic Overhaul," *Congressional Quarterly Weekly Report*, vol. 39 (February 28, 1981), p. 373.

FIGURE 7-1. *Commodity Credit Corporation Outlays on Price Support Programs, Dairy and All Farm, 1971–86*

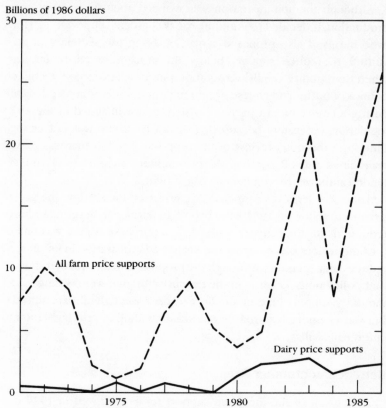

Billions of 1986 dollars

SOURCES: CCC outlays for farm price supports from *The Budget of the United States Government, Historical Tables, 1986,* table 8-1, and *Historical Tables, 1989,* table 8-1. Net outlays for dairy price support program from U.S. Department of Agriculture, Agricultural Stabilization and Conservation Service, *1983–84 Dairy Price Support Program* (USDA, 1984), table 8, and *1986–87 Dairy Price Support Program* (USDA, 1987), table 8.

which had traditionally absorbed only a small share of farm price supports, took almost 37 percent of those expenditures in fiscal year 1980 and close to 47 percent in 1981 (figure 7-1). This massive expenditure growth caused serious strains in the agricultural coalition: other commodity interests felt that dairy was getting too large a share of severely constrained resources.

Clearly some action was necessary to reduce production, but finding a politically acceptable means to do so would not be easy. Reducing the support price would drive many small family farms out of business. Moreover, while price support cuts would lead to lower production in the long run, they might actually increase production in the short run, as desperate marginal producers struggled to cover their fixed costs by milking to capacity. Providing incentives to dairy farmers to reduce production (or capacity, by cutting their herds) was another option, but the Reagan administration saw production controls as increasing government involvement in the industry when they wanted to get government out.

The Reagan administration and many consumer groups fought for cutbacks in price supports. Many economists also criticized the parity index, arguing that the calculation method did not accurately reflect the increases in productivity of producers. A coalition of consumer groups and milk users (for example, chocolate manufacturers and the Pizza Hut chain) argued that the parity index should more accurately reflect dairy production costs. The National Milk Producers Federation discussed a modified version of the 1979 Carter plan to decrease production. Their version would have set the minimum price support on a sliding scale between 75 and 85 percent of parity, depending on the amount of milk purchased by the government.[20]

Changes in Congress resulting from the 1980 election increased the administration's leverage in winning cuts in agricultural programs. The most important change was the new Republican control of the Senate. In the past the Senate had been the farm lobby's stronghold, because small rural states are overrepresented and all senators have at least some rural constituents. But the new Republican Senate majority had been won in part on Reagan's coattails and was reluctant to deviate too far from the president's program. The cohesion of the agricultural coalition was also hurt by the defection of many southern Democratic "boll weevils" in the House to support the President on budget and tax issues. As a result, many northern Democrats refused to acquiesce in farm programs of interest to Southern members as they had in years past.[21]

First Steps

The administration's first action was to propose legislation eliminating the April 1, 1981, semiannual adjustment in the support price.

20. Ibid., pp. 373, 375; and Robert G. Kaiser, "Reagan Budget-Cutting Passes First Hill Test on Dairy Bill," *Washington Post,* March 27, 1981.
21. See Richard E. Cohen, "Living by the Sword," *National Journal,* vol. 13 (October 31, 1981), p. 1956; and Carl L. Infanger, William C. Bailey, and David R. Dyer, "Agricultural Policy in Austerity: The Making of the 1981 Farm Bill," *American Journal of Agricultural Economics,* vol. 65 (February 1983), p. 7.

(The outgoing Carter administration had also suggested skipping this adjustment.) The April increase was scheduled to add 90 cents to the support price, from $13.10 to 14.00 per hundredweight.[22] The administration claimed that semiannual adjustments had contributed to the overproduction of dairy products. Elimination of the increase would save the federal government $147 million, and consumers would not face an increase in dairy prices.[23] This legislation was the first of the Reagan administration's economic bills considered by Congress, and the administration lobbied hard for passage, hoping that a victory against the powerful dairy lobby would provide momentum when more important legislation was introduced later in the session.

The dairy lobby was divided over how to deal with this proposal. Many cooperatives argued that the inflation adjustment was necessary and claimed that overproduction was due not to overly generous price supports but to low feedgrain prices (which encourage farmers to sell grain, "processed" by cows, as milk) and to relatively low beef prices (which discourage sale of less productive cows for slaughter).[24] But the National Milk Producers Federation, an umbrella organization to which most dairy cooperatives belong, had anticipated the cut for some time, and decided to neither oppose nor support it. By making concessions now, the federation felt, it would be in a stronger position to fight cuts that might be proposed later in the omnibus farm bill.[25] But dairy state legislators and dairy interests were reluctant to move forward on the legislation until they knew what dairy provisions were to be included in the administration's four-year farm bill. The administration, on the other hand, sought to delay submitting its four-year

22. The support price is in fact not a single national amount. It increases directly with distance from the center of U.S. dairy production in Wisconsin and Minnesota. This system is intended to prevent low-cost producers in that region from dominating other markets.
23. See the testimony of Deputy Secretary of Agriculture Richard E. Lyng in *Milk Support Price Adjustment,* Hearings before the Subcommittee on Livestock, Dairy and Poultry of the House Committee on Agriculture, 97 Cong. 1 sess. (Government Printing Office, 1981), pp. 28–39. See also Elizabeth Wehr, "Reagan Bill Canceling Dairy Support Clears," *Congressional Quarterly Weekly Report,* vol. 39 (March 28, 1981), p. 561.
24. Senators from dairy states also argued that it was unfair to (1) give dairy farmers such short notice of the elimination of an inflation adjustment, and (2) consider dairy separately, rather than as part of a general farm bill, where cuts were more likely to be spread evenly. See the testimony of Senators William Proxmire, Robert Kasten, and Patrick Leahy in *Semiannual Milk Price Support Adjustment,* Hearing before the Subcommittee on Agricultural Production, Marketing and Stabilization of Prices of the Senate Committee on Agriculture, Nutrition and Forestry, 97 Cong. 1 sess. (GPO, 1981), pp. 5–19.
25. Elizabeth Wehr, "Dairy Bill Advances Despite Complaints," *Congressional Quarterly Weekly Report,* vol. 39 (March 21, 1981), p. 505.

proposal until after the House and Senate had cut the semiannual adjustment, fearing that proposals for additional cutbacks would weaken congressional support for eliminating the April adjustment.[26]

Congress eventually gave the administration a victory on the semiannual adjustment, but many members, including Republicans, were reluctant collaborators. The Republican-controlled Senate Agriculture Committee acted first, passing its bill 14–2. Rudy Boschwitz, Republican of Minnesota, was one senator in a difficult position. He was reluctant to oppose the president but was equally disturbed with voting against the dairy industry. He voted with the president, and said, "I told the people of Minnesota to hang in there with President Reagan—and I hope they hang in with me."[27] In the full Senate, dairy interests sought to protect the program by attaching amendments that would make the bill unacceptable to either the president or the House, delaying enactment until after the April 1 increase went into effect. This would allow dairy state Republicans (and others) to scuttle the president's plan without voting directly against him on a budgetary issue.[28] After difficult battles to defeat these amendments, the Senate then passed the bill by an overwhelming 88–5 vote.

Dairy supporters in the House followed a different strategy. The Agriculture Committee's Livestock, Dairy and Poultry Subcommittee first passed a four-year authorization to try to foil the administration's strategy of gradually chipping away at dairy price supports. The subcommittee bill would have set supports at a minimum of 75 percent of parity through 1985, while retaining semiannual adjustments. It was a clever strategy: it provided most of the short-term savings of the administration's plan (inflation had driven support levels down to about 74 percent of parity since the last semiannual adjustment), but its real

26. "House Panel Reluctant to Cut Dairy Supports," *Washington Post*, March 13, 1981; and Ward Sinclair, "Administration Delays Farm Bill; Worry About Dairy Votes Cited," *Washington Post*, March 24, 1981.

27. Elizabeth Wehr, "Senate Panel Votes to Block Milk Price Support Increase But House May Stymie Plan," *Congressional Quarterly Weekly Report*, vol. 39 (March 7, 1981), p. 428.

28. The first vehicle used by dairy state senators was an amendment to limit imports of casein, a processed dairy product. The second was a series of amendments opposing the grain embargo to the Soviet Union. The latter amendments had been intended by dairy industry supporters to attract wider support from grain state legislators, and in so doing to slow down action on price supports, since similar resolutions had previously failed to pass the House. The Reagan administration lifted the grain embargo just before final action by the Agriculture committees on the 1981 farm bill. See Wehr, "Reagan Bill Canceling Price Support Clears"; and Infanger, Bailey, and Dyer, "Agricultural Policy in Austerity," pp. 3–4.

purpose was to preempt consideration of further cuts when the omnibus farm bill was considered later in the year. But subcommittee chairman Tom Harkin realized that he did not have enough votes to win in the full committee, so he backed down, suggesting the 75 percent floor for only the next six months. This would have led to a very modest April adjustment and to spending only about $20 million above the president's request. But Agriculture Committee members felt heavy pressure not to erode the first Reagan administration budget-cutting measure; they rejected the revised Harkin plan by a vote of 16–25. The same forces were at work during the floor debate. House Speaker Thomas P. O'Neill urged Democrats not to block the bill, and it was approved on a voice vote.[29]

The administration had its first victory. The vote seemed to prove that when made to stand alone or in opposition to other commodity and nutrition programs, individual commodity interests could be defeated.

Making Long-Term Changes

When the omnibus farm bill was introduced later in 1981, it contained more bad news for dairy interests. The administration proposed dairy support rates of 70 percent of parity. Most other commodity support programs were also cut in a variety of ways. This was part of a deliberate administration strategy to break the monopoly on agenda setting long held by the coalition of producer groups and their legislative allies. As David Stockman later put it, "My strategy is to come in with a farm bill that's unacceptable to the farm guys so that the whole thing begins to splinter."[30] And the stakes were much higher than in the spring dairy vote: these provisions would not be temporary ones, but would presumably have the normal four-year life span of agricultural reauthorizations.

Dairy interests managed to stave off budget cuts in the reconciliation bill passed by Congress in July. The big battles were over finalizing the omnibus farm bill. Both the House and Senate Agriculture committees had approved farm bills with overall price tags well above both the administration's proposal and the first budget resolution.[31] In Sep-

29. Wehr, "Dairy Bill Advances Despite Complaints," pp. 505–06. For background see *Milk Price Support Adjustment*, Hearings.

30. William Greider, "The Education of David Stockman," *Atlantic Monthly* (December 1981), p. 35.

31. The House committee bill set payments at 75 percent of parity with only an annual adjustment. The original Senate bill proposed by Senator Robert Dole had set the

tember, one month before authorization expired, the administration offered a substitute bill. The dairy component allowed support prices at 70 to 90 percent of parity, with annual adjustments for inflation. An additional floor was set at the then-current support price ($13.10 per hundredweight). But the secretary of agriculture was given discretion to forgo the inflation adjustment when expenditures were above $750 million in a year.[32] The administration focused on selling this substitute to the Republican-controlled Senate, which passed it by a voice vote.[33]

Faced with a restrictive bill from the Senate and threats from the tobacco lobby that it would defect to support the administration's restrictive dairy program unless dairy groups came to its aid, dairy groups sought ways to rally the farm coalition. Dairy industry representatives met with Tom Harkin, chairman of the House dairy subcommittee, and presented a combination of provisions for dairy and other agriculture groups. The dairy component was the same as the Senate bill's in fiscal year 1982 but more generous in later years. Thus its incentive to farmers to reduce herds (and production) was a weak one: if they hung on to their bovine investment for one lean year, they would benefit from higher support prices in later years.

To get this passed, farm interests arranged floor consideration so that their legislation appeared as a moderate alternative to two extreme proposals. The plan worked in the following way: first Berkley Bedell, Democrat of Iowa, submitted the "compromise" package as an amendment to the Agriculture Committee's original proposal, with the endorsement of committee and subcommittee leaders of both parties. Farm state representatives were urged to pass the Bedell amendment first and later introduce more liberal amendments specific to their in-

---

minimum at 70 percent of parity. The committee accepted a Boschwitz amendment that restored the 75 percent target in theory, but allowed it to be overridden if targets for either expenditures or quantity of milk purchased were surpassed. Because these targets were certain to be reached, the 75 percent threshold had no practical effect in the short term, but it kept the 75 percent level in law, which might be helpful to dairy interests in later bargaining rounds. See Elizabeth Wehr, "Senate Panel Revises Farm Bill; House Waits," *Congressional Quarterly Weekly Report,* vol. 39 (May 16, 1981), pp. 857–58; and Robert G. Kaiser, "Despite the Industry's Record, the Federal Cow May Be Drying Up," *Washington Post,* June 28, 1981, p. A5.

32. Elizabeth Wehr, "Block Seeking Compromise on Farm Bill," *Congressional Quarterly Weekly Report,* vol. 39 (September 5, 1981), p. 1674.

33. Two floor amendments more favorable to the industry sponsored by Senator Boschwitz were rejected. *Congressional Record* (September 15, 1981), pp. 20543–60; and Elizabeth Wehr and Ross Evans, "Senate Farm Bill Reflects Budget Pressures," *Congressional Quarterly Weekly Report,* vol. 39 (September 19, 1981), p. 1806.

terests. The amendment passed 400–14, with the support of 104 Republicans. Next, Representative Barney Frank, Democrat of Massachusetts, introduced the administration-backed package passed by the Senate. A line of dairy program supporters rose to deride the Frank amendment as too tough on dairy farmers. Although this was the administration's package, the White House failed to send official notification of its position, thus leaving House Republicans uncertain of where Reagan stood. Representative James Jeffords, Republican of Vermont, submitted a more liberal dairy program to replace Frank's amendment. By prior arrangement, dairy state representatives split on this proposal in the floor debate, with several claiming that it was too liberal. Both the Frank and Jeffords amendments were defeated by wide margins.[34] By the time the administration caught on to what had happened, it was faced with a House bill that would substantially exceed budget restrictions in out-years.

Although the House-passed bill had little prospect of gaining acceptance by the Senate, it increased the dairy industry's prospects for gaining a favorable compromise in conference with the Senate. The dairy provisions of the final farm bill were indeed a compromise between the two chambers' bills. The bill retained a support price freeze at $13.10 per hundredweight in fiscal year 1982 and price increases in each of the three succeeding fiscal years. But support minimums were set in dollar rather than parity terms, and the support prices were tailored to meet spending targets. By fiscal year 1985, the minimum support price would have equaled less than 60 percent of the projected parity figure.[35] Parity was not completely discarded, however. The statute contained a dual set of upward triggers: support prices would rise to a minimum of 70 percent of parity if government purchases fell below specified levels and to 75 percent if they met more stringent targets.[36] The legislation was a blow to the dairy interests, and they were the strongest opponents of accepting the conference

34. See *Congressional Record* (October 7, 1981), pp. 23507–16; and Robert G. Kaiser, "Lobby Scores a Major Victory," *Washington Post,* October 9, 1981, p. A4.

35. See Infanger, Bailey, and Dyer, "Agricultural Policy in Austerity," p. 8; Elizabeth Wehr, "High Cost, Sugar Threaten Compromise," *Congressional Quarterly Weekly Report,* vol. 39 (November 7, 1981), p. 2197; and Wehr, "House Passes Farm Bill by Two-Vote Margin," *Congressional Quarterly Weekly Report,* vol. 39 (December 19, 1981), pp. 2481–82.

36. Beginning in 1983, the minimum support level would be 70 percent of parity in any year that federal purchases were expected to be less than $1 billion. The minimum would be 75 percent of parity if net purchases were less than 4 billion pounds in fiscal 1983, 3.5 billion in fiscal 1984, and 2.69 billion in fiscal 1985. P.L. 97-98, sec. 103.

report on the agriculture bill. It was, however, passed by both houses of Congress.[37]

Despite the cuts in the real purchasing value of price supports (which had not been increased since October 1980), dairy surpluses and federal purchases continued to mount. Federal outlays rose from $46 million in fiscal 1979 to $1.93 billion in fiscal 1981.[38] In May 1982 the administration announced a proposal to do away with the minimum support levels legislated in 1981 and allow the secretary of agriculture to set the minimum support price. Agriculture Secretary John Block promised to use this discretion to freeze the support level at $13.10 per hundredweight until January 1, 1983, eliminating a scheduled increase of 15 cents per hundredweight on October 1. Supports would then be lowered significantly if supplies did not drop. Harkin said the dairy plan was "laughable and ludicrous"; dairy organizations opposed it as well.[39] Several legislators proposed alternatives that would provide increased price supports in exchange for production controls on individual farms to lower dairy output. These proposals gained substantial support from dairy interests, but were opposed by the Reagan administration.

With Congress unwilling to give the administration complete discretion over support levels, and the Reagan administration unwilling to accept production controls, the result was incremental cutbacks. Congress froze price supports at the $13.10 level for fiscal 1983 and fiscal 1984 in the 1982 reconciliation bill. The fiscal 1985 level was set to equal the parity level to which $13.10 corresponded on October 1, 1983.[40] In addition to the freeze, the act contained two downward triggers: the secretary of agriculture was authorized to make deductions from the support level in years that purchases were above levels specified in the statute.[41]

Despite the reduced support levels, both milk production and herd

37. Wehr, "House Passes Farm Bill by Two-Vote Margin," p. 2482. The Senate passed the bill 68–31. The House vote was a very close 205–203.

38. *Dairy Price Support Proposals,* Hearing before the Subcommittee on Livestock, Dairy and Poultry of the House Committee on Agriculture, 97 Cong. 2 sess. (GPO, 1982), p. 20.

39. Elizabeth Wehr, "Administration Dairy, Sugar Plans Draw Fire," *Congressional Quarterly Weekly Report,* vol. 40 (May 8, 1982), p. 1071.

40. This was projected to be 61.2 percent, which would convert to $14.05. Elizabeth Wehr, "New Farm Support Plans, Food Stamp Changes Push Savings Totals Over Top," *Congressional Quarterly Weekly Report,* vol. 40 (August 21, 1982), p. 2050.

41. Starting in 1982, 50 cents per hundredweight would be reduced from farmers' support price if the government purchases were greater than 5 billion pounds annually. In October 1983 an additional 50 cents would be assessed through 1985 if purchases

sizes grew in 1983, reflecting large grain crops (and low prices) and low beef prices.[42] Thus the administration continued to press for further legislation to stop overproduction and reduce costs, which reached $2.5 billion in fiscal 1983. Meanwhile, other commodity program expenditures were also exploding, further increasing pressures for cutbacks (see figure 7-1).

The dairy industry remained divided over how to counter the program reductions. A majority of the industry, including the National Milk Producers Federation, supported production limits for individual farmers. But some producers—especially those in the Southeast—and most user groups wanted cuts in the levels of price supports rather than production limits. The industry split led to stalemate on a House bill that included production quotas.[43] Six months of maneuvering followed, including a belated administration effort to substitute a simple cut in price supports for the proposal to pay dairy farmers to reduce production. But Congress did enact a temporary, voluntary program to lower production backed by most of the dairy industry. In addition to this diversion program, the legislation also froze prices paid to farmers at the reduced levels established by the 1982 act (an effective level of $12.10 per hundredweight). It also contained additional downward triggers for 1985 if purchases exceeded levels in the law.[44] Despite

---

were more than 7.5 billion pounds annually. The second assessment was to be rebated to farmers who cut their production. P.L. 97-253, sec. 101.

42. For analyses of the reasons for the production increases, see Ward Sinclair, "Reagan to Judge Hill Decision to Stem Flow of Milk and Money," *Washington Post,* November 25, 1983, p. A2; Andrew H. Malcolm, "Dairy Output Rises Despite Efforts to Curb It," *New York Times,* November 11, 1983, pp. A1, B6; and Michael T. Belongia, "The Dairy Price Support Program: A Study of Misdirected Economic Incentives," *Federal Reserve Bank of St. Louis Review,* vol. 66 (February 1984), pp. 5–14.

43. Elizabeth Wehr, "Split Within Dairy Industry Frustrates Compromise Effort," *Congressional Quarterly Weekly Report,* vol. 41 (May 21, 1983), p. 1018.

44. The final legislation (P.L. 98-180) reduced the support price from $13.10 to $12.60 per hundredweight through fiscal year 1985. In addition, it continued through March 1985 one of the two 50-cent assessments enacted in 1982, and authorized further price support reductions if purchases were projected to exceed specified levels. A price increase of at least 50 cents per hundredweight was also authorized in July 1985 if purchases fell below 5 billion pounds and the secretary felt that a production stimulus was needed. While the categories were juggled and prices depended on purchase amounts, the presumed (and actual) outcome was an effective support level of $12.10 through June 1985 and $11.60 thereafter. The paid diversion program was authorized to begin in January 1984. Participants in the diversion program were required to cut production by 5 percent to 30 percent from their previous yields and were paid a rate of $10 per hundredweight. The statute also provided for an assessment of up to 15 cents per hundredweight to pay the costs of a national dairy promotion program. For a comparison of the House, Senate, and final provisions, see *Dairy and Tobacco Adjustment*

strong veto threats from Office of Management and Budget Director David Stockman, the president signed it because he feared that failure to do so might endanger Republican control of the Senate.[45]

Indexation Revived?

Congress revised the dairy support program five times in the first Reagan administration—three times in 1981 alone. Support prices were cut, and the link between price supports and the parity indexing mechanism was broken. But as Congress began to debate a new four-year agricultural authorization bill in 1985, it was clear that further changes were in store. Agriculture policy had become a budgetary disaster area: farm programs that had been projected in 1981 to cost $11 billion between fiscal years 1982 and 1985 were now projected to cost more than $60 billion over that period. But the farm economy was in desperate shape, with a high dollar hurting exports and a debt crisis driving many farmers into bankruptcy. And the farm lobby was more divided than ever before on how to deal with agricultural problems.[46]

The dairy industry had specific problems of its own. The diversion program led to a slight dip in dairy production and purchases. But by early 1985, when the diversion program expired, production and outlays for milk removals began creeping back up toward record levels.[47]

Act of 1983, H. Rept. 98-556, 98 Cong. 1 sess. (GPO, 1983). See also Elizabeth Wehr, "Industry-Supported Dairy Bill Is Turned Back in the House," *Congressional Quarterly Weekly Report,* vol. 41 (October 22, 1983), p. 2167; and Ward Sinclair, "Hill Conferees Approve Bill to Cut Milk Surplus," *Washington Post,* November 16, 1983, p. A7.

45. In addition to dairy provisions, the bill contained tobacco sections that led David Stockman to dub it the "Jesse Helms Reelection Act of 1984." Stockman argues that in signing the legislation, "the single cleanest, easiest, and most justified shot at budget cutting during the entire Reagan presidency was kicked in the ditch." David A. Stockman, *The Triumph of Politics: Why the Reagan Revolution Failed* (Harper and Row, 1986), p. 386. On the political pressures leading the president to sign the bill, see Ward Sinclair, "Reagan to Judge Hill Decision to Stem Flow of Milk and Money," *Washington Post,* November 25, 1983, p. A2; Ward Sinclair and David Hoffman, "President Signs Bill to Reduce Milk Production," *Washington Post,* November 30, 1983, p. A1; and Seth S. King, "How the Dairy Lobby Put the Squeeze on the White House," *New York Times,* December 4, 1983, p. E5.

46. On the political background to the 1985 farm bill, see Jonathan Rauch, "Writing a Blank Check," *National Journal,* vol. 17 (March 23, 1985), pp. 625–31; Bruce Stokes, "A Divided Farm Lobby," *National Journal,* vol. 17 (March 23, 1985), pp. 632–38; and Stokes, "Behind the Farm Bill Muddle: Farmers Divided," *National Journal,* vol. 17 (May 11, 1985), pp. 1007, 1030–31.

47. Milk production in 1984 fell 2.5 percent below the previous year, but rose 6.1 percent in 1985 over 1984. U.S. Department of Agriculture, Economic Research Service, *Dairy: Situation and Outlook Report,* no. D5-405 (USDA, 1986), p. 6.

In part, the problem was one of program design: the short-term nature of the diversion program led many farmers to withhold milk from the market without actually reducing herd sizes; once the program expired, this four-legged productive capacity was brought back into the market.[48]

The debate on the 1985 farm bill began with the protagonists farther apart than ever. The administration proposed a major shift toward a market focus in agriculture policy. Dairy price supports, for example, were to be further reduced over the next two years. Beginning in fiscal year 1988, price supports would be replaced by direct payments to producers for the difference between the current market price of milk and a declining percentage of the market price in the preceding three years.[49] Adoption of these proposals would have gutted the dairy support program, but they represented such a radical change from current policy that they were not taken seriously by Congress.

The National Milk Producers Federation, on the other hand, wanted to resurrect indexing of dairy price supports, which had fallen into disuse as ad hoc cutbacks stated in dollar terms had gradually replaced automatic increases stated in parity terms. The federation proposed a new dairy-specific index that more adequately incorporated productivity increases and included a stabilizer for periods of excessive supply. The federation also proposed permanent standby authority for diversion programs like the one just ending.[50]

Neither the House or Senate Agriculture committees wished to take the lead in proposing program cuts or budget-busting legislation, and both had tremendous difficulties developing a bill that could command a majority of committee support, let alone win on the floor. Neither reported legislation until the farm law was nearing expiration in September. The bills that were eventually reported retained past differences between the committees. The House bill was far more gener-

48. In addition, the diversion program caused serious price disruptions, especially in the Southeast, where production costs are higher. This led a higher percentage of Southeast producers to participate in the program than in other regions, forcing imports of milk from the Midwest. On problems with the diversion program, see *Reauthorization of the Agriculture and Food Act of 1981,* Hearings before the Senate Committee on Agriculture, Nutrition and Forestry, 99 Cong. 1 sess. (GPO, 1985), pt. 1, pp. 140–67.

49. On the administration's proposal, see Elizabeth Wehr, "Administration's Farm Bill Aims to Reverse Course Set in 1930s," *Congressional Quarterly Weekly Report,* vol. 43 (March 2, 1985), p. 398.

50. For an outline of the federation's proposal, see *Reauthorization of the Agriculture and Food Act of 1981,* Hearings, pt. 1, pp. 448–62.

ous.[51] Its dairy provisions reflected a philosophy of higher support prices and nonmarket production controls: it included the dairy industry's indexing plan, a standby diversion plan, and a new program to purchase entire dairy herds and get them out of production (known as the "cow-killing" program). As House Dairy subcommittee chairman Tony Coelho, Democrat of California, summarized the strategy, "We decided to put as much as possible in the House bill, knowing we could give up some things and still not give away the guts of the program."[52]

The Senate bill reflected the extreme nervousness of farm state Republicans whose seats were at risk in the 1986 election. The committee reported a Democratic-sponsored package that proposed no diversion programs and additional purchase triggers for price support reductions that did not begin until 1987.[53] An administration-backed effort to impose immediate downward price support triggers was rejected on the Senate floor, and the conference committee reached a predictable compromise with no clear philosophical basis. Indexing remained dead. The standby diversion program was rejected as well. But the "whole herd buyout" was accepted on a temporary basis. A combination of assessments (ostensibly to pay for the herd buyout) and support reductions reduced the effective support price almost immediately. Downward price triggers (roughly half the magnitude of those in the Senate bill) were also included, to take effect beginning in 1988.[54]

51. A Republican counterproposal in the House, backed by the administration, would have cut support prices further instead of imposing production controls. It was defeated by the House on a vote of 244–166. Seventy-four Republicans defected to support the more generous Agriculture Committee plan. See Ward Sinclair, "House Rejects Reagan's Lower Farm Supports," *Washington Post,* September 27, 1985, p. A5.

52. David Rapp, "Farm Bill Offers Limited 'Win' for All Sides," *Congressional Quarterly Weekly Report,* vol. 43 (December 21, 1985), p. 2676.

53. On the provisions of the House and Senate bills, see David Rapp, "House Panel Votes Farm Bill with 'Protectionist' Provision," *Congressional Quarterly Weekly Report,* vol. 43 (September 14, 1985), pp. 1828–33; and Rapp, "Farm Belt Republicans Courted to Pass Senate Agriculture Bill," *Congressional Quarterly Weekly Report,* vol. 43 (September 28, 1986), pp. 1921–23.

54. Price supports were set at $11.60 per hundredweight through the end of 1986, $11.35 through September 1987, and $11.10 thereafter. In addition, farmers were assessed a fee of 40 cents per hundredweight from April through December in 1986 and 25 cents for the first nine months of 1987 to pay for the buyout program. This yields an effective support rate of $11.60 through April 1986, $11.20 through the end of 1986, and $11.10 thereafter. Beginning in 1988 and effective through 1990, an additional 50 cents per hundredweight would be cut from the support rate then in effect each January if purchases for the year were projected to surpass 5 billion pounds. P.L. 99-198, title I.

FIGURE 7-2. *Milk Production and Consumption, 1970–87*

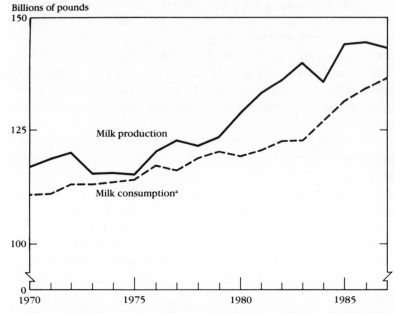

SOURCES: Gordon C. Rausser and Kenneth R. Farrell, Eds., *Alternative Agricultural and Food Policies and the 1985 Farm Bill* (Berkeley: University of California, Giannini Foundation of Agricultural Economics, 1985), p. 262; and U.S. Department of Agriculture, Economic Research Service, *Dairy Situation and Outlook Report,* various issues. Data on implicit price deflator for GNP from *Economic Report of the President, 1988* (Government Printing Office, 1988), p. 252.

a. Commercial disappearances from domestic sources.

Consequences

The dairy price support program provides several valuable lessons about the consequences of indexing. It shows, first of all, how application of indexing to price support and other purchase programs can have severe distortive effects on markets and government outlays, especially when it is accompanied by open-ended purchase requirements. Instead of adjusting supply quickly to demand, the structure of the dairy price support program tended to reinforce disequilibrium because real prices to producers remained at levels that elicited an excessive supply of milk (figure 7-2).

Indexing gave the dairy industry a very strong bargaining position. For the most part, it needed only to block new legislation to preserve its position. And if it did have to endure price support cuts, they would be from indexed levels rather than nominal ones. This strong bargaining position is reflected in budget trends: net outlays by the Commodity Credit Corporation for dairy price supports in fiscal years 1981–84 were 360 percent higher than in the preceding four years.

Cutbacks did eventually take place in the dairy program, if somewhat belatedly, gradually, and haphazardly. Thus the dairy case also reinforces very clearly the finding in the congressional pay case that indexing does not necessarily take benefit levels off the political agenda. Photographs of caverns full of government-owned cheese have performed the same function for dairy price supports that declining reserves did for the social security system: they have made nonspecialist policymakers aware that something is seriously wrong with the system, such that clientele demands to "stay the course" can no longer be tolerated. This sort of good-policy objective is not nearly so powerful as the blame-generating pressures that have scuttled many congressional pay raises, but it did help to tip the balance in favor of cutbacks.

Conclusions

Dairy price supports before 1981 were a classic case of credit-claiming and vote-trading politics in action. Because the group was relatively weak in isolation and agricultural coalitions were very fragile, dairy interests favored automatic escalation of price supports rather than taking their chances on ad hoc increases. Policy specialists in the legislature supported and facilitated this procedure by building logrolling coalitions. But the dairy case also illustrates the limits of coalition politics: it depends ultimately on retention of autonomy by legislative specialists and the existence of enough resources to satisfy all claimants. A majority of legislators do not have strong blame-avoiding incentives to declare dairy price supports off limits to cuts.

In the early 1980s dairy price supports became a special target of the OMB and the White House. The huge growth of expenditures and immense overproduction—a very visible by-product of price supports—made price supports vulnerable in Congress as well. Specialists in the House attempted to use their power over the agenda to defend the dairy program and its indexing provisions against administration attacks and more restrictive Senate bills, but they had to retreat in the face of these initiatives.

Viewing the dairy industry as a loser because its indexing provisions were stripped away is obviously an oversimplification, however.

Congress lowered support prices and moved away from the parity index. But it firmly rejected dismantling the program or giving the secretary of agriculture wide discretion to set price supports. To understand dairy price politics, one must explain not only the demise of indexing, but also why the program was not transformed or support prices cut even more.

Perhaps the most important reason the basic dairy support program remained intact is that while the power of legislative specialists was weakened, it was never broken. Only on the first 1981 dairy vote (on stopping the semiannual adjustment) was President Reagan able to define the terms of the debate, focusing blame on legislators who refused to back him. In later battles, the authorizing committees adapted to the new environment and retained much of their ability to control their chambers' agendas.

To maintain agenda control, committee leaders have had to juggle at least four kinds of pressures: responding to individual commodity interests, keeping the agricultural coalition together, developing a bill that could pass their chamber, and avoiding a presidential veto.[55] Responding to individual commodity interests is clearly a major priority. No matter how much Jesse Helms, as chairman of the Senate Agriculture Committee, might have privately disliked dairy price supports on principle, he did not want dairy state legislators taking retribution against tobacco programs later on. Thus specialist leaders must protect dairy state legislators' fundamental interests, which they define to include the basic integrity of the price support program and to exclude administrative discretion that could be used to gut dairy supports.

However, when the claims of one commodity program get out of line, adjustments must be made—especially when there is an overall budgetary ceiling. Dairy programs were certainly in this situation in the early 1980s. The major dairy organizations (notably the National Milk Producers Federation) knew this. They still tried to get the best deal that they could for dairy farmers, using agenda control mechanisms (such as the House "compromise" ruse in the 1981 farm bill) to achieve this end. But they were also careful not to jeopardize their position in the policy process by appearing obstructionist; it is better to compromise and be consulted than to be obstructionist and be by-

55. On leadership in congressional committees, see Steven S. Smith and Christopher J. Deering, *Committees in Congress* (Washington, D.C.: Congressional Quarterly Press, 1984), pp. 167–202.

passed. (Many dairy state legislators were more prone than the lobbyists to take a hard line, at least in roll call votes, but the fact that these
legislators "voted their districts" could be forgiven by colleagues as a
blame-avoiding political necessity, especially since such posturing
rarely obstructed compromise on outcomes).[56] Thus the inevitability
of cutbacks in the dairy program was accepted by dairy interests and
by committee members; the debates focused instead on the form,
magnitude, and timing. Suspension of automatic increases was a first
step in the cutback process; the ad hoc cutbacks that followed less-
ened the immediate practical significance of parity and thus lowered
the benefits to dairy interests of defending it.

While legislative specialists must respond to individual commodity
interests, they must also keep the agriculture coalition together. In the
1980s, this task has involved allocating cutbacks across various commodity programs. Cutback management caused major strains within
the coalition; achieving "absolute, complete, and total agreement" was
no longer possible. But David Stockman's hope that he could shatter
the coalition was never achieved either. Committee members were
able to "circle the wagons" around the basic structure not only of dairy
price supports but the other commodity support programs as well.

The shape of the specialists' cutback proposals was further limited
by the need to take into account targets set by the two chambers'
Budget committees and by the need to win chamber majorities. Given
tight budgets and obvious expenditure overruns, legislative specialists
received less deference on the floor than in previous years. Agriculture
bills in the Reagan period routinely exceeded budget targets, in part
because farm problems were far worse than anticipated. But the Agriculture committees did cut programs to meet Budget committee targets, knowing that they would be open to challenge on the floor if
they did not. As long as they made that effort, their expertise advantage was so great that major changes to committee bills proposed on
the floor had little chance of passage.

Finally, leaders of the authorizing committees have to produce bills
that will not be vetoed by the president. This challenge is particularly
important in conference committee negotiations. Reducing the likeli-

56. Of course, dairy organization leaders face blame-avoiding pressures of their own:
rank-and-file dairy farmers tend to be less aware of the limitations on what can be
achieved and the necessity to be perceived in Washington as a reasonable player in
policy debates. As a result, they pressure interest group leaders to take a harder line than
the leaders think is wise.

hood of a veto often involves accommodation on specific policy questions. It may also include coming up with strategies to make it difficult for a president to veto a bill he does not like—that is, forcing him to jump on the bandwagon to avoid personal blame or losses for allies. This can be a powerful incentive, as the 1983 dairy bill shows.

Dairy policymaking in the 1980s, in short, suggests forms of blame avoidance that are both more subtle and more complex than in the social security and congressional pay cases. Dairy state legislators often postured to show that they were doing their best for constituents. But they knew when to compromise to avoid even greater losses (and political recriminations). Specialist leaders sought to allocate cutbacks in a way that would keep the agricultural coalition intact. And the president, sensitive to his own agricultural base and that of many of his allies, refused to use a veto strategy to force the more radical changes sought by his advisers.

8

Minimum Wages

For the most part, indexing mechanisms have been applied to expenditure and revenue programs rather than regulatory ones. But one important regulatory program—the minimum wage—came close to being indexed in 1977. The indexing proposal won the support of the Carter administration as well as the congressional committees with jurisdiction over the measure. But unlike the social security case, where nonspecialists in Congress intervened to push reluctant policy specialists to adopt indexing, in this case nonspecialists overturned the committee's recommendation for indexing. This failure was not preordained by the alignment of political forces, however. It resulted as well from clever maneuvering by opponents of indexing.

Background

The Fair Labor Standards Act of 1938 established a wage floor and criteria for which types of business establishments and jobs would be covered by the minimum wage requirement.[1] Over the next thirty-six years, the minimum wage was raised in a series of steps, rising to slightly over 50 percent of the average manufacturing wage after each increase and declining thereafter as inflation eroded its value. The trend in employment coverage was much more consistent: the percentage of nonsupervisory, private, nonagricultural jobs covered by the federal minimum wage requirement nearly doubled, from 43.4 percent in 1938 to 83.7 percent in 1974.[2]

On the surface, indexing the minimum wage would seem to have

Alice Keck Whitfield is coauthor of this chapter.

1. An earlier minimum wage under the National Industrial Recovery Act was overturned by a Supreme Court decision that the act was unconstitutional.

2. Finis Welch, *Minimum Wages: Issues and Evidence* (Washington, D.C.: American Enterprise Institute for Public Policy Research, 1978), p. 3.

much the same appeal as indexing income transfers to the poor and aged—namely, it protects individuals who have the least market power to maintain their own income. Indexing may also prevent low-income workers from dropping out of the work force if it keeps their real wage from declining relative to public assistance payments. But most economists believe that the minimum wage increases unemployment, especially among low-wage workers. The effect of the minimum wage on low-income workers, they argue, is a complex one: those who are able to obtain employment earn more than they otherwise would, but fewer of them are employed.[3] Workers (notably first-time workers) who lack skills may be excluded from the work force altogether, since the value they can contribute to a product may be less than the wage floor. Pricing low-skill workers out of the market, in turn, contributes to the development of a permanently unemployed underclass. To combat this problem, a number of economists and policymakers have proposed instituting a subminimum wage for teenagers that would allow firms to employ workers, usually for a limited period, at a wage that corresponds to their productivity. But this proposal has been vigorously opposed by organized labor, which fears that it would lead firms to fire adult workers and replace them with teenagers. The minimum wage may also have regional effects, tending to protect jobs and firms in the relatively higher-wage northern states from competition by lower-paid southern workers.[4]

Organized labor has been the strongest supporter of a single minimum wage, even though most unionized workers already earn wages exceeding that amount. The reason is that a high minimum wage helps to keep firms using low-wage, low-skill workers from competing with more productive (but more expensive) unionized workers.[5] This phe-

3. Economists have shown great puzzlement as to why the minimum wage is popular among low-wage workers, since it increases unemployment among these workers. There are two reasons. Many low-wage workers who do find jobs—and most of them do—would be worse off without the minimum wage. Those who do not find jobs do not attribute this to the minimum wage and would like to have a wage at or above the minimum when they do gain employment. See Frank G. Steindl, "The Appeal of Minimum Wage Laws and the Invisible Hand in Government," *Public Choice*, vol. 14 (Spring 1973), pp. 133–36.

4. See Thomas Rustici, "A Public Choice View of the Minimum Wage," *Cato Journal*, vol. 5 (Spring–Summer 1985), pp. 123–28.

5. In addition to their labor substitution effects (of high-priced for low-priced labor), minimum wage laws also encourage substitution of capital for labor by raising the relative price of the latter. On the economic effects of the minimum wage, see generally Minimum Wage Study Commission, *Report* (Government Printing Office, 1981), vols. 1, 6.

nomenon also splits the business community to some extent, with firms employing high-wage workers gaining protection from competition by lower-wage firms.

Obviously, the strength of each of these effects varies with the level of the minimum wage in relation to other wages and with the extent of its coverage of the labor force. It is thus not surprising that the debate over indexing has been entangled with conflict over the base from which it should be indexed, and which workers, if any, should be exempt.

Political Alignments

The interest group lines in the battle over minimum wage indexing are clear: organized labor is for it and business groups are generally against it, believing that an ad hoc process places them in a stronger strategic position to resist both real and nominal increases in the minimum wage. Policy experts, in this case economists, are also largely opposed to indexing, and their position is used by opponents of minimum wage indexing to strengthen their own case.

But an examination of the strategic positions of the major participants within Congress reveals a more complex story. Legislative specialists (or in this case the Democratic majority among them) tend to be closely allied with organized labor, and thus support minimum wage indexing even though it means a reduction in their own discretion and opportunities to claim credit by enacting ad hoc increases in the minimum wage.

The choice facing legislative nonspecialists was relatively painless for some, but difficult for many others. Where legislators' constituencies consist overwhelmingly of either business or labor interests, they can presumably vote with those interests and claim credit for doing so. Many southerners will be reluctant to index the minimum wage unless it is at a very low base, because they fear a loss of competitiveness for their region. And some legislators, notably those representing agricultural districts made up of family farms, might face few direct pressures at all.[6] They can afford to vote their policy preferences or, as they have

6. The minimum wage was extended to certain agricultural workers under the 1966 amendments to the Fair Labor Standards Act. However, farms hiring fewer than 500 man-days in their peak employing quarter were exempt from minimum wage requirements. The minimum wage for covered agricultural workers was lower than that for other workers until passage of the 1977 Fair Labor Standards Act amendments. However,

done in the past with minimum wage legislation, use the issue as a vote-trading opportunity. Both farm state and southern Democrats have traded support for the minimum wage and food stamps for urban legislators' support for commodity price supports. The vote-trading interests of these legislators suggest that indexing the minimum wage should be resisted; once increases became automatic, urban legislators would no longer have to trade with rural legislators to obtain those increases. A valuable bargaining chip would be lost. But if they did reject indexing, they would prefer to do so in a way that minimizes blame from their vote-trading partners.

For many legislative nonspecialists, however, any vote on the minimum wage presents a stark and unpleasant choice between business and labor interests. While there is credit to be gained, there is blame as well. This group of legislators might prefer to get minimum wage decisions off the agenda through indexing. An automatic process would prevent them from having to choose between constituencies in future votes on minimum wage increases. Indexing has a definite "pass-the-buck" appeal for this group. But as with the congressional pay case, legislators cannot pass the buck in the long term without an initial vote to authorize indexing. And a vote to index the minimum wage has a blame-generating potential of its own. Business interests, in particular, are certain to oppose such a move. If this cross-pressured group of legislators is forced to vote on indexing the minimum wage, they are likely to seek to redefine the issue or make their own position on it obscure, minimizing blame from both sides. The motivations and strategies of the legislative participants are summarized in table 8-1.

This situation presented several opportunities for Republican opponents of mimimum wage indexing in the 1970s. They could not keep the issue off the congressional agenda because the legislative specialists opposed them. And they could not hope to win in Congress on a straight party vote. So long as there was a Republican in the White House, they could probably depend on a presidential veto. But when this was no longer a possibility, they would need to develop a legislative strategy to defeat indexing of the minimum wage. More specifically, they could attempt to sway Democrats, especially southerners and those from agricultural districts, whose policy ideas and interests were often similar to their own, who faced weaker pressure from or-

under 1974 amendments to the act, the wage differential had dropped to 10 cents an hour—$2.20 compared with $2.30—and would have disappeared in 1978 even without congressional action in 1977.

TABLE 8-1. *Legislators' Objectives and Strategies in Indexing the Minimum Wage*

Player	Dominant objective	Strategy
Democratic legislative specialists	Credit claiming	Press minimum wage onto agenda, win support of legislative nonspecialists and president
Legislative conservatives	Good policy, credit claiming	Offer legislative nonspecialists option to redefine issue in a way that does not index the minimum wage but minimizes blame from labor
Farm state legislators	Vote trading	Oppose indexing to preserve opportunity for future vote trading on farm issues
Southern Democrats	Vote trading, blame avoiding	Oppose indexing to prevent job losses and preserve vote-trading opportunities
Most other legislators	Blame avoiding	Select option that minimizes blame from both business and labor

ganized labor, and who did not want to let go of the vote-trading opportunity presented by periodic decisionmaking on the minimum wage. Moderate Democrats (and Republicans) might be swayed by a counterproposal that offered some concessions to labor without actually granting indexing. Such an initiative might appear to these cross-pressured legislators to be the best opportunity to minimize blame from both business and labor. A strategy appealing to both these groups could potentially win away enough legislators to deny indexing a legislative majority. And that is precisely what happened.

The Push for Indexation

The idea of indexing the minimum wage is hardly a novel one; Australia and New Zealand did it in 1914, and a number of industrialized countries have done so since then.[7] But it entered the U.S. agenda as a result of the high inflation of the early 1970s and the increasing diffi-

7. *Fair Labor Standards Amendments of 1977*, S. Rept. 95-440, 95 Cong. 1 sess. (GPO, 1977), p. 22.

culties labor had in obtaining ad hoc increases. After a wage floor hike in 1967, there was a seven-year delay until the next one was passed. This occurred despite dominance of the House Education and Labor and the Senate Human Resources committees by allies of organized labor. The delay may even have been due to such dominance: this close alliance led legislative nonspecialists, who felt that the specialists were captives of labor, to refuse to defer to the committee specialists. In 1972, for example, both committees reported minimum wage bills, but the House bill was overturned on the floor by an alliance of Republicans and southern Democrats. The House then refused to allow the committee to go to conference with the Senate, fearing that the committee would defer to the Senate bill, which was closer to the committee's original proposal.[8] In 1973 the two houses of Congress managed to agree on a minimum wage bill, but President Nixon vetoed it, and the House (again led by a coalition of Republicans and some southern Democrats) sustained the veto.[9] In 1974 Nixon signed a bill very close to the 1973 plan when it became clear that he did not have enough votes to sustain a veto.[10]

Early in October 1975, the constitutional convention of the AFL-CIO called on Congress and the president to increase the federal minimum wage from $2.10 to $3.00 per hour. Although the minimum wage legislation enacted in 1974 included increases that were to be effective in 1976, Andrew Biemiller of the AFL-CIO claimed, "The wage floors established by the bill have been overtaken by inflation and the rates are now too low to meet the objectives of the act."[11] As in the social security case, organized labor sought to link benefit indexing to an increase in the base. By the end of October, Representative John Dent, Democrat of Pennsylvania, chairman of the House Education and Labor Committee's Subcommittee on Labor Standards, convened hearings on the minimum wage. His bill sought to increase the minimum wage to $3.00 by 1976 and to index it to the Consumer

8. *Congressional Quarterly Weekly Report,* vol. 31 (June 9, 1973), p. 1459; and *Congressional Quarterly Almanac,* vol. 28 (1972), pp. 361–71.

9. For an analysis of the veto and the House vote to sustain it, see *Congressional Quarterly Weekly Report,* vol. 31 (September 15, 1973), p. 2452, and (September 22, 1973), pp. 2534–35. Republicans and southern Democrats did not vote solidly in favor of the president. Eastern Republicans and southern Democrats voted almost two-to-one to override the veto, but they provided enough favorable votes to sustain it.

10. *Congressional Quarterly Almanac,* vol. 30 (1974), pp. 239–44.

11. *Fair Labor Standards Amendments of 1975,* Hearings before the Subcommittee on Labor Standards of the House Education and Labor Committee, 94 Cong. 1 sess. (GPO, 1976), p. 6.

Price Index so that when prices rose more than 3 percent, the minimum wage increased by that amount plus 1 percent. This was the same formula then used for the federal employees' retirement program and later repealed because it overcompensated those retirees.[12]

At the 1975 hearings, business interest groups opposed indexing generally and the CPI mechanism specifically. The National Restaurant Association representative said, "Congress should not abdicate the important responsibility of weighing the many factors not reflected in the CPI."[13] William C. Dunkelberg, an economist, provided analysis showing the inflationary and disemployment effects of an increase in the minimum wage. When asked about the indexing scheme, he said that he did not think the CPI was an appropriate index because it did not take into account productivity changes.[14] Department of Labor representatives pointed out that the "kicker" of 1 percent above inflation compounded to eventually give increases greater than the actual price rise.

Although Dent's proposal did not go anywhere in 1975, it laid the ground for a second attempt at indexing in 1977. In that year, the AFL-CIO, tired of waging continuous battles for minimum wage increases and fully aware of organized labor's contribution to the 1976 Democratic victories, anticipated smooth sailing for its legislative initiatives. Increasing the minimum wage to 60 percent of the manufacturing wage and indexing it at that level was one of labor's primary objectives. Dent introduced legislation including an immediate increase in the minimum wage from $2.30 to 55 percent of the average hourly earnings in manufacturing, or $2.85. By 1979 the minimum wage would be maintained at 60 percent of the average hourly earnings in manufacturing. In proposing to index to the average manufacturing wage, Dent withdrew his support for the CPI linkage he had proposed two years earlier.[15] In hearings held in March many business interest groups and labor economists again expressed opposition to indexing.

12. Without the 1 percent kicker, the CPI linkage would prevent low-wage workers from joining in the general growth in real wages that characterized the period up to the early 1970s. Ad hoc changes between 1950 and 1975 increased the minimum wage more than a CPI linkage would have. See Sar A. Levitan and Richard S. Belous, *More than Subsistence: Minimum Wages for the Working Poor* (Johns Hopkins University Press, 1979), p. 133.

13. *Fair Labor Standards Amendments of 1975,* Hearings, p. 92.

14. Ibid., p. 142.

15. *Fair Labor Standards Amendments of 1977,* Hearing before the Subcommittee on Labor Standards of the House Committee on Education and Labor, 95 Cong. 1 sess. (GPO, 1977), p. 10. On the 1977 debate generally, see Levitan and Belous, *More than Subsistence,* chap. 5.

Representatives of the American Hotel and Motel Association, for example, questioned the appropriateness of basing service industry wages on the wages in manufacturing. They pointed out that the wage increases due to productivity gains in manufacturing often could not be justified in a service industry.[16]

Chamber of Commerce representatives claimed the proposals would eliminate over 2 million full- and part-time jobs and increase consumer price levels 3 percent. Industries from agriculture to amusement parks would be damaged, they warned. One spokesman for the chamber encouraged Congress to maintain control for setting the minimum wage level. He said, "If you feel a responsibility to provide a minimum wage, . . . then you certainly ought not to forego that responsibility now by tying to some index and getting yourself off the hook."[17]

For the most part, the economists who testified were against the minimum wage and indexing. Finis Welch argued that the indexing plan would have a "ripple effect" in the economy. Because the average wage in manufacturing is affected by the minimum wage, an increase in the minimum wage would in turn increase the average wage, which would increase the minimum and so on.[18] Edward Gramlich, who claimed he was not as opposed to the minimum wage as most economists, was frequently cited during the hearings. Gramlich argued that an increase in the minimum wage could be beneficial in terms of income redistribution, but an increase as large as that proposed in the Dent bill would cause unemployment and inflation. He suggested indexing at 50 percent of the manufacturing wage.[19]

Meanwhile, there was a serious split on this issue in the Carter administration. Secretary of Labor Ray Marshall supported Dent's plan, while some members of the Council of Economic Advisers wanted smaller increases. The administration reached a compromise in March and proposed an increase to $2.50 in July. After one year, the wage

16. *Fair Labor Standards Amendments of 1977*, Hearing, p. 57. In fact, however, use of the manufacturing wage as an indexing mechanism would have a more conservative effect than other measures, such as the retail wage index. Since many retail workers are employed at the minimum wage, each inflation adjustment would have an upward "ratchet effect" on the wage base being indexed. Because the vast majority of manufacturing workers earn more than the minimum wage, the ratchet effect would be lower. See the discussion in *Congressional Record* (September 15, 1977), p. 29434.
17. *Fair Labor Standards Amendments of 1977*, Hearing, pp. 306, 325.
18. Ibid., p. 95.
19. Ibid., p. 296.

would be maintained at 50 percent of the manufacturing wage.[20] This plan was much less liberal than that supported by the AFL-CIO, and it was counted as a major defeat for organized labor. George Meany called the proposal "shameful" and said, "This is a bitter disappointment to everyone who looked to this administration for economic justice for the poor."[21] Nevertheless, the administration had agreed to the principle of indexing. In order to fight for a higher wage floor, the AFL-CIO joined civil rights, minority, and religious groups in forming the Coalition for a Minimum Wage. The coalition was dedicated to winning "a minimum wage increase sufficient to lift America's lowest-paid workers out of poverty and keep them off the street."[22] The stalemate between the Carter administration and labor led to a four-month delay in further action.

A cold war between the administration and the AFL-CIO obviously benefited neither, however. Thus in July President Carter agreed to support a more generous package, increasing the wage to $2.65 with the level to be set at 53 percent of the average manufacturing wage by 1980. Organized labor pronounced the plan acceptable.[23] These proposals were approved by the House Education and Labor Committee on a 29–7 vote. A majority of committee Republicans were opposed to indexing but planned to fight the provision on the floor.[24]

In September, Dent's bill was brought to the House floor. Consideration took place one day before the House was to vote on the conference report on the four-year extension of the farm bill—an issue of critical importance to rural members, and one on which they often engaged in vote trading with urban members on issues such as the minimum wage. Representative John Erlenborn of Illinois, the ranking

20. The administration's proposal was based on "straight-time" (that is, excluding overtime) hourly earnings, rather than gross hourly earnings as in the Dent bill. The former figure is about 4 percent lower than gross hourly earnings. See *Fair Labor Standards Amendments of 1977,* Hearing, pp. 474–76; and Levitan and Belous, *More than Subsistence,* p. 123.

21. See Philip Shabecoff, "Minimum Wage Bill Is Reported to Divide the Administration," *New York Times,* March 23, 1977, p. A20; and Shabecoff, "$2.50 Minimum Wage Proposed by Carter in Setback to Labor," *New York Times,* March 25, 1977, p. A1.

22. Philip Shabecoff, "Unemployment Rate Fell to 7.3% in March as Cold Wave Eased," *New York Times,* April 2, 1977, p. 12.

23. As in the Carter administration's original proposal, the link was to straight-time earnings. Philip Shabecoff, "Carter and Labor Back a 35¢ Rise To Make the Minimum Wage $2.65," *New York Times,* July 13, 1977, p. A1; and A. H. Raskin, "Carter and Organized Labor," *New York Times,* July 14, 1977, p. 28.

24. Mary Eisner Eccles, "House Panel Approves Minimum Wage Hike," *Congressional Quarterly Weekly Report,* vol. 35 (July 23, 1977), p. 1520.

TABLE 8-2. Congressional Votes on 1977 Minimum Wage Amendments to H.R. 3744, by Party and Region

| | Amendments | | | | | |
| | Substitute ad hoc increases for indexing | | Institute subminimum teen wage | | Vote switching between amendment on indexing and amendment on subminimum wage | |
Party and region	Percent supporting	Total number voting	Percent supporting	Total number voting	Number switching to prolabor position	Number switching to antilabor position
Republicans	89.4	141	91.6	142	1	2
Democrats	35.3	275	28.7	279	44	21
Northern Democrats	15.8	190	17.5	189	20	19
Southern Democrats	78.9	85	52.2	90	24	2
Agriculture Committee Democrats	60.0	30	25.8	31	10	0

SOURCE: *Congressional Quarterly Almanac*, vol. 33 (1977), pp. 148-H to 151-H.

Republican on Dent's subcommittee, submitted an amendment providing for a three-stage increase in the minimum wage through 1980 without indexing. Republican strategists believed that unless they offered a positive alternative such as the phased increase, the committee's proposal would win. As its key architect said in a later interview, the proposal "gave cover" to many representatives: "They could go home and say to labor, 'I voted for an increase,' and say to their friends in business, 'I voted to protect you against a mindless, thoughtless rule for mandating an increase.' "[25] In offering his amendment, Erlenborn cited the civil service retirement program's indexing features as an example of a bad indexing scheme. He also questioned the use of the manufacturing wage to index the minimum wage, and he concluded that indexing would "signal a surrender by this Congress and by this administration to inflation as a way of life and to inflation that cannot be reduced."[26]

The Erlenborn amendment lowered legislators' political costs of opposing indexing, regardless of the roots of that opposition. The amendment passed by a vote of 223–193. Labor narrowly avoided a second major defeat the same day, as the House rejected another Erlenborn amendment to create a teenage subminimum wage by a single vote. Speaker Thomas P. O'Neill broke what had been a tie vote.[27]

A comparison of the two roll call votes reveals some important differences in support for the anti-indexing and subminimum wage amendments (table 8-2). Republicans voted overwhelmingly in favor of both amendments; about five-sixths of northern Democrats voted against both. Among both these groups, however, support for the subminimum wage was actually higher than for the anti-indexing amendment. But the latter won and the former lost because two overlapping groups of Democrats—those from the South and those serving on the Agriculture Committee—shifted massively toward a prolabor position on the subminimum wage vote after taking an antilabor position on the anti-indexing provision.[28] Only two southern Democrats and no Agriculture Committee Democrats moved in the opposite direction.

Why did southern and agriculture-oriented members shift in this

25. Interview with John Erlenborn, November 23, 1987.

26. *Congressional Record* (September 14, 1977), p. 29181.

27. Ibid. (September 15, 1977), pp. 29436, 29463–64; and Philip Shabecoff, "House Votes Minimum-Wage Rise and Rejects a Lower Youth Rate," *New York Times,* September 16, 1977, p. A1.

28. Of the ten Agriculture Committee Democrats who shifted to a prolabor position on the subminimum wage issue, four were northerners and six were southerners.

way? Erlenborn's anti-indexing amendment increased the minimum wage but did not establish permanent annual adjustments. Thus in the short term it allowed these members to vote their interests while limiting blame from labor and from their legislative partners in the urban-rural vote-trading coalition. In the long term it kept their urban partners dependent on rural support for future minimum wage increases—a dependency that would have been lost if a permanent escalator had been put into the minimum wage legislation. In the subminimum wage vote, however, support for the labor position did not threaten long-term vote-trading interests. Moreover, there was no middle ground that allowed these members to support conservative policy preferences while minimizing blame from urban allies. Vote-trading (and blame-avoiding) concerns therefore dominated, and many members—the bare minimum needed to defeat the subminimum wage—defected.

After the House defeated indexing of the minimum wage, George Meany pledged to work for a better bill in the Senate. However, the Carter administration dropped support for the provision.[29] And when the Senate considered a Human Resources Committee bill that included indexing, the bill's cosponsors, Harrison Williams and Jacob Javits, feared that it would be subject to the same attack as the House bill. They decided to preempt their opponents and offered an amendment to their own bill that would delete indexing and raise the minimum in four steps to $3.40 by 1981—roughly the same level as that anticipated under the Senate committee's indexing proposal, but to slightly higher levels and for one more year than the Erlenborn substitute. In announcing this about-face, Senator Williams acknowledged the House defeat and the concerns of others against indexing. This retreat allowed proponents of a minimum wage hike to defeat a series of Republican amendments providing less liberal increases. The Williams-Javits amendment was then passed, 76–14.[30] In conference, a compromise was reached to increase the wage in four stages to $3.35 by 1981.[31] Reconsideration in that year would once again coincide with the farm bill reauthorization, facilitating renewed logrolling. It would also coincide with the report of a Minimum Wage Study Commission created by the 1977 act. One of the commission's mandates was to investigate the probable consequences of indexing the mini-

29. *New York Times,* September 24, 1977, p. 19.
30. *Congressional Record* (October 6, 1977), pp. 32696–724.
31. P.L. 95-151.

mum wage. In its final report, issued in 1981, the commission recommended linking the minimum wage to an index of average hourly earnings in the private economy (including both the farm and nonfarm sectors).[32]

The political environment was even less favorable to minimum wage legislation in 1981 than it had been in 1977, however. The Reagan administration was clearly hostile to the minimum wage, and Republicans had gained a majority in the Senate. Organized labor had to concentrate its waning political resources on fighting other battles, notably resisting the subminimum wage. After passage of the 1977 legislation, increases in and indexing of the minimum wage virtually disappeared from the public agenda for a decade.[33]

Congress finally took up the minimum wage again in 1987, after Democrats regained control of the Senate. The AFL-CIO once again led the push for indexing the minimum wage. But it took more than a year before the proposal began to move in Congress. The House moved first, in March 1988. House Education and Labor Committee Chairman Augustus F. Hawkins included indexing in his bill to raise the minimum wage to $4.65 an hour over a three-year period. But a decade had done nothing to ease business and Republican opposition to the proposal. From the outset, it appeared that indexing had little chance of passing the House and no chance of getting President Reagan's signature. Nevertheless, Hawkins and AFL-CIO lobbyists favored keeping indexing in the bill as long as possible to use as a bargaining chip—something that could be given up on the floor of the House or in conference with the Senate.[34]

These machinations placed Democrats on the Subcommittee on Labor Standards, who were the first to have to vote on the proposal, in an awkward position. Most of them did not want to go out on a limb for a potentially blame-generating proposal that was unlikely to become law and might well sink any prospects for an increase in the minimum

32. The commission supported indexing by a vote of 5–2, with one commissioner not voting. See Minimum Wage Study Commission, *Report*, vol. 1, pp. 74–84, 165, 234–38. The commission's report was essentially ignored. See Mary Eccles and Richard B. Freeman, "What! Another Minimum Wage Study?" in *American Economic Review*, vol. 72 (May 1982, *Papers and Proceedings, 1981*), pp. 226–32.

33. See Kenneth B. Noble, "Now, Maximum Interest in the Minimum Wage," *New York Times*, January 7, 1987, p. A18.

34. See Frank Swoboda, "The Minimum Wage: A Democratic Conflict," *Washington Post*, February 29, 1988, p. A15; and Patrick L. Knudsen, "Bill to Boost Minimum Wage Encounters Resistance, Delays," *Congressional Quarterly Weekly Report*, vol. 46 (February 27, 1988), p. 506.

wage. Despite Hawkins's protests, most of them defected, and indexing died in the subcommittee by a vote of 7–2. The full Education and Labor Committee added a replacement bargaining chip in the bill it reported to the floor—an additional forty-cent increase in the minimum wage in a fourth year—but indexing was once again dead for the near future.[35]

Consequences

Since 1977 the minimum wage has fallen further and further behind the average manufacturing wage (figure 8-1). The small phased increases scheduled by the 1977 act went into effect as planned, but no increases have been legislated since then. By 1987 the federal minimum wage had fallen to 34 percent of the average manufacturing wage, far below both the original Carter administration proposal and the poverty line for a three-person family.[36]

It is impossible to know what the consequences would have been if organized labor had succeeded in obtaining indexing of the minimum wage in 1977, when political conditions were most propitious. But one can make some educated guesses based on experiences with other indexed programs and with proposals for the subminimum wage. The Reagan administration would have tried to repeal minimum wage indexing when it came into office. But the administration's strategic position would have been difficult. Without indexing it is necessary only to block legislation in order to erode the real value of the minimum wage. Under Republican control of the Senate from 1981 to 1986, this was relatively easy. If minimum wage indexing had already been in place, the administration would have been forced to get a repeal through Congress. If the experience with entitlement programs (especially those with strong clienteles) is any guide, they probably would not have succeeded entirely. The major rollbacks of indexing in

35. See Frank Swoboda, "Panel Votes to Raise Minimum Wage," *Washington Post,* March 4, 1988, p. A15; Patrick L. Knudsen, "House Panel Agrees to Minimum-Wage Hike," *Congressional Quarterly Weekly Report,* vol. 46 (March 5, 1988), p. 578, and Knudsen, "House Labor Adds 4th Year to Minimum-Wage Increase," *Congressional Quarterly Weekly Report,* vol. 46 (March 12, 1988), p. 679.

36. Through most of the 1960s and 1970s, a person working full–time all year at the minimum wage had earnings roughly equivalent to the poverty line for a three-person family. By 1985 these earnings were less than the poverty threshold for a two-person family. See Nadine Cohodas, "Minimum Wage Getting Maximum Attention," *Congressional Quarterly Weekly Report,* vol. 45 (March 5, 1987), pp. 403–07; and Ralph E. Smith and Bruce Vavricek, "The Minimum Wage: Its Relation to Incomes and Poverty," *Monthly Labor Review,* vol. 110 (June 1987), pp. 24–30.

FIGURE 8-1. *Ratio of Minimum Wage to Average Manufacturing Wage, 1947–87*

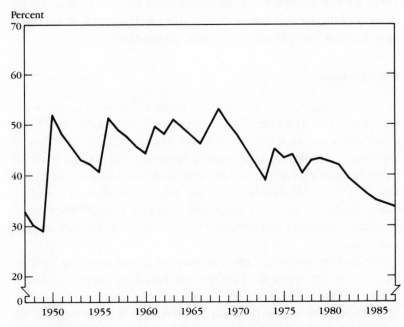

SOURCES: Minimum wage data from Finis Welch, *Minimum Wages: Issues and Evidence* (Washington, D.C.: American Enterprise Institute for Public Policy Research, 1978), p. 3. Average hourly earnings in manufacturing from *Economic Report of the President, 1988* (Government Printing Office, 1988), p. 298.

welfare state programs occurred in the Reagan administration's first year and consisted mostly of temporary freezes and some cuts in program bases, rather than outright repeals of indexing. Some of these losses have been recovered in later years. There is little reason to believe that the situation would have been dramatically different with an indexed minimum wage.

Similarly, the failure of the Reagan administration to win congressional approval of a teen subminimum wage despite years of trying shows the difficulty that even a popular conservative president has in changing the legislative status quo when faced with determined opposition from organized labor.

The 1977 defeat, in short, almost certainly put the minimum wage at a much lower level today than it would otherwise have been. The prolonged decline of the minimum wage over the last decade may in turn make it difficult to restore its historic relationship to the average manufacturing wage when the minimum wage is eventually raised. Since expectations about a program's base tend to be based on recent experience, a restoration of the minimum wage to a level above 50 percent of the average manufacturing wage would appear to be a very large increase, out of step with current expectations.

Conclusions

It is tempting to view the outcome of the battle on minimum wage indexing either as a case of conflicting good-policy ideas, which opponents won because they created serious doubts about the inflationary effects of indexing, or as a simple interest group conflict in which business defeated labor. But these interpretations would be simplistic as well as simple. Both sides in the indexing debate showed great flexibility, tailoring their own proposals to attract support from crosspressured legislators and minimize blame toward themselves and potential allies.

The Carter administration's ambivalent stance on indexing the minimum wage, for example, clearly represented an attempt to find a middle ground between the pressures it was receiving from both sides. The administration's first proposal adopted the AFL-CIO's proposal for indexing, but at a base more acceptable to business interests. This seemingly clear-cut attempt to minimize blame from all sides satisfied no one. As a result of pressure from organized labor, the administration proposed a more liberal indexing bill to replace its initial plan. But the administration failed to support the proposal strongly after announcing it, and when the House dropped indexing, the administration did not launch a hard sell in the Senate to save it.

It was in Congress that the decisive battles occurred. Unlike their counterparts in the case of social security, Democratic members of the House and Senate committees with jurisdiction over the minimum wage did not resist efforts to cut their discretion over minimum wage increases. In fact, they led those efforts. The minimum wage case, like that of dairy price supports, suggests that when legislative specialists are closely allied with and monitored by a highly organized constituency, they will sacrifice discretion if the clientele wants them to do so. But as was the case with the dairy price supports, the minimum wage case points up some serious potential disadvantages to dominance of congressional committees by strong advocates for particular clienteles: if legislative nonspecialists perceive that a committee represents the interests of a specialized clientele to the exclusion of those of the larger body, the nonspecialists may overturn the committee's recommendations. In the case of minimum wage legislation, this occurred in both 1972 and 1977.

But the potential for a rebellion by nonspecialists does not fully explain why policy nonspecialists in Congress intervened to block indexing of the minimum wage, when they had done precisely the opposite with social security in 1970. Many of the policy arguments made against indexing, most notably that it gave a signal that the federal government was surrendering to inflation, were similar in both cases. Nor can a rebellion by nonspecialists explain why Republicans won in both cases despite being a minority in the House.

The most obvious reason that social security benefits were indexed and the minimum wage was not is that Republicans voted cohesively (97 percent of those voting) in favor of indexing social security benefits and were almost as solid (89 percent) against indexing the minimum wage. Democrats split on both votes. Only about one-third of Democrats favored the winning position; these defectors furnished the Republican margins of victory. But why were Republicans in favor of indexing in the first case and opposed in the second? And how were they able to maintain such cohesion when Democrats could not?

Expectations about future changes in the program in the absence of indexing were important in shaping Republican preferences. In the social security case, ad hoc changes appeared likely to surpass inflation; in the minimum wage case, the opposite appeared to be the case. Moreover, the minimum wage vote in 1977 was correctly perceived as a Democratic measure and as a payoff to organized labor. The 1970 vote on social security in the House had neither of these attributes.

The high level of Republican cohesion on the two votes resulted from the fact that almost all Republican members perceived the party position as politically safe (blame-minimizing). Protecting social security benefits by indexing them was an easy position to defend with constituents, even those who wanted higher benefits. Opposing indexation of the minimum wage had a somewhat higher risk (and led to a higher defection rate), although labor is not a normal part of the electoral base of most Republican legislators. But the staged, nonindexed increases in the Erlenborn amendment offered Republicans (and many Democrats) who were concerned about offending labor a politically acceptable alternative to voting for the combined benefit increase and indexing proposal: it allowed them to reconcile their good-policy and blame-avoiding instincts.

Democratic unity on the two votes was lower not just because of greater diversity within the party, but also because cross-pressures on individual members were often higher and there was no single blame-minimizing position that all of them could accept. Heavy majorities of southern Democrats opposed indexing in both cases. Their reasons for opposing indexing differed in the two cases, however. Southern Democrats opposed indexing social security benefits because they wanted to preserve credit-claiming opportunities and support specialists; they rejected indexing the minimum wage because they wanted to preserve jobs and vote-trading opportunities. Northern Democrats favored indexing the minimum wage because a vote against it would be difficult to explain to their labor constituency. They split on indexing social security because it created conflicts between credit-claiming and blame-avoiding objectives.

For a majority of legislators, indexing the minimum wage never attained the "impossible to vote against" status of social security indexing. Nor was it likely to do so, given the adamant opposition of the business community. In this conflict, labor managed in 1977 to win its minimum objective of a simple short-term increase in the minimum wage level, but was unable to ensure stability of that gain through indexing.

9

Federal Income Taxes

The federal income tax is hardly one of the most popular of federal programs. But it is not without its credit-claiming opportunities, especially in a period of high inflation.[1] Without either indexing or ad hoc changes, inflation has an effect on taxpayers similar to its effect on social security beneficiaries: they are worse off, and the treasury is better off. In the case of the personal income tax, this results from the progressive nature of the tax structure. As nominal wages are adjusted upward for inflation, they are taxed at higher marginal rates. This effect, known as "bracket creep," leaves individuals with less real after-tax income. Inflation also erodes the real value of provisions of the tax code (notably the personal exemption) that reduce individuals' tax burdens. Thus its effects are likely to be especially severe at lower income levels, where the personal exemption is relatively more important. Inflation may also change the distribution of tax liabilities across income groups, because different sources of income often do not rise at the same rate during inflationary periods.

The effects of inflation on income taxes also have important budgetary implications. Bracket creep gives government extra revenue without raising tax rates—the "fiscal dividend." Legislators can use the fiscal dividend to increase spending levels or to cut deficits without legislating a tax increase. Politicians can also use the fiscal dividend to cut tax rates without reducing real long-term revenue levels. This is where the potential for credit claiming comes in. Voting for tax cuts, like voting for social security benefit increases, is a popular stand. As

Karl M. Knapp provided research assistance for this chapter.
1. On the effects of inflation on the income tax, see Congressional Budget Office, *Indexing the Individual Income Tax for Inflation* (Background Paper) (Government Printing Office, 1980), pp. ix–x. On the political effects of tax buoyancy (that is, whether revenues from a specific tax rise faster than inflation and economic growth), see Richard Rose, "Maximizing Tax Revenue While Minimizing Political Costs," *Journal of Public Policy*, vol. 5 (August 1985), pp. 289–320.

192 l AUTOMATIC GOVERNMENT

Senator Russell Long noted, "It has never really been difficult to pass a tax cut if the situation were such that it is justified. I say that as one who served as chairman of the Finance Committee for 14 years. If we can justify a tax cut, it is easy to accomplish. In fact, it is easy enough to pass one even if it is not justified."[2] Maintaining discretion over tax brackets also allows officeholders to channel tax cuts toward particular groups.

This is precisely what Congress has done. From 1960 to 1975, for example, Congress used the opportunity provided by bracket creep to enact frequent tax cuts, which resulted in lower taxes than would have been the case if 1960 tax provisions had been indexed. At the same time, Congress redistributed the tax burden toward higher-income taxpayers.[3] Despite these tax cuts, both marginal and average tax rates rose significantly in the 1960s and 1970s for families at median income levels. (Admittedly, real incomes were rising as well.) The same was true for families at one-half and twice the median income level.[4] Bracket creep helped to make these increases politically possible because legislators did not have to vote for tax increases.

Bracket creep is not the only way inflation distorts the tax structure. It also tends to overstate capital gains (income from the sale of assets held for a long period) because part of the increase in the value of the asset is an illusory gain due to inflation. The same is true of interest from savings accounts. Debtors, however, benefit from a nonindexed tax code because the decline in the real value of their debt caused by inflation does not count as income.

It is bracket indexing, however, that has sparked the most interest and congressional action. Most workers have incomes subject to the personal income tax, but a much smaller number (disproportionately those with high incomes) have substantial capital gain and interest income. Indexing the latter provisions might be seen as a tax break for the rich, giving them protection from inflation not enjoyed by other taxpayers. Moreover, bracket indexing is relatively simple to administer centrally, requiring only annual changes in tax tables. Indexing of

2. *Congressional Record* (July 16, 1981), p. 16125.
3. Emil M. Sunley, Jr., and Joseph A. Pechman, "Inflation Adjustment for the Individual Income Tax," in Henry J. Aaron, ed., *Inflation and the Income Tax* (Brookings, 1976), pp. 158, 165. Congress cut rates more than simple indexing would have allowed because the yield from progressive income taxation is increased by rising real income as well as nominal income.
4. U.S. Department of the Treasury data, published in *Congressional Record* (July 15, 1981), p. 15792.

savings and capital gains, on the other hand, would require complex calculations by taxpayers, opening up new potential for error and fraud.

Political Alignments

The lines of conflict on indexing of tax brackets are likely to be somewhat similar to those on the initial indexing of social security, pitting legislative specialists in Congress versus conservatives, with other players as the swing vote. In general, congressional specialists on tax matters—members of the Senate Finance and House Ways and Means committees—will presumably oppose indexing. After all, they have the most influence over tax policy and thus can make the most credible claims with constituents and clientele for having aided their causes. This credit-claiming motivation is bolstered by a desire to maintain power within their respective chambers. Putting the personal income tax base on automatic pilot drastically reduces the committees' room to maneuver on tax policy. Maintaining discretion on tax policy allows members of these committees to do favors for their colleagues.

For congressional conservatives (largely Republicans), however, indexing income tax brackets is above all an issue of good policy: they believe that it is not fair that government should benefit from inflation while individuals suffer, nor is it a good idea that government should have an automatic source of rising revenues. Support for indexing also offers conservatives opportunities for claiming credit and for generating blame. Conservatives can claim to be protecting workers' incomes, while portraying those who oppose indexing as using inflation to "steal" from taxpayers. Making this case to the public is not as easy as in the social security case, however. The concepts of a progressive tax structure and bracket creep are complex and rather difficult to grasp.

Moderate and liberal legislators face a more complex set of incentives. On the one hand, they share with the policy specialists (although to a lesser extent) the opportunity to claim credit with constituents for supporting ad hoc tax cuts. As Senator David Durenberger, Republican of Minnesota, put it in 1979:

> Congress has widely taken credit for tax reduction in 1975, 1976, 1977, and 1978, yet the average taxpayer has not benefited from a real reduction in income tax liability.

Mr. President, I can only conclude that indexing has been opposed by Congress because we get credit only once.[5]

Nonspecialists may also wish to defer to policy specialists so that they can maintain a good working relationship with powerful committees. It is not for nothing, after all, that U.S. senators said of longtime Finance Committee Chairman Russell Long that "when you beat Senator Long, you lose." A nonindexed income tax bracket system also fits the blame-avoiding needs of legislative nonspecialists: if an ad hoc tax cut causes a greater revenue loss than anticipated, bracket creep should eventually take care of the problem by generating additional revenue. Under an indexed system, on the other hand, legislators have to vote to increase tax rates or eliminate tax breaks—very painful blame-generating situations—in order to raise revenues.

For liberals in particular, a nonindexed income tax system allows them to fund increased expenditures without voting for tax increases—that is, it helps to achieve their policy preferences in a way that minimizes blame. But if conservatives manage to raise public awareness of the issue, indexing may become difficult to vote against. Liberals and moderates may, in short, be forced to jump on the bandwagon and support indexing.

In this political environment, the level of public awareness of the issue and the ability of the various players to manipulate the public agenda are likely to have a profound impact on which motivations dominate policymakers' decisions and thus on policy outcomes. Policy specialists will want to keep the issue off Congress's agenda so that nonspecialists will not have to take an open stand on it. Conservatives will want to get it on the agenda. These motivations and strategies are summarized in table 9-1.

Indexing is not likely to be adopted so long as the following conditions are met: (1) the issue does not have high public salience; (2) there are high barriers to prevent conservatives from getting the issue on the agenda; and (3) policy specialists do not have strong conservative good-policy—that is, proindexing—views that overwhelm their credit-claiming interests.

Once indexing of tax brackets is in place, however, the strategic advantage shifts to its proponents. Now proponents can claim that those who favor repeal are threatening to *take away* something that

5. *Congressional Record* (December 6, 1979), p. 34916.

TABLE 9-1. *Legislators' Objectives and Strategies in Indexing Individual Income Taxes*

Player	Dominant objective	Strategy
Policy specialists	Credit claiming, power in chamber	Keep issue off agenda in order to maintain discretion and prevent defection by rank-and-file
Legislative conservatives	Good policy, credit claiming	Raise visibility of tax indexing and force it onto agenda, making nonspecialists defect to support it
All other legislators	Blame avoiding, credit claiming	Take credit for tax cuts, but defect to support indexing if increased issue salience requires it

taxpayers already enjoy: protection against automatically rising tax bills. Voters do not have to have a very sophisticated knowledge of the tax system to understand the message: it appeals directly to their loss-avoiding instincts. If legislators are indeed blame avoiders, few will want to sponsor a repeal of bracket indexing, and not many more will want to vote for it.

Origins of Indexation

Tax indexation began to gain support in the United States during the early 1970s, when inflation levels increased. The adoption of indexing by Canada in 1974 stirred further interest in the United States.[6] The first indexing bill was introduced in Congress in 1974 by Senator James Buckley, Republican of New York. Efforts to attach indexing amendments to Senate tax bills failed by wide margins in both 1975 and 1976.[7]

Indexing amendments began to gain momentum during the Carter

6. On the Canadian experience, see Jane Probyn, "What Indexing Income Taxes Produced in Canada," *New York Times,* August 23, 1981; and Advisory Commission on Intergovernmental Relations, *The Inflation Tax: The Case for Indexing Federal and State Income Taxes* (GPO, 1980), pp. 24–25.

7. The votes were 63–27 in 1975 and 63–22 in 1976. *Congressional Record* (March 20, 1975), pp. 7815–17; and (August 3, 1976), pp. 25216–24.

administration. Senate Republicans introduced floor amendments proposing tax indexing in 1977, 1978, and 1979. In the first year it lost badly—24–63. No Democrat supported the amendment and ten Republicans opposed it. In 1978, in the wake of California's Proposition 13, a similar amendment did much better. Proposed as an amendment to the Revenue Act of that year by Senator Robert Griffin of Michigan, the amendment was defeated by a vote of 53–37—still a comfortable margin. But despite the fact that there was very little turnover of seats (only three) between the two votes, there was substantial movement based on "conversion" of sitting senators. Thirteen senators—eight Democrats and five Republicans—changed their minds and decided to vote for indexing. Only two senators (both Republicans) switched to oppose indexing.[8] No longer was tax indexing strictly a Republican partisan issue in the Senate. Senate proponents of indexing came even closer to victory in 1979, when Senators William Armstrong and Robert Dole tried to attach an indexing amendment to the windfall profits tax. They failed by only six votes (41–47).[9]

Less progress was made on the House side, where stricter rules against floor amendments to Ways and Means legislation stymied Republican efforts. Republicans offered amendments within the Ways and Means Committee to index the personal income tax, but they were unable to win committee support for those proposals. In 1978, for example, Representative Willis Gradison, Republican of Ohio, offered an amendment to index the individual income tax, but it was defeated by the committee on a 13–23 vote along party lines.[10] The only tax indexing measure to gain House approval was passed in the same year. Representative Bill Archer, Republican of Texas, proposed indexing the base value of assets used in calculating the capital gains tax. The Ways and Means Committee accepted the measure by a vote of 21–16 because of Democratic defectors (some of whom were voting strategically, in the hope that this provision would help to sink the entire tax bill). It was opposed on the floor by committee Democrats, but adopted by a vote of 249–167. Republicans voted overwhelmingly for it (142–1), while a majority of Democrats opposed it (107–166). But the provision lacked support from Ways and Means Committee lead-

8. In addition, there was one seat change where the new senator supported indexing and his predecessor had not.

9. *Congressional Record* (December 6, 1979), p. 34927. Only eleven Democrats supported indexing, while forty-two opposed it.

10. *Congressional Quarterly Almanac*, vol. 34 (1978), p. 229.

ership, and was viewed by many specialists as both costly and unfair (since taxes on earned income were not indexed). It was dropped in conference.[11]

While indexing of tax brackets was enjoying mixed success in Congress, the external political environment was becoming more favorable to indexing. Real policy change was taking place at the state level. Spurred by the tax revolt and by the large budget surpluses caused by bracket creep, nine states, mostly in the West and Midwest, adopted indexing in the late 1970s.[12] Tax indexing often coincided with limitations on total spending growth.

Public opinion was changing as well. Through most of the 1970s, the federal income tax was in a rough tie with the local property tax in Americans' minds as "the worst tax—that is, the least fair." About 30 percent of Americans gave that honor to each tax. Between 1978 and 1979, however, the percentage of Americans viewing the federal income tax as "worst/least fair" jumped to 37 percent and stabilized near that level.[13] This change was spurred by very high rates of inflation in the final years of the Carter presidency, which exacerbated bracket creep. Support for bracket indexing was also growing among opinion leaders such as the *New York Times,* which endorsed indexing of tax brackets in 1980.[14]

The Triumph of Indexation

Despite changes in public opinion and state law, tax bracket indexing still seemed a long way from enactment before the 1980 election. Although the Senate vote on indexing had been close in 1979, it had not even been considered on the floor of the House. Even after the 1980 election, the Democrats maintained a majority in the House. Moreover, House Democrats passed new rules overrepresenting their

11. Ibid., pp. 245–46. The Carter administration also opposed tax indexing generally and capital gains indexing specifically. See *Tax Notes,* vol. 7 (July 31, 1978), pp. 99–100.

12. The nine states are Arizona, California, Colorado, Iowa, Minnesota, Montana, Oregon, South Carolina, and Wisconsin. *Congressional Record* (July 15, 1981), p.15782; Robert Kuttner, *Revolt of the Haves: Tax Rebellion and Hard Times* (Simon and Schuster, 1980), pp. 145, 207–08, 224–29; and ACIR, *The Inflation Tax,* pp. 21–24.

13. Advisory Commission on Intergovernmental Relations, *Changing Public Attitudes on Governments and Taxes, 1983* (Washington, D.C.: ACIR, 1983) pp. 1, 8, 40–43.

14. *New York Times,* November 25, 1980.

majority on the Ways and Means Committee. It appeared that agenda control in the House would remain with the Democrats.

The 1980 election did have four critical effects, however. First, it transferred chairmanship of the Senate Finance Committee from an opponent of tax indexing to one of its strongest advocates. Thus proponents would probably control the Senate agenda. Second, it gave Republicans a Senate majority. Unless they failed to unite, they could pass the Finance Committee's bill—and they had a strong incentive to unite to show that they were capable of governing. Third, the election placed Ronald Reagan, who also was a supporter of tax bracket indexing, in the presidency. And last, it threw control of the House floor up for grabs. Although the Democratic majority could control what Ways and Means recommended to the House, they might not be able to pass it.

The 1980 Republican party platform had supported indexing as part of its tax reform measures, the centerpiece of which was the Kemp-Roth tax cut.[15] President Reagan did not include indexing in his tax bill, however, although he had supported it as a candidate. The president proposed only a three-year, 30 percent tax cut (later cut to 25 percent). He wanted a "clean bill" to facilitate quick passage of the tax cut. All other reform measures were to be included in a separate bill later so that the tax cut bill did not get bogged down and lose momentum.[16] It was hoped that the promise of a second bill would forestall an endless series of special interest amendments that might not only stall the tax cuts but also turn them into a bigger revenue drain than the administration wanted. Moreover, there was opposition within the administration to the severe revenue losses resulting from indexing of tax brackets. Treasury Secretary Donald Regan opposed indexing in testimony before the Finance Committee, arguing that it would, in the now standard refrain, be a sign that government was giving up the fight against inflation.[17]

Senator Robert Dole, the new chairman of the Senate Finance Committee, did not share the administration's doubts about the wisdom of indexing personal income taxes. Dole had been one of the strongest supporters of indexing in the Senate for many years. On the first day of the new session he introduced a bill providing for the indexing of tax

15. *Congressional Quarterly Almanac,* vol. 36 (1980), p. 59-B.
16. *Congressional Quarterly Almanac,* vol. 37 (1981), p. 91.
17. *Tax Reduction Proposals,* Hearings before the Senate Finance Committee, 97 Cong. 1 sess. (GPO, 1981), pt. 1, pp. 39–40.

brackets, the personal exemption, and the zero bracket amount to the percentage change in the Consumer Price Index for the previous year. Indexing was to begin in 1982 and continue for four years, at which time it could be reviewed.[18]

The former chairman of the committee, Russell Long of Louisiana, had been a determined foe of indexing and had wielded very strong control over the committee.[19] Now that Dole held the chair, this obstacle was removed. Moreover, Dole was reinforced on the Finance Committee by staunch Republican supporters of indexing—notably Senators William Armstrong, David Durenberger, Charles Grassley, and Steve Symms—who had not been on the committee in 1978. Democrats on the committee were also beginning to support tax indexing. In 1978 all the committee's Democrats voted against indexing when the measure was considered on the Senate floor, while all but one of the Finance Republicans voted for it. In 1981 three Finance Democrats would vote for indexing on the floor.[20] Dole did not hold separate hearings on tax indexing, however, and the issue surfaced only intermittently in hearings on the Reagan administration's tax proposals.

The Senate Finance Committee gave proponents of indexing a powerful platform from which to help set the 1981 tax agenda. And they believed that controlling the agenda would be important if they were going to push the House in the direction of theirs and the president's proposals. But the Constitution posed an important obstacle to seizing the initiative: all revenue measures are supposed to originate in the House. To get around this problem, Dole decided to use a House-passed bill to raise the debt ceiling as a vehicle for a Senate tax bill.

Dole did not include indexing in the committee's main tax package, however. Instead, indexing was proposed as an addition to the tax bill by Senator Armstrong during markup.[21] Indexing was approved by the committee but was submitted to the Senate as a committee amendment to the bill, rather than as part of the bill. Presenting it in this manner avoided putting Dole in the awkward position of openly op-

18. *Congressional Record* (January 5, 1981), pp. 14–15.
19. Alan Ehrenhalt, "Senate Finance: The Fiefdom of Russell Long," *Congressional Quarterly Weekly Report*, vol. 35 (September 10, 1977), pp. 1905–15.
20. The defectors were Senators Max Baucus, David Boren, and Daniel Moynihan. Three Finance Republicans also defected to vote "nay": John Chafee, John Heinz, and Malcolm Wallop. The vote in committee on the indexing proposal was 9–5.
21. *Congressional Record* (July 16, 1981), p. 16121; and Pamela Fessler, "Finance Committee Clears President's Tax Plans; House Panel Sets Timetable," *Congressional Quarterly Weekly Report*, vol. 39 (June 27, 1981), pp. 1130–31. The Armstrong proposal was almost identical to Dole's tax indexing bill.

posing the president's desire to have a "clean bill" and the administration's concerns about huge out-year revenue losses. But Hill veterans like Dole were certainly skeptical that Congress would be able to pass a second major tax bill in the near future, especially one that reduced taxes further. The tax cut bill was likely to be the only train leaving the station; if indexing was not on board, it was not going to go anywhere.

David Stockman claims that Dole agreed to let Armstrong's indexing amendment come before the Senate in order to win Armstrong's support for the tax package, while assuring the administration that the amendment would not pass.[22] Dole loyalists deny any duplicity. But Dole's assurance, if it was given, was certainly not fulfilled. He pushed hard for indexing. In Senate debate on the amendment, Dole and other supporters of bracket indexing portrayed it as a measure of simple tax justice, intended to protect the income of Americans not only from inflation, but also from Congress. It was, in the words of Senator Durenberger, "nothing more than a windfall profits tax on government. It proceeds from the philosophy that any windfall income created by inflation should remain with the income earner and taxpayer . . . rather than passing to the Federal Government."[23] Supporters argued that indexing was an effective mechanism to force expenditure restraint on Congress by forcing it to raise tax rates when it wanted to increase spending. They also portrayed indexing as a means of preventing Congress from taking credit for tax cuts that had no effect on real income.

Opponents of the bill, notably Russell Long, argued that if indexing had been enacted, Congress could not have given previous cuts or the one it was presently considering. Nor would Congress have the fiscal room it needed to target tax cuts where they were needed most. (Presumably "need" in this context could refer to political needs as well as to economic ones.) Worst of all, indexing tax brackets at that time might force senators to vote on a tax increase in the future if the 1981 tax cuts caused a severe revenue shortfall. Long cited the near bankruptcy of the social security system as an example of the problems that indexing could create.[24] Opponents of the amendment also argued that it would contribute to inflation by fueling the deficit, and that it would lessen opposition to inflation by making it less painful.

22. David A. Stockman, *The Triumph of Politics: Why the Reagan Revolution Failed* (Harper and Row, 1986), p. 254.

23. For Senate debate, see *Congressional Record* (July 15, 1981), pp. 15780–95; and (July 16, 1981), pp. 16119–27, 16137–38.

24. Ibid., p. 15783.

Supporters of indexing responded that because government benefited from high inflation through the fiscal dividend, it was necessary to adopt indexing so that inflation would no longer be in government's interest. Tax bracket indexing was, therefore, an anti-inflationary measure rather than a stimulant to inflation. In addition, limiting government revenues by indexing tax brackets would give Congress increased incentives to cut wasteful spending.

The arguments made in 1981 were not that different from those made in prior years. And the arguments made by the sponsors of tax bracket indexing do not sound very politically appealing: for example, that indexing would place increased pressure on themselves to make difficult expenditure-cutting decisions. But this time, indexing of tax brackets passed the Senate by a vote of 57–40. Why the change? Indexing won on this round in large part because the new political climate of fiscal conservatism had allowed the election of many conservative senators since 1978. Of the members of the Senate who voted on indexing in 1981, 60 were elected before 1978. A comparison of the votes of this group and the votes of the group elected in the interim period (table 9-2) shows that the newer group generated the support that was needed for passage of indexing. In 1981 the more senior group voted 25 in favor of indexation and 35 against. The group elected in 1978 and 1980 voted 32–5 in favor, however. Of course, the party makeup of these groups was markedly different. Of the group elected before 1978, 24 were Republicans, 35 were Democrats, and 1 was an independent. The post-1978 group was composed of 27 Republicans and 10 Democrats. But it should also be noted that voting in the earlier group was closer to party lines in 1981 than in the post-1978 group. In the newer group, a majority of Democrats voted for indexing, compared with a better than four-to-one ratio of Democrats opposed in the older group.

A more detailed comparison of the 1978 and 1981 Senate votes underscores the importance of turnover, rather than conversion, in explaining the adoption of income tax indexing in 1981. The number of senators present for both the 1978 and 1981 votes who changed their position from opposition to support exactly balanced those who changed from support to opposition (5 each). But there were 16 new members voting in favor of indexing in 1981 whose predecessors in the same seat had voted against it; none of the new members made the opposite switch. Senate passage of tax bracket indexing, in short, seems to owe less to blame-avoiding behavior than to a change in the

TABLE 9-2. Senate Votes on Income Tax Indexing in 1981, by Party and Year of First Election

	Republicans		Democrats		Total	
Year of first election	Percent supporting	Total number voting	Percent supporting	Total number voting	Percent supporting	Total number voting
Before 1978	75.0	24	19.4	36[a]	41.7	60
1978 or later	92.6	27	70.0	10	86.5	37
Total	84.3	51	30.4	46	58.8	97

SOURCE: Congressional Record (July 16, 1981), p. 16138.
a. Harry F. Byrd, Jr., of Virginia, who was elected as an Independent, is counted as a Democrat.

composition of that body and its new members' notions of good policy. Defection by senators who had previously opposed indexing but were prepared to jump on the bandwagon was quite limited.

The story is quite different in the House. Representative Willis Gradison, Republican of Ohio, introduced a bill to index personal income taxes on the first day of the 1981 House session. It had more than 130 cosponsors at that time, and 218—a majority of the House—by the time of the Senate indexing vote.[25] But Democratic policy specialists in the House still opposed indexing. The tax bill reported by the Ways and Means Committee did not include indexing, nor did debate on the floor of the House focus on it.[26] Rather than attempt to alter the bill through floor amendments, opponents of the Ways and Means tax cut proposed their own substitute to the committee bill. This bill (the Conable-Hance substitute) was negotiated by House Republicans, "boll weevils" (conservative southern Democrats), and the Reagan administration. It reflected less a consistent philosophy than the result of a fierce bidding war between the administration and House Democrats to demonstrate who controlled the floor of the House. The Conable-Hance bill included indexing, despite the continued reservations of many officials in the administration, in order to win the support of Ways and Means Republicans (notably Barber Conable and Willis Gradison) who strongly favored it.[27] Debate was over the entire package, and the final vote was essentially a measure of support for the president's position, which was influenced greatly by Reagan's televised appeal two days before the vote. The administration won convincingly—238–195—with 48 Democrats defecting to support the president.

The passage by the House of a tax bill that included bracket indexing for the first time, and despite the fact that that the chamber still had a Democratic majority, suggests blame avoidance at work. It was not tax indexing that had the major blame-generating potential, however. It was rather the tax rate reductions that were to precede it and were supposed to produce an economic boom. Voting against this macroeconomic "free lunch" to taxpayers, as well as the personal appeal of the president, would indeed be difficult to explain. Most members did not wish to try.

It is perhaps ironic that tax bracket indexing, which had never been able to get on the agenda of the House, passed without ever really

25. Ibid., p. 15781.
26. *Tax Notes*, vol. 13 (August 3, 1981), pp. 315–16.
27. Stockman, *The Triumph of Politics*, p. 260.

appearing on that agenda. But it passed because it was part of the Republican alternative package, which circumvented normal House agenda control procedures, just as it had failed earlier because it was not part of the Ways and Means Committee packages.

Staying the Course?

Initial passage of the tax indexing measure did not guarantee that it would actually be implemented, however. It was not scheduled to go into effect until after the third year of the tax cut. Congress thus had plenty of time to change its mind. Even backers of the bill admitted that this was a possibility: as Representative W. Henson Moore, Republican of Louisiana, said shortly after passage, "We all agreed at the time that if something terrible should happen to the economy, we could take it out of the law."[28] And as the magnitude of emerging budget deficits became clear, second thoughts about the combination of a massive tax cut and indexing did indeed emerge in both Congress and the Office of Management and Budget. As early as 1982, Senate Finance Committee Chairman Dole suggested forgoing the third year of the tax cut and moving up indexing of tax brackets by a year instead; he dropped the idea when the president opposed it.[29]

In 1983 House Ways and Means Committee Chairman Dan Rostenkowski, Democrat of Illinois, took the lead in proposing repeal of bracket indexing.[30] The chairmen of the House and Senate Budget committees and Senate Majority Leader Howard Baker, Republican of Tennessee, expressed support for repeal or delay. Even Dole said of bracket indexing, "I'm still committed to it, but I don't know how long we can hold on to it."[31] By the end of the year, Senator Dole included

28. Pamela Fessler, "1985 Indexing Change Looms as Watershed for Tax Policy," *Congressional Quarterly Weekly Report,* vol. 39 (August 22, 1981), p. 1532.

29. Dale Tate, "Keys to Budget Compromise Emerge from Leaders' Talk," *Congressional Quarterly Weekly Report,* vol. 40 (April 10, 1982), p. 788.

30. Rostenkowski's proposal to repeal bracket indexing was part of a broader package to repeal all tax cuts enacted in 1981 that did not take effect before the beginning of 1984. However, his plan was opposed by Speaker O'Neill, who favored an immediate tax increase in the form of a cap on the 10 percent tax cut scheduled for July 1983. See Thomas B. Edsall, "Rostenkowski Asks Tax Freeze," *Washington Post,* February 9, 1983, pp. A1, A6; and Edsall, "Rostenkowski Enrages O'Neill on Tax Stance," *Washington Post,* February 10, 1983, p. A4.

31. See "How Strong a Recovery?" *Business Week* (January 31, 1983), p. 92; "The Budget Battle Begins," *Business Week* (February 7, 1983), p. 90; and "Now the Horse-trading Begins," *Business Week* (February 14, 1983) p. 35. Dole expressed some willing-

a cap on indexing of tax brackets in his proposed deficit reduction package.[32]

Despite support from legislative specialists and budget guardians, the apparent opening for repeal of indexing closed quickly. President Reagan made it clear that any tax package including repeal of either the last year of the tax cut or of indexing would be vetoed.[33] The 1982–83 recession made legislators even more reluctant than usual (on good-policy grounds) to risk choking off a recovery with a tax increase. And Democrats were reluctant to back a measure that would place its biggest percentage increase on lower- and middle-income taxpayers.[34] Neither the Senate Finance Committee nor the House Ways and Means Committee adopted repeal of bracket indexing, and neither committee was able to bring a tax increase package (except the one related to the social security rescue package) to a floor vote in its chamber in 1983.

The story the next year was not very different. Once again, the two tax-writing committees failed to include changes to indexing in their tax programs. An amendment proposing a three-year delay in bracket indexing came to a Senate vote in 1984 and was defeated by a 19-vote margin.[35] A month later, a proposal to cap adjustment of personal income tax brackets as well as a number of federal payments to individuals at 3 percent lost by the overwhelming margin of 23–72.[36] In 1985

---

ness to consider a repeal or delay of bracket indexing if absolutely necessary to reduce the deficit, however, and two moderate Republicans on the Senate Finance Committee, John Danforth of Missouri and Chafee of Rhode Island, urged that it be delayed or abandoned. *Administration's Fiscal Year 1984 Budget Proposals,* Hearings before the Senate Committee on Finance, 98 Cong. 1 sess. (GPO, 1983), pp. 58, 68, 71.

32. Dole would have rounded indexing of both income tax brackets and social security benefits down to the next full percentage point, while increasing the zero bracket amount. Dale Tate, "Deficit Reduction Moves Fail As Torn Congress Shies Away from Tax, Spending Mandate," *Congressional Quarterly Weekly Report,* vol. 41 (November 19, 1983), pp. 2408–09.

33. See the interview with the president in *Business Week* (February 14, 1983), p. 121.

34. On the effects of the repeal of bracket indexing on different income groups, see Joel Havemann, "Tax Indexing and Deficits—The Cure May Have Become Part of the Problem," *National Journal,* vol. 15 (February 12, 1983), pp. 320–21.

35. The amendment was sponsored by Republican Finance Committee member John Chafee, but Republicans voted overwhelmingly (46–7) for a motion to kill it. Democrats voted against killing the motion by a margin of 31–11. Pamela Fessler, "House, Senate Approve Tax Hike Measures," *Congressional Quarterly Weekly Report,* vol. 42 (April 14, 1984), p. 829.

36. Dale Tate, "GOP Leaders in Senate Rebuff Attack on Deficit-Cutting Plan," *Congressional Quarterly Weekly Report,* vol. 42 (May 12, 1984), p. 1080.

Senator Ernest Hollings, Democrat of South Carolina, the ranking minority member of the Budget Committee, proposed in that committee's budget debates a package of tax increases including a one-year freeze on tax brackets and adjustment thereafter only for inflation exceeding 3 percent. The motion was defeated 18–4.[37]

Policy debates since bracket indexing took effect in 1985 have confirmed its relatively secure status. The Gramm-Rudman-Hollings deficit reduction plan left automatic inflation adjustments in tax brackets untouched. The tax reform bill enacted by Congress in 1986 also included indexing of tax brackets, the personal exemption, and the standard deduction.[38] Because the reform effort was defined at the outset as a revenue-neutral measure rather than a revenue-raising one, repeal of indexing did not even surface as an issue during the debate.[39]

President Reagan deserves most of the credit or blame for the repeated failure of efforts to repeal bracket indexing. (The same is true, of course, for other initiatives to increase revenues.) The certainty of a presidential veto has limited legislators' incentives to propose or support a repeal, since there would be no policy benefits to offset the political costs. Thus, although leaders of the tax-writing committees personally have favored some retrenchment on bracket indexing, they have seen no point in including a provision that would doom the entire package. And Democrats in particular did not wish to give President Reagan an issue with which he could bash their party.[40] Indeed, much of the fiscal policy history of the Reagan presidency can be written as an attempt by congressional leaders of both parties and some executive branch officials to get the president to accept some responsibility and blame for a tax increase—and his refusal to do so.[41]

The long-term future of tax indexing is somewhat more open to question, however. The Congressional Budget Office has suggested that repeal or modification of indexing would be one of the most effective means of reducing the federal deficit: in January 1987 the CBO

37. Helen Dewar, "Senate Unit Votes Down Tax Boosts," *Washington Post,* March 13, 1985, pp. A1, A6.
38. Brackets and the standard deduction are set by statute in 1987 and 1988 and indexed in later years. The personal exemption is indexed beginning in 1990.
39. However, an early reform plan developed by the Treasury Department included a proposal to index capital gains. See Jeffrey H. Birnbaum and Alan S. Murray, *Showdown at Gucci Gulch: Lawmakers, Lobbyists, and the Unlikely Triumph of Tax Reform* (Random House, 1987), p. 54.
40. David Broder, "Tax Indexing: A Tough Fight," *The Washington Post,* February 20, 1983, p. C7.
41. See Stockman, *The Triumph of Politics,* chap. 12.

estimated that repeal would add $75 billion to federal revenues over the four-year period from fiscal year 1989 to fiscal 1992.[42] Certainly a new administration open to tax increases would seriously consider repeal as a device with relatively low political costs to raise increased revenues. (Indeed, the Conservative government elected in Canada in 1984 has partially deindexed taxes for precisely this reason.)[43] And while tax indexing has some of the "impossible to vote against" attributes of social security COLAs, it remains a bit more difficult for the common person to grasp. An end to tax indexing might also win support from fiscal conservatives concerned about budget deficits.

The symbolic resonance of income tax bracket indexing is strong enough that, like social security COLA cutbacks, it is likely to win congressional support only if legislators are given political protection. The most effective form of protection would be the same sort of presidential appeal that helped win approval of tax indexing in the first place. Failing that, a delay in the effective date of the repeal of bracket indexing for a few years or a slow phase-in of the repeal might provide enough distance that some legislators who otherwise could not vote for a repeal might be able to do so. But such a move would not solve immediate budget problems and would thus weaken the policy incentive to vote for it.

Consequences

Indexation of income tax brackets has been in place a very short time. But several consequences already seem clear. First, in concert with the 1981 tax cut, indexing has dramatically altered the politics of budget projections. In the past, presidents were able to project dwindling deficits over the next few years without changing the tax laws: bracket creep would ostensibly provide the needed revenue boost. It did not, of course. Instead, Congress voted tax cuts (especially in selective tax expenditures or loopholes) and increased spending. With the end of the "fiscal illusion" of disappearing deficits, pressure for real deficit reduction increased. Under pressure from the Budget commit-

42. Congressional Budget Office, *Reducing the Deficit: Spending and Revenue Options, A Report to the Senate and House Committees on the Budget—Part II* (CBO, 1987), p. 203.

43. Beginning in 1986, personal exemptions and tax brackets in Canada are indexed only for inflation exceeding 3 percent a year. See Canada, National Council of Welfare, *The Impact of the 1985 and 1986 Budgets on Disposable Income* (Ottawa: Supply and Services Canada, April 1986).

tees, the agenda of the tax-writing committees shifted dramatically from creating tax expenditures to closing them.[44]

Unlike the experience in many other indexed programs, indexing of tax brackets did not remove the program base—the tax rate on a given level of real income—from the policy agenda. Dissatisfaction with the tax system continued, culminating in the Tax Reform Act of 1986, which drastically simplifies the tax bracket structure but retains indexing.

The failure of indexing to limit the tax policy agenda is probably best explained by the nature of taxation as a loss-imposing activity. If there is anything as certain as death and taxes, it is dissatisfaction with taxes. In this situation, it is unlikely that there will ever be a minimal consensus that the tax structure should be left alone, and there will always be credit for politicians to claim (and blame to generate) by arguing that the current tax structure is unfair to some or all taxpayers.

It is harder to make definitive judgments about the consequences of indexing for program clientele and the federal deficit. The answer inevitably involves speculation about what would have happened if there had been no indexing. But it seems likely that personal income tax rates and revenues would be higher today if indexing had not been enacted in 1981. Bracket indexing has certainly increased the hurdles that a real tax increase must go through in order to take effect. Before the 1981 tax cut and indexing, legislators needed only *not* to act— keep tax cut initiatives off the agenda—to increase real tax burdens. A tax increase could occur without changing current law and thus without attracting a presidential veto, which has proven to be the most intractable obstacle to a tax boost in the Reagan years.

Current concern over deficits presumably strengthens the bargaining position and resolve of proponents of a tax increase, so long as they are provided with some political protection. An unindexed bracket system, which would only require a Democratic-controlled Congress to block tax cut initiatives, would probably provide enough protection for a "backdoor" tax increase through bracket creep.

A repeal of tax bracket indexing would probably have a more important effect on clientele than a repeal of social security indexing. In

44. See Kenneth J. Kies, "The Current Political, Budgetary and Tax Policy Environment Suggests the Possibility of Major Federal Tax Legislation in the 100th Congress," *Tax Notes*, vol. 35 (April 13, 1987), pp. 179–91. This change was unanticipated in part. Because inflation dropped more rapidly in the early Reagan years than had been anticipated, the real value of the 1981 tax cuts was also greater.

the latter case, pressures for ad hoc adjustments (perhaps even exceeding inflation) would likely be irresistible, despite budget deficits. Certainly there would be credit-claiming incentives to propose them, and neither Congress nor the president has shown much ability to resist these pressures. The tax bracket clientele is much more heterogeneous and less well organized than social security recipients. Thus, it would be easier to avoid ad hoc tax cuts in a period of high deficits, thereby imposing real losses on taxpayers.

Conclusions

Indexing personal income tax brackets is contrary to the credit-claiming interests of legislative specialists and nonspecialists. It takes away free room for both tax cuts and expenditure increases. Yet both houses of Congress voted for it in 1981. Both long-run and short-term factors led to this decision. Tax revolts at the state level increased the visibility of the tax issue and made politicians more aware of its blame-generating potential. This in itself is important: politicians are motivated to blame-avoiding behavior only when there is some likelihood of being blamed. Tax limitation measures enacted at the state level and abroad also made the idea more credible as a policy proposal. Both of these factors helped to move indexing from an almost exclusively Republican issue to one with bipartisan support in the late 1970s. But its adoption required more than increased visibility and was far from consensual. Neither the Senate Finance Committee nor the House Ways and Means Committee investigated indexing thoroughly in hearings in 1981 and neither included it in their tax bills, although the Finance Committee did approve it as a committee amendment.

Several factors helped proponents of indexing overcome the many obstacles in their path. The most important was the change in control of the Senate. Control over the tax agenda passed from opponents of indexing to proponents and allowed them to put the House (and the president) on the spot by including it in the Senate tax bill. On the House side, the single up-or-down vote on the tax bill meant that members who wished to ensure a fiscal dividend to make room for future tax cuts (and the resultant credit claiming) would have to risk substantial blame by voting against the entire package endorsed by a very popular president. Indexing itself was not a highly salient issue in the House vote; it floated in on the high tide of tax cuts.

Indexing of tax brackets almost certainly would not have been enacted within the next few years if it had not been included in the 1981 tax cut package. This is not just because the unusual 1981 loss of agenda control placed opponents of indexing at a serious disadvantage. It is also because the 1981 tax cut changed decisionmakers' calculus once again. It became clear almost immediately after the tax cuts were enacted that the federal government faced massive deficits in coming years. If indexing had not been included in the 1981 package, this deficit growth would have relieved blame-generating pressures on legislators to enact indexing separately. "We need the money" would have been a very plausible excuse for voting against indexing in the mid- and late-1980s. Legislators would have been much more aware that voting for indexing now probably means voting for tax increases later. And budget guardians—in both the OMB and the congressional budget committees—would presumably have lobbied very hard against indexing because of the need to reduce the deficit.

But indexing of tax brackets was enacted in 1981, and once embedded in law, it quickly acquired something close to the sacred cow status of social security benefit indexing. To oppose it could be portrayed by future election opponents as voting for a backdoor tax increase. And that is not an image that many legislators wish to project.

10

Indexation as a Political Choice

This study began with the question, Why do politicians agree to index programs when it may require sacrificing discretion and credit-claiming opportunities? The cases examined here suggest that the simple answer to this question—indexing is a response to decision-making overload—is not adequate. Politicians did face pressures to index, but decisionmaking overload does not appear to be prominent among them. Neither politicians nor clienteles view indexing simply as a neutral technique for reducing decisionmaking costs, and many indexing decisions have been far from consensual. Public choice theory, which focuses on politicians' efforts to develop and exploit credit-claiming opportunities, does no better as an explanation of indexing choices than does a focus on overload. In making indexing decisions, politicians are concerned both with retaining credit-claiming opportunities and with avoiding blame for unpopular actions. Clienteles are concerned with whether specific indexing proposals will provide greater or lesser benefits than they would get from ad hoc changes.

The problem with all single-objective theories of politicians' behavior is not that they are altogether wrong, but that they are incomplete. These theories focus on one aspect of politicians' objectives and extrapolate it to all of their behavior rather than trying to understand when politicians will stress a particular objective. But politicians' objectives change depending on the pressures and opportunities they confront.

This chapter utilizes this broader perspective on politicians' objectives in making indexing decisions. It begins by outlining the major hurdles that confront proponents of any plan to index federal programs. It then discusses the strategies that proponents have used to advance indexing and that opponents have used to block it, along with some shortcomings of each of these strategies. Next it shows how changing political and economic constraints have altered strategic choices in recent years. Finally, the analysis is used to help explain the positions taken and roles played by the major participants in the six case studies of indexation policy examined here.

Hurdles

Indexing proposals must clear a common set of hurdles to win adoption. But there are several "paths" across those hurdles, and several strategies that proponents of indexing can use to clear the hurdles. Four hurdles emerge from the six case studies as critical to the enactment of any indexing proposal.

—Hurdle I is establishing a base of support among participants in the policy process. Some individuals or groups must view indexing as being in their own policy or political interests and must be willing to expend the resources needed to get the issue on the agenda and gain the support of others.

—Hurdle II (usually the easiest) is establishing the plausibility of indexing—proponents must be able to give a respectable argument in policy terms for making automatic adjustments in the program. If an indexing proposal cannot pass this minimal good-policy test, it is not likely even to make it onto government's agenda.

—Hurdle III is tailoring proposals to index to make them compatible with clientele interests or building enough support among policymakers to overcome clientele opposition. This test is much more concrete than the second one, for client groups are very concerned about the specifics of the base to be indexed and the mechanism used.

—Finally, Hurdle IV is making a proposal to index consistent with the political interests of policymakers who have the power to advance or block it. This last hurdle is in fact a series of barriers, usually involving, at a minimum, legislative specialists, chamber majorities in both houses of Congress, and the president. Failure at one of these barriers is usually sufficient to stop a change in policy. And a strategy that is helpful in securing the support of one set of policymakers (such as legislative specialists) may alienate others (such as nonspecialists or budget guardians). But this final hurdle is also highly malleable: policymakers are especially likely to change their position if new blame-generating pressures are brought to bear on them. And Hurdle IV is obviously related to Hurdle III: if interest groups oppose a specific indexing proposal, they will likely pressure policymakers to do so as well.

Establishing Plausibility

The plausibility hurdle is fairly distinctive, so it is useful to consider it separately. Establishing the plausibility of indexing is in fact a twofold process. The first task is getting indexing onto the policy agenda. Indexing must occur to some participants in the policy process as a reasonable response to a policy problem, and they must be able to convince other participants that it is in fact appropriate. This is easiest where program standards are set in nominal dollar terms by statute and thus become distorted over time. Once indexing has been used successfully for several programs in a sector and specialists have become familiar with it, they are more likely to consider it as an option in additional programs. Nonspecialists may also be less resistant as they too gain experience with indexing.

When indexing is being actively considered for a program, its adherents must complete a second task: establishing the plausibility of specific proposals. Many issues are likely to surface as proposals are developed. Do the particular base and index being used make sense, for example? What are the chances of unanticipated perverse consequences? Are there sufficient safeguards against such an occurrence? The various participants in the policy process are likely to put differing spins on these questions. For clientele, these questions may mean: how advantageous can we make the base and index to our own interests and still sell the idea to policymakers? Policy specialists may have the same concerns, but these will generally be tempered by their reluctance to propose a plan that their chamber will reject. For nonspecialists and budget guardians, on the other hand, the plausibility hurdle may mean: are we getting the full story about the consequences of this proposal from clientele and specialists? Obviously, the more familiar the indexing linkage being considered, and the more credible the proponents of the proposal (for example, legislative specialists who do not appear to have slavishly served the interests of specific clienteles in the past), the more likely a proposal is to clear this plausibility hurdle.

Political Strategies

The other three hurdles that indexing proposals must clear reflect participants' interests more directly. The strategies that proponents of indexing choose to clear these hurdles—and that opponents choose to prevent them from doing so—reflect the distinctive political dynamics of the program. Indexing in some cases means sacrificing credit-claiming opportunities; in others it is a welcome relief from potential blame. Strategies also reflect the participants' own interests and resources. Proponents of a position are unlikely to base their strategy on mobilization of a program's constituency if they know that the clienteles are weak or divided. Moreover, strategies take account of the political and policy objectives of other participants. Those designing a strategy must be willing to tailor the policy agenda, the payoffs in their proposals, and voters' perceptions in ways that will make their position compatible with the interests of others.

Several distinctive strategies or "paths" to clear—or raise—these hurdles to indexing emerge from the case studies. These strategies can be divided into those that appeal primarily to politicians' credit-claiming interests, those that appeal to nonpolitical interests, those that appeal to their interests in avoiding blame for themselves and generating it toward political opponents, and those that are a hybrid. Each of these paths has distinctive disadvantages as well as advantages.

Credit-claiming Strategies

Appeals to politicians' credit-claiming interests work best when some or all of the participants see political benefits to be gained from a particular policy choice, and the remainder are at least neutral and hence willing either to cede discretion to those who are most interested or to engage in vote trading to get something that they themselves want. Strategies based on credit-claiming objectives do not necessarily lead to consistent positions or outcomes with respect to indexing, however. In the early debates on social security and personal income tax brackets, for example, most legislative specialists initially resisted indexing in order to preserve the credit-claiming opportunities that they believed came with discretion. In the minimum wage and dairy price cases, on the other hand, credit-claiming legislative specialists favored indexing.

These differences reflect differences in clienteles and legislative specialists and in their relationship to each other. They give rise to two distinctive credit-claiming strategies or paths. The first path reflects politicians' incentives to retain discretion over programs because they believe that ad hoc adjustments can provide political rewards. This path can be called simply the *credit-oriented* strategy. The political base (Hurdle I) here is usually established among legislative specialists, who are in the best position to affect inflation adjustments. Obviously, this strategy is used almost exclusively to oppose indexing. It can be seen in the early debates on indexing both social security and income tax brackets. But this strategy is unlikely to work unless specialists feel enough independence from clienteles to resist their demands or the clientele is too poorly organized to press its demands effectively. Clienteles cannot be too politically marginal or divided, however; otherwise politicians would not seek credit from them in the first place.

The credit-oriented strategy certainly has its attractions. But it has distinctive problems that often prevent specialists from attempting it or that cause it to fail when it is tried. Specialists may split, especially if some of them have strong good-policy views on the issue and do not feel that they need the credit that they can accrue through discretion. Without a united political base, a credit-oriented strategy is likely to fail. This occurred in both the social security and income tax cases. In addition, clienteles may be mobilized against specialists if they believe that discretion is hurting them (Hurdle III). And either legislative nonspecialists or the president may reject specialists' decisions (Hurdle IV). They are especially likely to do so if continued support for discretion places them in a blame-avoiding position.

To defeat a credit-oriented strategy, legislative specialists must be either pressured to alter their own strategy or beaten outright in political combat. One way to accomplish the first is with an alternative strategy appealing to specialists' credit-claiming interests. In this second *clientele-led* strategy, well-organized clientele groups take advantage of a high degree of mutual dependence and cooperation with the specialists to coopt them to their own position, whether it be for or against indexing. Such a strategy can be seen in both the dairy and minimum wage cases. Obviously, it is not very practical where the clientele is weak or divided.

If a clientele can indeed coopt specialists in this fashion, it obviously is in a strong position to clear both Hurdle I (establishing a political base) and Hurdle III (clientele acquiescence). But there are problems. First, a clientele may have trouble arriving at a clear position on the intertwined questions of whether indexing is in its interests and what base and index are acceptable. This problem was clearly evident in the later dairy debates and surfaced in the minimum wage debate as well. Second, proposals that are acceptable to clientele and specialists may rouse opposing clienteles, as clearly occurred in the minimum wage debate. And finally, nonspecialists and budget guardians may not accept proposals that are built on the interests of a specific clientele. They lack the close ties of mutual interest to the clientele, are often cross-pressured by other interests, and may feel resource constraints more keenly. Thus legislative specialists need to maintain control of the agenda. This Hurdle IV problem was, of course, the downfall of minimum wage indexing. This hurdle often causes clienteles to lower their sights in their proposals, as did organized labor (unsuccessfully) and dairy farmers (mostly unsuccessfully in the 1980s). It may also lead them to develop a supplemental strategy (for example, logrolling or blame generating) to win the approval of nonspecialists.

Nonelectoral Strategies

Another pair of strategies evident in the case studies appeals to politicians who do not have a strong direct stake in the issue at hand. A first strategy appeals directly to politicians' *good-policy* objectives. The political base for such a strategy may be established by the president, legislative specialists, experts, or a variety of other sources. Such a strategy is likely to be attempted, and to be successful, when (1) clientele groups are relatively weak or uninterested in the program, (2) specialists either share similar good-policy ideas or are willing to compromise, and (3) budget guardians and policy nonspecialists see the stakes as being fairly low.[1] In indexing politics, these conditions are most likely to be met in decisions over relatively small programs.

Among the cases examined here, this situation is most closely approximated in the adoption of automatic adjustments for food stamps. While food stamps encountered severe political difficulties in the 1970s with respect to other issues, the adoption of indexing occurred with little political debate. Adoption was facilitated by a compromise on the size of the base to be indexed and the index to be used. The program clientele was too weak to have a major influence over the

1. Of course, policymakers may disagree about what constitutes good policy. The important thing is that they do not see major political gains and losses resulting from pressing their positions.

form of indexing or the base to be indexed. Most policy specialists on the Agriculture committees had a limited political stake in the program in this period, with a majority viewing it as a logrolling vehicle to build support for commodity programs. Program advocates saw it as a worthwhile improvement in the program, although they preferred a higher base. And program costs at this point were too low to provoke serious concern by budget guardians. While the political dynamics of the indexing debate on food stamps are atypical of the cases examined here, it is probably fairly typical of the smaller benefit and social services programs.

The good-policy strategy has important shortcomings, too. The most important is the difficulty in overcoming political inertia to get a proposal through the many stages of the policy process (Hurdle IV) without having strong political incentives to offer.

A second strategy to get around the lack of direct political incentives is to build vote-trading coalitions. This *logrolling* strategy is usually used as a supplement to another strategy, most often a clientele-led one. It is found particularly with programs that have a narrow but intense political appeal and clientele (such as commodity price supports). A coalition of legislative specialists and clientele establishes the political base (Hurdles I and III) and ensures the cohesion needed to make deals with representatives of other programs (Hurdle IV). Such a strategy was clearly present in the dairy case; it has also been used with the minimum wage. But as these cases show, logrolling has shortcomings, too. Clientele groups and legislative specialists face differing pressures: the former feel pressure from their members to maximize benefits, while specialists want to develop a package that they are certain they can sell to nonspecialists. These pressures occasionally lead to a breakdown of the political base, as can be seen within the dairy industry. Second, logrolling coalitions may be particularly vulnerable when resources are tight, as potential coalition partners feel that any resources devoted to another group's problems take resources away from themselves. Finally, there is a problem distinctive to using logrolling to promote indexing: coalition partners may believe that indexing will make the program less dependent on their support in the future and thus lower their bargaining power.

Blame-oriented Strategies

Blame-oriented objectives and strategies are prevalent where an issue offers little credit but substantial blame, where policymakers are cross-pressured, or where there is substantial opposition to a proposal but policymakers want to do it anyway for reasons of policy or personal interest.

Three clearly blame-oriented strategies emerge from the case studies. The first is the *pass-the-buck* strategy. Here politicians try to persuade others to adopt automatic procedures in order to avoid politically unpleasant decisions in the future, such as voting for congressional pay increases. While this strategy may be used to facilitate the adoption of indexing, it can also be used to facilitate cuts in indexed programs. The major problem with this strategy, however, is that it requires a quiescent clientele and strong agenda control by those who are attempting to pass the buck. If these conditions are absent, politicians may incur blame as they try to institute and maintain pass-the-buck mechanisms. They thus have strong incentives to defect and avoid blame in the short term, casting aside potential for long-term blame avoiding.

Much the same is true of the *circle-the-wagons* strategy. This involves situations in which politicians have taken, or are considering taking, politically dangerous positions, usually for good-policy reasons. They seek to obtain a consensus to diffuse blame broadly: if almost all policymakers support the position, it can be portrayed as both courageous and responsible, rather than as reckless and unresponsive to constituents. The social security cuts of 1983 are a good example of this phenomenon. Again, opposition from affected clientele (Hurdle III) and policymaker defections resulting from fear of incurring short-term blame (Hurdle IV) are serious problems with this strategy. Once defections begin, politicians may jump on the bandwagon, and the circle-the-wagons process collapses.

The precarious nature of the pass-the-buck and circle-the-wagons strategies is due in large part to the fact that politicians have incentives to generate blame against opponents as well as to avoid it themselves. Interest groups may also generate blame to achieve their policy and political objectives. The political base for such a *blame-generating* strategy is often outsiders who have few positive incentives they can offer to persuade others and who feel that they have been excluded from the decisionmaking process (for example, congressional Republicans in the case of congressional pay). It may also be used by "insiders," however—such as the president in the 1981 tax reform act. The purpose is to force opponents to jump on the bandwagon and abandon their real preferences in order to avoid blame. Weak agenda control by specialists facilitates use of this strategy.

Hybrid Strategies

Two other strategies seen in indexing politics are hybrids, appealing to mixtures of good-policy and blame-avoiding objectives. In the *"stop me before I kill again"* strategy, policymakers attempt to remove items from the agenda that provide attractive credit-claiming opportunities that they find dangerous in policy terms. Successful pursuit of this strategy allows them to achieve their true policy preferences without having to take positions that incur blame. This strategy was used by both a Republican president and Republican legislative specialists to promote indexing in the case of social security. But such a strategy is unlikely to succeed unless agenda control by credit-oriented legislative specialists can be overcome. Moreover, the lure of credit-claiming opportunities is strong even for fiscal conservatives. Thus this strategy is usually accompanied by supplementary strategies—especially blame generating—to get proposals over Hurdle IV (acquiescence by policymakers).

A final hybrid strategy evident in the cases is *scarcity driven.* This strategy may be used for or against indexing. Its central tenet is the reduction of government spending. Here the political base is often established among institutional budget guardians, often joined by presidents and fiscal conservatives in the legislature. These actors are usually drawn to the strategy by good-policy beliefs, but they attempt to persuade opponents largely by blame generating—portraying them as fiscally irresponsible. Obviously, this strategy is likely to encounter opposition both from clientele and from legislative specialists.

Changes in Politicians' Incentive Structure

The strategies used by politicians in indexing decisions have not been static over time. Politicians' objectives and strategies reflect the kinds of choices they confront—for example, whether discretion allows them to allocate benefits or forces them to allocate losses. Changes in the economy and fiscal climate, in the way political campaigns are run and the way political institutions operate, as well as the enactment of indexing itself, can force politicians to alter both their objectives and their strategies in making indexing decisions. These broader institutional changes can, like specific choices, be manipulated by politicians; but they are usually more difficult to influence. The bulk of these broader changes in recent years—although by no means all of them—have increased the pressures for policymakers to engage in blame-avoiding behavior and to use blame-oriented strategies.

The coming of high, persistent, and uneven inflation in the late 1960s clearly increased public awareness of the resulting erosion of program standards (especially in income transfer programs). It dramatically altered the policy agenda: instead of intermittent appearances on the agenda, there were almost constant pressures for inflation adjustments. The slowdown of economic growth that began after the first oil shock also made it more difficult to provide increases that outpaced inflation. The combination of these two developments undercut the credit-claiming opportunities formerly available in ad hoc adjustments and may have made policymakers fear that by maintaining discretion over programs they were likely to attract blame rather than credit. If policymakers' attitudes toward indexing did shift as a result of this potential incentive to pass the buck, however, the effect was a subtle one. It does not appear clearly in the two cases, social security and income tax brackets, where one might expect to see it. More evident in the social security case are fears by conservative legislators that constant pressures to adjust benefits would be too expensive. In the tax case, conservatives feared that bracket creep furnished too easy a source of revenue for government expansion.

The onset of severe budgetary stress in the early 1980s further altered the choices and pressures confronting politicians. There is now even less room left for program expansion (and credit-claiming strategies) in most sectors of government activity. The need to preserve their benefits in a period of budgetary stress increases the attractiveness of indexing for program clienteles. But budgetary stress has also led budget guardians to become more involved in indexing decisions and more sensitive to measures that require automatic spending increases. These developments have undercut the ability of clienteles and policy specialists to keep decisionmaking within a narrow (and favorable) policy subsystem needed to maintain credit-claiming strategies. Direct competition between programs for limited federal dollars has also mobilized clientele groups to defend existing indexing mechanisms. Increasingly, policy change means allocating losses—and that is the stuff of which blame is made.

Policymakers did not move toward blame-avoiding behavior willingly—quite the opposite. Legislators have been especially vociferous in pressing for resources that would improve their ability to claim credit with constituents. Increased legislative staff, especially in district offices, allows legislators to improve their performance of constituency service functions (for example, helping retirees get their social security checks).[2] Senators and representatives also use newsletters to constituents to claim credit for the collective benefits they provide (such as voting for social security benefit increases). Newsletters have the added advantage of allowing the legislators to explain their policy views in areas where constituents are relatively united, while skirting issues where they are not.

On the other hand, challengers have developed new tools to use in generating blame, notably television advertisements that present quick, simple, negative images in voters' minds to undermine confidence in the incumbent. The increased popularity of such "negative campaigning" reinforces legislators' reluctance to vote against positions held by even small but vociferous constituencies. For programs with large clienteles, like social security, it has made cutbacks in indexing almost impossible.

Political and institutional changes have also stimulated blame-oriented strategies and behavior within Congress. Legislators are less dependent on their party's apparatus to win the party nomination and on the party's funds or image to win the general election. As a result of the decline of norms of apprenticeship in Congress and the growth of formula funding for federal grant programs, junior members are less dependent on the largesse of more senior members to win benefits for their constituents. In this environment, members are less likely to forgo opportunities to generate blame against their colleagues if it suits their own political interests. If their colleagues do not like to take an open stand on such classic blame-generating issues as congressional pay raises, federal funding of abortions, and a balanced budget amendment to the Constitution, that is just too bad.

At the same time, a series of congressional reforms has undercut the ability of legislative specialists to control the legislative agenda. Rules changes enacted in 1970 made it easier for House members to gain

2. Morris Fiorina, *Congress: Keystone of the Washington Establishment* (Yale University Press, 1977), chap. 7.

floor consideration of amendments.³ Thus issues like indexing, which might not have reached the floor in prior years because they did not fit the credit-claiming and blame-avoiding interests of the specialists, are reaching the floor. The institution of recorded teller votes in the House in 1970 (followed by electronic voting in 1973) dramatically increased the number of issues on which representatives were forced to take recorded positions, further intensifying the pressures for blame-avoiding behavior.⁴ And because legislators often know little about the precise amendment they are voting on and cannot predict which issues may be raised and cast in a blame-generating light by a challenger in a future election, they search for politically safe solutions.

A final factor that has changed policymakers' objectives is the operation of indexing itself, especially as it has interacted with budgetary pressures. Once indexing mechanisms are in place, it becomes more difficult to cut a program surreptitiously by letting inflation erode nominal program standards. Politicians must act visibly to impose losses by changing statutes rather than simply acquiescing as inflation does it for them. Politicians' fear of attracting blame for imposing losses insulates most indexing mechanisms from change.

Participants

In the six cases examined here, there was no single institutional base for the adoption of indexing or for later modifications of it. Participants who were the major force behind the drive for indexing in some cases were most reticent or much less involved in others. The preceding analysis has shown why this is so. Participants' positions and roles grew out of very different political incentives and policy objectives of those participants in varying situations.

The roles of five types of participants in indexing decisions—policy experts, clienteles, legislative specialists, legislative nonspecialists,

3. See Steven S. Smith, "Revolution in the House: Why Don't We Do It on the Floor?" Brookings Discussion Paper no. 5 (Brookings, September 1986).
4. See Walter J. Oleszek, *Congressional Procedures and the Policy Process,* 2d. ed. (CQ Press, 1984), pp. 140–42. Policymakers have not been indifferent to these increasing blame-avoiding forces, however. In the past few Congresses, increasing use has been made in the House of restrictive rules that limit the introduction of "hard to vote against" amendments. The House has also responded to another consequence of increased roll call voting—increased pressures to be present for many votes—in a blame-avoiding fashion. Most roll call votes are now scheduled on Tuesdays through Thursdays, lessening pressures to be in Washington and freeing members for time in their home districts.

and budget guardians—will be briefly reviewed here in light of this analysis.

Policy Experts

Policy experts, generally economists, have been the participants least directly affected by political incentives. But the effectiveness of their input has varied depending upon the political salience of the issue. Experts have had varying opinions on indexing. Many favored it, especially in benefit programs, as a way of evening out benefits over time and depoliticizing the process. But others, both liberals and conservatives, have argued that indexing weakens resistance against inflation.

The influence of policy experts is felt primarily at Hurdle II: establishing indexing as a plausible policy option. Policy experts often preceded interest groups in their discussion of indexing; economists in particular were familiar with it from other contexts. Once indexing made it to the public agenda, however, a very different dynamic usually took over. While the indexes themselves generally remained the realm of experts, disputes arose over the base to be indexed. Groups lobbied for or against indexing and for or against specific bases. Policy specialists often opposed the invasion of their discretion and power that indexing would create. In short, the free (both uninhibited and politically costless) flow of ideas ran hard against the reality of political and economic interests. In this environment, experts' arguments generally became just one more element in the cross-pressures facing legislative nonspecialists. These arguments were not ignored, but they usually were not decisive. Perhaps the most significant role for experts came in the fight over indexing of the minimum wage. Most economists opposed it, and they in turn were opposed by the most powerful interest group involved (organized labor) and supported by business interests. Expert opposition to the minimum wage provided cross-pressured legislators with a blame-avoiding excuse to vote against the committee proposal.

Expert opinion was also important in later decisions about modifying or repealing indexing. Again, it was felt largely in establishing the plausibility of various options. In the social security case in particular, actuaries' reports made it clear that cuts were necessary to keep the trust funds solvent; the system in place was no longer plausible for the future. Experts also helped to determine the size of cuts needed to keep the system afloat. In so doing, expert opinion helped policymakers circle the wagons around a social security rescue package that included cutbacks, providing an excuse for supporting the package and thus relieving blame-generating pressures. But experts often affected the specific form of cutbacks as well. In the food stamps case, for example, the fact that program advocates controlled much of the technical expertise on the program helped them to shape cutbacks in ways that limited the long-term effects of the cuts.

Clienteles

Clientele groups have been far from united on the desirability of indexing. Their opinions were heavily influenced by whether they believed that they could do better under a system of ad hoc policy adjustments. Indeed, the cases show that it is almost impossible to separate interest group or policymaker opinions on indexing as a procedure from their beliefs about its substantive effects. Conflicts over indexing have almost always revolved around plans for specific benefit bases and indexing mechanisms. Groups have generally tried to get significant ad hoc gains and then to lock them in place with indexing. Groups have become substantially more risk averse (and hence more favorable to indexing) as budgetary stress has increased.

Even when they are mobilized, interest groups do not always dominate the policymaking process. The battle over the minimum wage can be seen as a straightforward battle between conflicting groups of organized interests and their legislative allies. But other conflicts, notably over the initial indexing of social security, are not easily interpreted in this manner. And in battles over indexing cutbacks, organized interests have suffered important defeats (most notably in the case of dairy price supports) when they are confronted by mobilized nonspecialists. Interest group activity is a major facet of the policy process, but groups are by no means universally dominant across time and across programs.

Legislative Specialists

Two findings about the role of legislative specialists (that is, authorizing committees) are particularly striking. First, specialists have not had a consistent position on indexing. A majority of legislative specialists initially opposed indexing of social security and personal income tax brackets. The opposite was true with respect to the minimum wage and dairy price supports. Second, the specialists often did not get their wishes. The indexing cases discussed here provide little evidence for the argument that "Congress can no longer check the narrow, provincial interests of its subunits as it once could."[5] In the social security and minimum wage cases, positions favored by the specialist committees were overturned on the floor of the House of Representatives. In both cases, committee leaders then adapted their own positions to those of the majority of legislative nonspecialists. Adaptation by legislative specialists is also evident in cutbacks in dairy price supports.

Differences in legislative specialists' support for indexing can be explained in large part by variations in specialists' objectives and in the nature of their ties to clienteles. Legislative specialists may be guided primarily by nonelectoral motives, especially when the political stakes are small. The adoption of indexing in the food stamp program is a good example. Legislators may also have strong policy convictions that prevail over their political interests. For example, strong good-policy convictions led Senate Finance Committee Chairman Robert Dole to lead the fight for tax indexing in 1981.

In addition, specialists often disagree among themselves on policy preferences. In the authorizing committees, as in Congress as a whole, there has often been strong division on indexing issues along partisan and ideological lines. It is usually the substantive effects of indexing rather than the procedure itself that have determined positions. Republicans and conservative Democrats have generally supported indexing when they believed that it would lower federal expenditures and revenues and aid the business community and usually opposed it when it would have the opposite effect. But these concerns have always been tempered by their desire to avoid blame for imposing visible losses on politically relevant groups.

Differences in committee clienteles can lead to differing outcomes even when politicians are able to act as credit claimers. The congressional finance committees, which have jurisdiction over social security and income taxes, have multiple clienteles and hence have less need to be responsive to the demands of any single interest. Members of these committees have generally been power-oriented, that is, focused on increasing their influence within their legislative chamber.[6] It is in

5. Kenneth A. Shepsle and Barry R. Weingast, "Legislative Politics and Budget Outcomes," in Gregory B. Mills and John L. Palmer, eds., *Federal Budget Policy in the 1980s* (Washington, D.C.: Urban Institute, 1984), p. 347.

6. On this topic, see Richard F. Fenno, Jr., *Congressmen in Committees* (Little, Brown, 1973), chaps. 1, 5; and John Manley, *The Politics of Finance: The House Committee on Ways and Means* (Little, Brown, 1970).

their interests to keep their own discretion high, so that members of their chamber will have to return to them repeatedly for favors. Indexing weakens their discretion and hence their freedom to maneuver. These specialists have tended to support indexing only when compelled to do so for blame-avoiding reasons.

The labor, agriculture, and civil service committees, on the other hand, have narrower and well-organized constituencies. Committee members have generally been highly attuned to the interests of these clienteles. Partly as a result, members of these committees have had a harder time getting their legislation through the full chamber; repeated requests for ad hoc increases require the expenditure of very scarce political resources. When these committees' specific clienteles became convinced that indexing was in their interests and settled on an appropriate base, these legislative specialists then tended to support that position.

Legislative Nonspecialists

Legislative nonspecialists have not ratified specialists' decisions on indexing issues blindly. They have two sets of expectations that authorizing committees (and party leadership) must satisfy if they are to endorse their decisions. Their first condition for deference is that the committees must not get too greedy in pursuing their own interests and those of their clienteles when they differ from those of majorities in the larger bodies. Many legislators, especially Republicans, felt that this criterion had been violated in the 1977 battle over indexing the minimum wage.

Legislative nonspecialists also expect the specialists to protect them from blame-generating choices by keeping those choices off the agenda. But the ability of committee majorities to control the agenda, which was never very strong in the Senate, has been weakened over the past twenty years in the House as well. This erosion of specialist control was clearly evident in the House votes on indexing of social security and income tax brackets and has occurred repeatedly on the congressional pay issue. As nonspecialists have gained in ability to get items on the floor agenda and have sought to cast them in blame-generating terms, legislators have been less able to defer to specialists, even if they would have liked to do so.

Nonspecialists are also more likely to be deferential if specialists are united. When specialists fail to arrive at a common position on indexing issues, nonspecialists face a more ambiguous set of decisionmaking cues. This is especially true for those (such as southern Democrats) who may not feel that their party's representatives on specialist committees reflect their own and their constituents' views. More important, divided views among specialists make it easier to get minority positions on the floor agenda. They may also presage a divided floor vote and thus the possibility that a future election opponent will use the vote as a blame-generating issue in a future campaign.

Budget Guardians

Several institutional budget guardians—notably the Office of Management and Budget and the House and Senate Budget committees—have been involved in the indexing policy conflicts described in this study.[7] The aggressive budget-cutting stance of the Reagan administration and the sharply higher budget deficits of the 1980s have led these actors to play a larger role than in the past.

Heightened participation has not been matched by success in engineering cutbacks, however. In particular, neither the OMB nor the congressional Budget committees have had much success in mounting across-the-board assaults on indexing, whether these take the form of freezes, COLA caps, or outright repeal. Such efforts have almost always foundered on the shoals of social security: no one wants to take the blame for cutting those benefits. The president has been reluctant to be identified with social security COLA cuts proposed by his budget agency, so most of these proposals have not seen the light of day. The congressional budget panels have also been reluctant to propose such cuts, knowing that they would alienate their colleagues, inevitably lead to blame-generating roll call votes, and almost certainly fail to pass. There have been two exceptions, both in the Senate. In 1981 the Senate Budget Committee agreed to a three-month social security COLA delay and a permanent shift in the COLA mechanism to the lower of wages or prices. But these proposals were dropped after the uproar surrounding the administration's May 1981 package of social security changes. In 1985 the Senate Budget Committee proposed and won brief floor support for a social security COLA freeze. But the committee was immediately sandbagged by the president, who refused to support the cuts. These outcomes do not encourage a recurrence, es-

---

7. An additional budget guardian, the congressional Appropriations committees, has played a lesser role in indexing debates, because most indexed programs are either entitlements (such as social security) or nonexpenditure programs (such as individual income tax brackets).

pecially now that both committees are under Democratic control again.

Executive and legislative budget guardians have been more successful in more pointed attacks on indexing mechanisms. Attacks by the OMB on specific targets—such as federal pay increases—have been implemented by Congress, especially in 1981. Less direct methods have also had some effect. Pressure to meet budgetary targets set by the congressional Budget committees has led authorizing committees to cut back on a number of indexing mechanisms—for example, in food stamps and dairy price supports. Indeed, the congressional budget process has added a new blame-avoiding dimension to the legislative process. Authorizing committees now attempt to avoid blame for "budget busting" by meeting, or at least coming close to, budgetary targets as calculated by the Congressional Budget Office. Committees that do so retain substantial discretion within their jurisdiction. Those that fail to do so will have their priorities challenged. Fortunately for the authorizing committees, the CBO has been relatively generous as a scorekeeper.[8]

Conclusions

The six cases of indexation policymaking reviewed in this study suggest that there is no single politics of indexation. Indexing proposals have come from a variety of sources. Proponents have used a variety of strategies to win enactment, as have opponents in their efforts to block or repeal indexing.

These motivations and strategies are by no means random, however. They reflect the very different opportunities and risks embedded in some programs, compared with others. Indexation politics for social security and individual income taxes, for example, is inevitably different than that for dairy price supports, because the clienteles are different and the potential for credit and blame is so much greater. The risks and opportunities that indexing presents vary over time as well as across programs.

The cases also suggest that blame-oriented objectives and strategies—when the political environment gives rise to them—are an especially powerful influence on policymakers' behavior. In some cases,

---

8. See Jonathan Rauch, "CBO's Wishful Thinking," *National Journal*, vol. 19 (March 7, 1987), pp. 550–54.

such as congressional pay, blame avoidance and blame generating are the obvious and overwhelming influences on policy outcomes. In other cases, such as social security, their effects are sometimes more subtle and they are intermixed with other policy objectives. In still other cases, such as food stamps, other objectives dominated initial decisions to index, but blame avoiding played a more important role in the way indexing has been modified. But in virtually every case, understanding policymakers' powerful incentives to avoid blame themselves and generate it toward opponents advances comprehension of why public policy has turned out as it has.

11

Explaining Indexation Decisions

The case studies in this study demonstrate repeatedly the effects of two successive developments—persistent high inflation and budgetary stress—on both policymakers' objectives and indexing policy choices. Inflation helped to put indexing on the policy agenda. But inflation's effects were felt differentially: some programs were indexed while many others were not. Budgetary stress placed cutbacks on the agenda and made policymaking more of a zero-sum game. New indexing virtually ceased after 1980, and existing indexing mechanisms came under attack. Again, however, some programs' indexing provisions were affected more than others. Increasing concern by policymakers over spending and deficits is not sufficient to explain the pattern of cutbacks, just as inflation alone cannot explain why indexing was employed in some programs but not in others.

This chapter examines why some proposals to index federal programs—and some proposals to reform existing indexing mechanisms—were enacted and others were not. It builds on the analysis of policymakers' objectives and strategies in chapter 10 to explain the scope of both original decisions to index federal programs and later decisions to modify those mechanisms or leave them untouched.

The Scope of Indexation

Chapter 10 suggested that indexing proposals face four hurdles in winning enactment: building a base of support, establishing plausibility, gaining approval or acquiescence of clientele, and gaining approval or acquiescence of policymakers. There are several possible paths over these hurdles. Which strategies are used—and whether proponents of indexing prevail—depends on the opportunities and risks specific to

230

individual programs. In some cases, political benefits are unimportant. Politicians may agree to give up discretion because they have a good-policy desire to protect beneficiaries (for example, food stamps and probably many other small income transfer and social service programs). In other cases, the wishes of a single clientele dominate policymaking. Indexing occurs if that clientele wants it and little opposition develops (for example, dairy price supports). In still other cases, politicians are motivated primarily by the desire to escape blame for unpopular decisions. They may seek to index in order to pass the buck (for example, congressional pay) or to avoid making decisions that are politically popular but irresponsible in policy terms; indexing proposals under these circumstances are almost certain to be contested, however. Finally, politicians sometimes support indexing, despite the required sacrifice of credit-claiming opportunities, because policy-motivated proponents forced the issue onto the agenda, and once lawmakers are forced to take a stand on the issue, they find it difficult to oppose it. Thus they jump on the bandwagon (for example, legislative specialists with social security and House Democrats with personal income tax brackets). Rarely do all politicians pursue the same strategy in particular choices, however. Instead, competing alliances of politicians with different objectives and strategies jockey for position.

As this analysis suggests, indexing proposals for some programs had lower hurdles to clear than others. It is these differences that explain why indexing is used more in some types of programs than others, and why there are differences in the use of indexing even within sectors. I will focus here on indexing decisions in five sectors: benefit and social service programs, purchase programs, grant programs, regulatory programs, and revenue and user charge programs.

Benefit and Social Service Programs

Indexing is very common in benefit and social service programs in part because these programs have a strong advantage in clearing the plausibility hurdle (Hurdle II). The effects of inflation on program clientele are direct, visible, and easily understood by policymakers.[1] Why should retirees' real social security benefits decline because of inflationary pressures beyond their control? Why should poor people

---

1. The effects of inflation are less severe, however, where recipients generally get short-term benefits, such as unemployment insurance. It is more difficult to establish the need for indexing in these programs because the plausibility hurdle is higher.

lose eligibility for legal services or free school lunches when their family income did not rise in real terms?

The high visibility of inflation's effects on benefit and social service programs also helps those programs in building a base of support and winning over program clientele: inflation causes direct short-term income losses (or, for means-tested programs, risk of losing eligibility), even if adjustments are made in the long term. And once some people's programs are indexed, the specter of relative deprivation arises: clientele may ask why their program is not indexed when others are. There may still be disputes among clientele about the best base and mechanism to use for indexing, however, and policymakers may be reluctant to sacrifice discretion.

The cases suggest several distinctive paths over these hurdles for benefit and social service programs. The first path is found in the large retirement and disability programs for federal employees, notably civil service retirement and military retirement pay. Initial indexing decisions in these programs followed a clientele-led logic, as well-organized constituencies worked closely with legislative specialists. In both cases, the clientele were able to obtain an increase in the annuity base as part of the indexing package and to improve on that package in following years. However, the new federal employees' retirement system, for federal employees hired after 1983, reflects the scarcity-driven logic of indexing politics in the 1980s: its inflation protection is substantially less generous than the civil service retirement system it partially supplants because the small clientele of the new program lacked the political clout to get a better deal.

The one major retirement and disability program in which indexing has not been enacted is compensation for veterans with service-connected disabilities. Politics in veterans' programs has also been clientele-led, but veterans' groups have opposed indexing of compensation, believing that they can do better through a system of annual ad hoc adjustments. The issue is not just COLAs, but a broader attempt to control the agenda in ways consistent with their interests. An annual COLA authorization bill provides a sacrosanct vehicle to make incremental improvements in related veterans' benefits that might not be able to get through Congress on their own. Legislative nonspecialists would not dare to oppose a bill that provides reasonable benefit increases to disabled veterans and to the survivors of those who gave their lives for their country; neither would the president veto it. As one participant in the process put it, the compensation COLA bill is an "unstoppable Christmas tree" on which a number of ornaments can be hung every year. Recognizing this problem, the Reagan administration proposed indexing veterans' compensation in its 1988 budget.[2] Veterans' organizations opposed the proposal, and it went nowhere.[3]

The story is quite different for pensions for veterans who do not have service-connected disabilities. This program, although run by the Veterans Administration, is not a retirement or disability program, but a means-tested or "welfare" program. Veterans' pensions were indexed in 1978 as part of a major reform of the program without opposition from veterans' groups. Veterans' pensions have never had the political unassailability that compensation has; many critics have long argued that they should be abolished.[4] Veterans' groups are happy to have the money for their constituencies, but once a satisfactory level of benefits was set by the 1978 act, they were content to have the issue off the agenda and have their adjustments tied to the seemingly invulnerable COLA for social security.

The clientele-led nature of veterans' pension politics is atypical of means-tested programs. Most means-tested programs do not have constituencies as politically powerful as the veterans' organizations. Indexing decisions on most other means-tested programs have been driven by good-policy rather than electoral considerations, and most of them have been indexed. The clientele support hurdle may not be a problem for these programs, ironically, because their clientele are politically weak; thus they generally are unable to dispute the terms of indexing, demanding an improvement in the benefit base before they will accept indexing. In addition, many means-tested in-kind programs have a defined benefit (such as access to head start or medicaid), rather than a graduated benefit. Thus only eligibility, not benefit size, has been involved in indexing disputes over many means-tested programs.

The relatively weak political clout of recipients of means-tested pro-

2. *The Budget of the United States Government, Fiscal Year 1988, Supplement,* p. 5-137.
3. *Analysis of Fiscal Year 1988 Budget Proposals for Veterans' Benefits and Services,* Committee Print 3, House Committee on Veterans' Affairs, 100 Cong. 1 sess. (Government Printing Office, 1987), pp. 2, 8; *Proposed Veterans' Administration Budget for Fiscal Year 1988,* Hearings before the House Committee on Veterans' Affairs, 100 Cong. 1 sess. (GPO, 1987), pp. 382, 387, 390, 411–12; and *Compensation and DIC Proposals,* Hearing before the House Committee on Veterans' Affairs, 100 Cong. 1 sess. (GPO, 1987), pp. 69, 114–15, 121, 145, 159, 160, 167.
4. See, for example, Gilbert Y. Steiner, *The State of Welfare* (Brookings, 1971), chap. 7.

grams may also give them some assistance in crossing the hurdle of policymaker support, for policymakers have little credit-claiming gain to reap by maintaining ad hoc increases. Thus the food stamp program was indexed before social security, not because its clientele was stronger, but because the Agriculture committees were willing to sacrifice discretion over program benefits.

Not all means-tested programs face low hurdles to indexing, however. Indexing of aid to families with dependent children has faced substantially higher barriers to both clientele and policymaker acceptance than many of the others. States set AFDC benefit levels, and these vary dramatically across states. As a result, there has been tremendous disagreement about the proper benefit level among the program's clientele, policy experts, and policymakers. Indexing AFDC would also necessitate massive overhaul of the program, either through a federal requirement that the states index benefits or through a federal takeover of benefits. (Indeed, indexing of benefits has been a part of many welfare reform proposals.) States have opposed a requirement that they index benefits; budget guardians and fiscal conservatives in Congress have resisted a federal takeover.

The social security program had a very different path across the clientele and policymaker hurdles than either means-tested or federal employee retirement programs. Of course it faced different challenges, including a huge clientele that would seem, at least in theory, to pose a classic collective action problem: its clients are likely to be poorly informed and poorly organized to defend their interests.[5] This would seem to be a perfect situation for credit-oriented strategies and for ad hoc adjustments that allow legislators to preserve their discretion over policy and claim credit for inflation adjustments.

The fact that social security is under the jurisdiction of the House Ways and Means and Senate Finance committees would also seem to reinforce tendencies to ad hoc adjustments. As noted earlier, legislators on these committees tend to be power-oriented rather than clientele-oriented and hence particularly anxious to preserve their discretion over programs. Both committees have broad jurisdictions and hence are less likely to be perceived by nonspecialists as captives of specific interests. And Ways and Means long enjoyed special protections against floor amendments by proponents of indexing.

5. On collective action problems, see Mancur Olson, *The Logic of Collective Action* (Harvard University Press, 1965); and Terry M. Moe, *The Organization of Interests* (University of Chicago Press, 1980).

How then did indexing win adoption in social security? Much of the answer lies in (1) a split among legislative specialists, (2) decreasing agenda control by legislative specialists, and (3) a substantial increase in benefits enacted simultaneously with indexing. Republican specialists became convinced that indexing fit their own policy and political interests and forced it onto the agenda. Once it reached the agenda, legislative nonspecialists could preserve their decisionmaking discretion (and credit-claiming opportunities) in the long term only by taking stands that might generate substantial blame in the short term. They chose to minimize blame, even though it was not clear when the initial 1970 House vote was taken that indexing was in the interests of social security beneficiaries. This should not be surprising. Large clientele groups are likely to be ill informed about the actual implications of indexing and possible alternatives. But they can understand appeals concerning protection of their benefits from inflation. On such issues, legislators must be concerned primarily with avoiding giving their opponents a popular election issue.[6]

Social security indexing was helped over the clientele and policymaker hurdles by its enactment in concert with major changes in the base that benefited clients and increased deficits. This was no coincidence. The change in the program base was a sweetener that made the legislative package, including indexing, more difficult to vote against. This occurred despite the fact that in the social security case indexing was placed on the agenda by fiscal conservatives precisely because they did not wish to vote for higher benefits. But once indexing got on the agenda, conservatives were not able to control the uses to which it was put. Indexing became one chip in a bidding war where deficit reduction was a low priority, and fiscal conservatives were unable to walk away from indexing—they had to match the highest bid by supporting the entire package.

The social security case suggests another lesson about indexing in federal benefit programs: efforts to institute indexing as a means to limit spending increases in these programs are likely to fail. The Reagan administration has had no more success in this regard than the Nixon administration did. In the medicare program, for example, the

6. This is not to say that interest groups were not active in the social security indexing debates: they were. But their influence was based less on their ability to deliver blocs of voters or financial contributions to specific candidates than on the likelihood of their raising the political profile of particular issues that might later be used by electoral opponents.

Reagan administration considered plans to replace the current benefit structure with an indexed voucher that recipients could use to purchase health care insurance.[7] The idea was to simultaneously limit expenditure growth and inject more competition into the health care market. But the idea was vehemently opposed by program clientele and faced a number of practical design problems as well. The administration eventually decided to concentrate on proposals that focused more directly on squeezing health care providers.

Purchase Programs

Purchase of goods and services covers a very broad range of programs, so it is not surprising that it is the category with the greatest internal variation in scope of indexing. Indexing is quite common in federal pay and commodity support programs and has also been used in medicare reimbursement, but is very rare in other sorts of purchase programs.

Indexing of purchase programs has some severe problems at the plausibility hurdle. Setting prices by statute and indexing them may upset the balance between supply and demand. These procedures may elicit a supply that is too high, especially when they are combined with an open-ended purchase requirement (for example, in the dairy price support program). Moreover, indexing prices lowers incentives to make productivity improvements. Indexing does not necessarily benefit providers of the goods and services, either. It is a question of alternatives, and in the case of government purchases, the alternative is generally not one of fixed, statutory payment levels (as would be the case with benefit payments), but flexible prices arrived at through a bargaining process. Moving to a system of indexed prices may result in a loss of bargaining power for providers.

Why then have some purchase program standards been set by statute and indexed? In the case of commodity support prices (such as dairy), clientele-led politics has been dominant. Individual commodity interests feared executive efforts to lower real price support levels; thus they preferred statutory rates to wide executive discretion. In addition, they saw indexing as a way to overcome the high coalition-building costs needed to get price support increases. They were closely allied with legislative specialists who saw maintaining links

7. See Linda E. Demkovich, "Reagan Takes on the Elderly Again as He Seeks to Slow Medicare's Growth," *National Journal,* vol. 13 (September 12, 1981), pp. 1616–20.

with agriculture as more important than claiming credit for ad hoc increases with individual voters. But they could not have succeeded without their ability to carry out a logrolling strategy.

In the case of white-collar federal pay, the plausibility hurdle was originally overcome by arguing that it was necessary to maintain salary comparability with the private sector. But why were clienteles and specialist committees willing to go along? At the time pay comparability was first used in 1962, federal white-collar employee unions were not a potent political force, but postal unions were. In seeking pay increases from Congress, white-collar workers were forced to piggyback on the demands of postal unions. Pay comparability gave white-collar unions a way to get more freedom from the postal unions; postal unions, for their part, agreed to pay comparability because the agreement gave most postal workers a much better deal than strict comparability provisions would have provided.[8] Specialist committees went along because they were more concerned with claiming credit with organized interests (federal, especially postal, employee unions) in the short run than in claiming credit over the long term with individual federal employees for helping to enact pay increases.[9] Postal workers abandoned the comparability process for collective bargaining in 1970 as part of a larger package of reforms including an immediate 14 percent pay increase, but they negotiate contracts with COLA provisions.[10] The main losers from this change were civil service workers, since postal workers were no longer interested in using their clout to push for full comparability pay increases for civil servants.

In military pay the plausibility hurdle for indexing was overcome by the use of comparability in civilian federal pay increases. Clientele were supportive because indexing lowered the political costs of getting pay increases that kept up with inflation. Jurisdiction over military pay remained in the favorable Armed Services Committee, however, so it was unlikely that comparability would keep real pay increases off the agenda. Moreover, the formula established by military pay compar-

8. *Congressional Quarterly Almanac,* vol. 18 (1962), pp. 355–69.

9. In the case of congressional pay, of course, the motive was essentially to pass the buck.

10. Pay for postal workers is still supposed to be comparable to private-sector pay, but the comparability pay process is not used. Most studies argue that postal workers are substantially overpaid in comparison with comparable private-sector workers. See, for example, Jeffrey M. Perloff and Michael L. Wachter, "Wage Comparability in the U.S. Postal Service," *Industrial and Labor Relations Review,* vol. 38 (October 1984), pp. 26–35; and Douglas K. Adie, *An Evaluation of Postal Service Wage Rates* (Washington, D.C.: American Enterprise Institute for Public Policy Research, 1977).

ability legislation clearly overcompensated many members of the armed services for inflation, especially those at higher ranks.[11]

The use of indexing in medicare reimbursement had a very different history and political logic than the other indexed purchase programs. As with the failed proposal for medicare vouchers, indexing of payment to providers was part of a broader response to rapid increases in program costs that forced policymakers to choose between the interests of providers and consumers. Unlike vouchers, however, indexing reimbursement squeezed only providers. Because of reluctance either to spend more or to raise medicare user fees further, indexing was one more ineffective tool in a battle to restrain costs without alienating providers too much.

Intergovernmental Grants

Indexing in federal grant programs, as discussed in chapter 3, is fairly limited. Indexing of overall authorization levels is especially unusual. In part this reflects a problem with the plausibility hurdle: it is far easier to understand why individuals' social security benefits should be indexed than why a program budget should be. Social problems change, after all, and spending priorities presumably should change with them rather than being fixed over time. It is especially hard to make a persuasive case for indexing project grants, which award funds on a competitive, nonrecurring basis. But a plausible argument can be made for indexing formula grants, which provide money to subnational units on a recurring basis according to a legislative formula: state and local governments need reasonable assurance of the funds that will be available if they are to plan effectively.

But the dearth of indexing in grants reflects two additional realities of grant politics. First, grants are a wonderful credit-claiming opportunity: they distribute benefits to a variety of specific clienteles, while costs tend to be ignored since they are distributed among the entire taxpaying public. This makes legislators reluctant to index grant budgets, since doing so would limit opportunities for both legislative specialists and generalists to vote in favor of popular programs.[12]

Second, most grants are subject to annual appropriation, and appropriators are loath to give up this control. The appropriators' role influ-

11. See Martin Binkin, *The Military Pay Muddle* (Brookings, 1975), pp. 62–66.
12. On grants as credit-claiming opportunities, see John E. Chubb, "Federalism and the Bias for Centralization," in John E. Chubb and Paul E. Peterson, eds., *The New Direction in American Politics* (Brookings, 1985), pp. 284–85.

ences calculations by clientele and program supporters on how to increase program budgets or at least hold them steady. Indexing grant program authorizations would make it harder for clientele and legislative specialists to get real increases in spending levels on the policy agenda in the absence of a crisis. And for the bulk of grant programs that have to go through the appropriations process, recurrent authorizations demonstrate to appropriators the continued interest of legislative specialists in obtaining funding (usually increased) for the program and provide a "hunting license" with which clientele and program administrators can seek increased appropriations. It is doubtful that an indexed authorization level would have the same credibility. Thus indexing authorizations might actually result in lower expenditures.

None of these obstacles to indexing grants is insurmountable. And both legislative specialists and clientele might be willing to try indexing if they feel that it could protect them in an unfriendly budgetary environment. Indeed, there are signs that such a shift was under way in the 1970s. Several grant programs, mostly in the education field, were indexed in this period. What might have been a major breakthrough came in 1980, when the authorization for the huge social services block grant was indexed.[13] Given the almost complete indexing in benefit and social service programs, grants might have become the next big growth area for indexing. Several precedents had been established, and that in itself tends to enhance the plausibility of the idea.

It was not to be, however. Any trend toward indexing of grants confronted a new obstacle, the strong push by the Reagan administration to reduce domestic spending. For the most part, the Reagan administration has been more interested in slashing grant spending and in limiting the federal role than in freezing grant spending at or near current levels. Even if legislative specialists and clientele had sought indexing of grant program budgets in light of the new political and budgetary realities, it is very unlikely that the Reagan administration and its conservative allies in Congress would have approved it. In fact the potential bellwether, the authorization for the social services block grant, was deindexed and cut in the Reagan administration's first year, as part of the 1981 reconciliation act.[14]

13. P.L. 96-272, sec. 201.
14. P.L. 97-35, sec. 2352.

There has been one major exception to the Reagan administration's reluctance to index grants, however. The administration, led by the Office of Management and Budget, has repeatedly proposed indexing the total budget of the huge medicaid program either to the Consumer Price Index or to health care inflation.[15] Currently medicaid is an open-ended program (that is, with no fixed ceiling) through which the federal government shares the cost of state programs to provide health care for the poor. In recent years, federal expenditures on medicaid have risen faster than both general inflation and the even higher rate of health care inflation. The administration's position is clearly an effort to cut program expenditures below what would occur under current law. But the administration's proposals have been vehemently opposed by Democratic legislative specialists, who see it as a threat to medicaid's nature as an open-ended entitlement, and by state officials, who believe that they would be stuck with huge increases in medicaid costs. The administration's proposal has never come close to overcoming these hurdles, for it is politically very unattractive to legislative nonspecialists.

Regulation

The case studies suggest both policy and political reasons why indexing has made so little headway in the regulatory arena. A first problem is the plausibility hurdle. As noted with purchase programs, fixing prices by formula can cause serious market distortions. Indexing proposals in the regulatory arena also have problems winning the support of program clientele. As the minimum wage case suggests, regulatory decisions often pit one clientele against one another (for example, producers versus consumers), making it difficult to arrive at a mutually acceptable base and mechanism for indexing. For those regulations where standards are currently written in nominal dollar amounts, there are usually some participants who have an interest in preventing those standards from keeping up with inflation. Organized labor, for example, wants to increase the number of federal contracts falling under the jurisdiction of the Davis-Bacon Act, so it opposes efforts to raise or index the minimum thresholds for coverage under the act. Even where prices are often adjusted on an ad hoc basis for inflation (as in most economic regulation), granting automatic adjustments

15. See, for example, *The Budget of the United States Government, Fiscal Year 1988, Supplement,* p. 5-107.

would end the short-term windfalls to those who benefit from temporarily lower real prices. It would also decrease their bargaining power to resist price increases in the long run. These beneficiaries are understandably reluctant to sacrifice these advantages.

Perhaps the greatest barrier to indexing regulatory programs, however, is in winning the support of legislative specialists. In most regulatory arenas, these specialists have a superior alternative to indexing: if they wish to simultaneously avoid blame for contentious decisions, avoid ceding power to the often mistrusted executive, keep some flexibility to respond to market conditions, and preserve possible indirect influence on decisions, use of a regulatory commission is a better buck-passing mechanism. And that is in fact what Congress has done.

Once again, however, these barriers to indexing are not insurmountable. Automatic inflation adjustments can be combined with discretion to waive those adjustments if they disrupt markets. And Congress may wish to provide some guidelines to regulatory commissions stated in constant dollars, as it did with the Natural Gas Policy Act of 1978 and the Staggers Rail Act of 1980. But these cases also indicate an important reason why indexing has not gone further in the area of economic regulation: the growth of indexing in this sector coincided with a movement toward deregulation. Congress substantially increased pricing freedom instead of indexing price movements. Indeed, indexing in both the railroad and natural gas cases was used as part of a transition to a freer pricing system.

Revenue and User Charge Programs

The general absence of indexing in taxes and user charges, despite buck-passing incentives to institute it, is due in large part to politicians' blame-avoiding instincts. The problem is Hurdle III (clientele opposition) and its effects on Hurdle IV (policymaker support). Politicians can escape blame once such a program is indexed, but affected groups are likely to oppose the enactment of indexing. Politicians have to incur short-term blame in order to avoid it over the long term. Since most politicians have a high discount rate when it comes to blame, indexing for these programs rarely makes it onto the agenda.

The two successful buck-passing indexations in this category—the OASDHI tax base and the medicare hospital insurance deductible—have much in common with each other and much that separates them from other revenue programs. Both were proposed by legislative specialists to finance the very popular social security-medicare programs.

This gave them a solid political base. And both were proposed as part of large packages (the creation of medicare and the 1972 social security benefit increase) that obscured the issue of future tax or user charge increases behind large and immediate benefit increases. This limited both clientele opposition and fears by nonspecialists that they would incur blame by voting for the proposals.

The dynamics of the other two major indexations in this category—income tax brackets and capping of medicare supplementary medical insurance premiums—were very different. They did not involve allocating losses; quite the opposite. The original medicare statute had implicitly indexed SMI premiums: they were set at a level that was supposed to yield one-half of program costs. The rapid increase in premiums under this procedure made an explicit indexed cap on premium increases a very popular measure. The cap gradually reduced medicare premiums to less than half the level they would have been if the cap had not been enacted.

The politics through which indexing of income tax brackets was adopted was even more complex and quite similar to the politics of social security indexing. A large but poorly organized clientele created opportunities for credit-oriented politics. But a split developed among legislative specialists, and specialists opposing indexing were unable to control the agenda. A cut in tax rates made the proposal very attractive to clientele. And at a critical stage in the process (in this case, on the House floor), politicians feared constituency blame if they voted against the proposal.

Maintaining Indexation

Once enacted, indexing alters the dynamics of the policymaking process for those programs, at least during a period of budgetary stress. It alters the base of expectations about future outcomes, and it transforms the process of making marginal cutbacks in programs (or increases in income tax revenues) from an automatic one driven by inflation to one where legislators must make a positive decision that can be used against them later. In short, it changes policymakers' role in loss allocation from invisible *acquiescence* in those losses to visible *imposition* of those losses.

Indexing has not been immune to broader social and economic trends, however. Indexing provisions have been trimmed for a number of federal programs, reflecting both the Reagan administration's priorities and the seriousness of the federal budget deficit. Several examples of indexing cutbacks have been discussed: the social security changes of 1977 and 1983, the food stamp and dairy price support revisions of the early 1980s, and the congressional pay debates of the last two decades. In each case, the beneficiaries of indexing mounted a spirited defense of existing provisions. And policy changes rarely involved complete abolition of indexing for a program. Instead, politicians have stretched out the periods between adjustments, made indexing formulas less generous, and imposed other incremental changes. Only in the dairy case does indexing appear to be a dead letter.

All programs have not been cut equally. Efforts to impose a freeze across all indexed programs have invariably failed because such a freeze would include politically sacrosanct social security. Indexing provisions for some programs have nevertheless undergone major changes, while others have been left relatively untouched.

Variations among programs in susceptibility to cutbacks should not be surprising. Proposals to repeal or modify indexing mechanisms must clear the same hurdles as proposals to index in the first place. The cases suggest three attributes—workability of the mechanism, strength and size of program clientele, and degree of automaticity—that make a program's indexing provisions more resistant to repeal or cutbacks.

Workability of the Mechanism

A first test for any revision of indexing mechanisms is obviously the plausibility hurdle. Indexing protects programs from change only so long as policymakers believe that it does what it was expected to do, without major flaws that cause a crisis in the program. The social security indexing mechanism in place until 1977 (and still in effect for recipients born before 1917) overcompensated for inflation, upsetting earnings replacement rates and threatening the financial viability of the system. This clearly put revision of the mechanism on the agenda, but the ensuing debate was limited to finding a new, more affordable indexing formula rather than questioning the desirability of indexing. Indexing of dairy price supports was abandoned because it was seen as contributing to a huge oversupply of milk. The dairy industry's efforts to devise a new index with stabilizer provisions for periods of excess production were in large part an effort to make indexing seem plausible again.

Clientele Strength

Efforts to cut indexing mechanisms must also gain clientele support (Hurdle III). It is not surprising that programs that can mobilize powerful constituencies on behalf of indexing provisions are more likely to maintain them intact or to modify them when it serves their interests. The contrast between social security and medicare user charges, on the one hand, and public assistance programs, on the other, is instructive.[16] The social security and medicare constituency has been able to limit cuts in social security COLAs by defending indexing, while keeping medicare part B premium increases, and more recently, part A deductibles, below what the original indexing mechanism would have provided. Food stamps and the social security minimum benefit, both of which cater to a smaller clientele with fewer political resources, have been dealt with much more severely.

What is more surprising is that programs with very large clienteles (such as taxpayers and social security recipients) have often been better at defending their indexing provisions than more compact, better organized clienteles (such as dairy farmers and legislators). And when policymakers have been forced to make cutbacks in indexed programs, they have generally done so through mechanisms other than permanent COLA cuts—often by targeting specific benefits and subgroups among the program's clientele. Both of these findings run counter to the precepts of pluralist theory, which argues that smaller groups will be more successful in defending their interests because they do not have as many problems in getting their members to contribute to the costs of political organization (the "free rider" problem). In short, one might expect the clientele support hurdle to be relatively low for attacks on programs with very large clienteles.

Blame avoidance can help explain both why policymakers make selective cutbacks and why large, diffuse clienteles are able to do relatively well in resisting cuts. The "free rider" problem is a more important constraint when groups must engage in common action to seek *new* benefits from government than it is in defending *existing* benefits.

16. The indexing mechanism for medicare part B premiums was altered when it threatened the real value of social security benefits. Medicare part A premiums were altered in 1986 after the historic relationship between the cost of a first day's hospital stay and total program costs was disrupted by the new diagnosis-related group system of hospital reimbursement.

Organization is helpful in these cases, both to pressure government officials to adopt the group's position and to assure those officials that information about their help will be effectively transmitted back to constituents, so those constituents can show their gratitude with votes and political contributions to their benefactors. Organization is much less important when policymakers—especially legislators—are considering actions that impose concentrated losses on a group or groups. Once indexing is in effect, government must take a positive step—impose rather than acquiesce—if it is to raise additional tax revenue or lower the purchasing power of benefits. In these cases, policymakers know that political entrepreneurs (notably future election opponents) will do the publicizing—that is, affix the blame. A vote in favor of such a change is something that is easily taken advantage of by an electoral opponent; it is a simple message, easily conveyed to a relatively uninformed electorate. And when social security or income taxes are involved, that message has a huge potential audience. As a result, repeal of indexing for these programs is far less likely than for a program such as dairy price supports, with its much narrower, though better organized, clientele. If clienteles have a negativity bias and will act upon losses once they have reached a certain threshold, it is better to pick on a small clientele than a large one.

The same logic helps to explain targeting of cutbacks. COLAs affect the entire clientele of a program. More narrowly focused cuts (such as food stamp eligibility or specific social security benefits) narrow the number of opponents. And when the cuts are aimed at recipients who are likely to be seen as least deserving (for example, those at the top of the income scale for means-tested programs), or who are politically weakest, even less blame is incurred by supporting cutbacks.

But if indexing provisions for benefit programs are generally difficult to cut, indexing mechanisms in other areas—such as user charges—are hard to sustain. For example, Congress has intervened repeatedly in both medicare user charges and in its own pay to impose new formulas and to freeze payments. The common denominator is that these are "pass-the-buck" indexations—which usually impose losses over what a huge program clientele might expect from the status quo. Some organized interest or political entrepreneur is likely to have both the incentive and resources to force reconsideration of such decisions. Once reconsideration makes it onto the agenda, it becomes very difficult to vote against.

Degree of Automaticity

The form of indexing is the third major factor affecting resistance to cutbacks. Less automaticity lowers the clientele hurdle by making it easier to get a change from the status quo onto the agenda. The president's authority to lower recommendations for congressional and civil service pay, for example, has shifted the scope of adjustments downward. Even more important, when congressional ratification of the scheduled adjustment is required, it is much more likely to be modified or overturned, especially when (as in the case of congressional pay) it is an unpopular one.

Similarly, contingent cuts have a somewhat easier time clearing the third hurdle. Legislators are understandably very reluctant to vote openly for permanent and immediate COLA reductions. It is politically more palatable to enact benefit cuts on an "as needed" basis, making the linkage between the legislators' vote and the unpopular change more obscure and more distant in time. This technique for avoiding blame is evident in the budget-cutting procedures adopted under the Gramm-Rudman-Hollings deficit reduction plan. Contingent cuts were also used in the 1983 social security rescue package, which required COLA cuts if the old age and survivors insurance trust fund fell below specified levels, and in several pieces of dairy legislation, which mandated cuts in support prices if government purchases of dairy products were above targets.[17]

Conclusions

Federal indexing policy choices have not been a simple technocratic response to the successive challenges of high inflation and budgetary stress. While these forces have played an enormous role in setting the policy agenda, the interests of policymakers and clienteles have mediated their effects. As a result, there have been substantial variations in indexing choices, both between and within sectors of government activity. The strength and interests of program clienteles and the degree of autonomy of legislative specialists have had an especially heavy influence on indexing choices. Indexing has hardly ever been imposed where a powerful clientele resisted it.

17. The linkage of the cutbacks to prevention of undesirable policy effects (irresponsible budget deficits, bankrupt social security trust funds, and runaway dairy expenditures) also made policymakers' actions more defensible in good-policy terms.

The opportunities and risks confronting policymakers have also changed over time. As indexing became more familiar, the plausibility hurdle shrank and indexing expanded into new sectors of federal activity. In sectors where indexing was already established, it became more difficult to resist it if powerful clientele demanded it. But new hurdles—notably the federal deficit and the determination of the Reagan administration to cut domestic spending—arose in recent years. These new barriers not only caused a virtual cessation of new indexing activity, they also led to a reconsideration of existing commitments to index. In these battles to preserve indexing, the ability of clientele and program supporters to generate blame against proponents of cutbacks was the most powerful protection against cuts.

12

The Consequences
of Indexation

Does indexing matter? Or does it simply regularize a process of inflation adjustments that were occurring anyway? Proponents and critics
of indexing have suggested a number of possible effects. The consequences are alleged to include increased security of benefits for recipients, increased budget deficits, and weakened resistance to inflation.
Perhaps most important, indexing is often said to lead to the substitution of automatic formulas for open deliberation in policymaking and
the erosion of accountability for policy decisions.

The evidence outlined in this study is not ideal for a thorough evaluation of the consequences of indexing. It is based on very few cases.
But the cases discussed here do account for most of the dollars in
indexed programs, and they are representative of the range of indexing
in the federal budget.

Lack of sufficient cases is not the major obstacle to assessing the
effects of indexing in any event. The real problem is that one cannot
know what decisions government would make (how it would adjust
social security benefits, for example) if program standards were not
indexed. Asking about the counterfactual case does make one crucial
point very clear, however. In assessing the consequences of indexing
one cannot simply compare the indexed level with a situation where
no inflation adjustments are made. Ad hoc inflation adjustments were
an important part of the policy process before adjustments were regu-
larized through indexing mechanisms; often those ad hoc changes
overcompensated for inflation. Abolishing indexing mechanisms
might curtail inflation adjustments in the short term, but it certainly
would not eliminate them in the long term.

Although one cannot know what would have occurred if programs
were not indexed, one can fruitfully ask what kinds of biases and con-

straints (if any) indexing builds into the policy process and how these biases influence policy outcomes. Here the study does suggest a series of tentative conclusions about the influence of indexing. The most general conclusion is that it *does* affect the policymaking process and, through this process, the clienteles of individual programs and the federal budget. Its effects on the economy, notably in reinforcing inflation, are less clear. But even where indexing does affect policymaking and outcomes, these consequences are by no means uniform across time and across programs. This chapter attempts to outline and explain the pattern of effects, employing the theory of policymakers' objectives and the case studies developed in this study.

Consequences for the Policy Process

Indexing affects both the size and content of policy agendas. In so doing, it also redirects political conflict. When a program has inflation-sensitive provisions, there is a presumption that policymakers will need to act on those provisions on a regular basis unless automatic adjustment mechanisms are in place. If there are indexing mechanisms, that presumption is reversed, except when an obvious flaw in the mechanism causes the program to malfunction. And when program standards have been set for a while and their value has been fixed by indexing, they tend to acquire a normative aura; they are seen as fair because they are familiar to both policymakers and clientele. Efforts to change the base are likely to be increasingly difficult, barring a major outside intervention (for example, a presidential initiative on welfare reform or a serious scandal in the program). Conflict is reduced because the prospects for winning a change from the status quo are slight.

Of course, the issues that indexing keeps off the agenda have changed over time. Before the onset of massive budget deficits, indexing probably limited changes that would have been expansionary in real terms. More recently, contractionary pressures have been more powerful, and it is these pressures that have been constrained. Indexing does not always limit the agenda, however. In particular, when attacks on automatic adjustments offer credit-claiming and blame-generating possibilities (as in the case of congressional pay), the base and mechanism for adjustments are likely to remain very controversial.

Indexing of benefit programs also tends to change the focus of policy initiatives by both supporters and critics of these programs. The benefit standard for food stamps, for example, had been a source of serious contention until indexing was adopted in 1971, with program advocates favoring a more generous plan. But the issue of the benefit base almost immediately disappeared from the public agenda. Program advocates moved on to other issues (notably ending the purchase requirement and expanding more narrowly targeted nutrition programs). Program critics have focused more on issues of eligibility (such as for strikers and recipients at the upper end of income eligibility) and fraud than on benefit standards.

As the food stamps case suggests, indexing may simply redirect conflict rather than suppress it. This is particularly true in a period of tight budgets: if one program or program standard is immunized from budget cuts, others will undergo even greater pressure.

Consequences for Democratic Accountability

The limitation and skewing of agendas and political conflict are not subjects that should be taken lightly. The American governmental process is ostensibly a democratic one in which elected representatives make policy decisions and are held accountable by the electorate. This image has always been an oversimplification: much decisionmaking authority is delegated to bureaucrats and regulatory agencies, for example. But indexing effectively delegates a whole new range of decisions away from elected officials—in this case largely to statisticians and legislative formulas. Indexing further undercuts the ability of nonexperts to understand and evaluate, let alone influence, proposals for policy change. Only experts are likely to understand how expenditures and clientele may be affected by a change in the period over which a COLA is adjusted or a change in caps on the indexed standard deduction for a means-tested program. Most policymakers—not just the public—may have to take experts' word on faith. As critical decisions are made, they are likely to be on the outside looking in.

Of course, politicians retain the authority to intervene and change program bases and indexing mechanisms. But even if they have the technical competence to do so, they rarely exercise this authority because they fear, on the one hand, imposing visible losses on program clientele or, on the other, appearing to be fiscally irresponsible. As this analysis suggests, indexing has a perverse effect on the accountability of policymakers. Indexing makes it more difficult to change program standards, especially to cut them, with low visibility. Politicians' accountability is increased, but it is accountability for maintaining specific policy outcomes rather than for making policy in a responsible manner. Increasing this kind of accountability can virtually require policymakers to exclude from public debate both specific program cuts and changes in the indexing mechanism. Policymakers' real discretion is slashed, and policy may be paralyzed. The clearest and most important example of this phenomenon is social security: policymakers are afraid even to appear to be considering cuts in current social security benefit levels, let alone actively push for cuts, because of the blame they will incur. A modification of social security benefits may or may not be desirable, but an exclusion of that issue from public discussion and debate almost certainly is not.

Consequences for Program Clientele

The effects of indexing on the welfare of program clientele flow from its effects on the policy process. First and most obvious, indexing does smooth out short-term differences across time in the real value of benefit programs, just as it was intended to do. No longer are benefits eroded by inflation without a conscious decision by government.

Second, indexing changes the strategic bargaining position of program clientele. Again, the nature of the effect varies with budgetary stress. When budget pressures are relatively weak, indexing makes it more difficult for affected groups to get requests for real increases on the agenda. Programs with strong clienteles generally won ad hoc increases in their benefit base simultaneously with the enactment of indexing.

When budgets become tighter, indexing strengthens the bargaining positions of affected clienteles by raising the hurdles to those advocating cutbacks. Proponents of cutbacks must force a reconsideration onto the agenda if they are to prevent inflation adjustments from occurring automatically and indefinitely. If program advocates can maintain agenda control, they are in a good position to defend their program. Moreover, indexing makes cutbacks in real benefits more visible, forcing policymakers to impose them rather than simply acquiesce in them. As Representative Leon Panetta has noted, "You have a real political problem when you try to control COLAs.... Benefit recipients consider COLAs as much a part of the entitlement as the benefit it-self."[1]

Even when indexing mechanisms are flawed, clientele are in a good strategic position to resist corrections and cuts. The slow, tortuous process of cutting the dairy price support mechanism was described in detail in chapter 7. Even more important from a budgetary stand-point are the flaws formerly existing in the Consumer Price Index, the primary inflation adjustment mechanism used in federal benefit pro-grams. The CPI clearly overcompensated for inflation for a number of years until it was corrected beginning in 1983. As a result, beneficiaries of many federal benefit programs (most important, social security) received excessive inflation adjustments.[2] The Social Security Admin-istration has estimated that 1981 outlays for social security (OASDI) and supplemental security income would have been 5 to 6 percent lower (almost $8 billion) if an index that more accurately measured housing costs had been employed since indexing of those programs began in 1975.[3] Because the indexing mechanism was not corrected retrospectively, individuals who retired before 1983 continue to be overcompensated.

The strengthening of clienteles' bargaining positions suggests a third consequence of indexing: it tends to limit real long-term changes either upward or downward in the base amount, simply taking that issue off the government agenda in many cases. And it is not at all clear that this was the intent of indexing's proponents (or at least some of them). The food stamp case has already been noted. A similar phenom-enon occurred with social security, even though the legislation index-ing the program had made explicit allowance for alternative increases.

The stabilizing effect of indexing is not consistent over time or across programs. Indexing mechanisms can and have been repealed or modified. Benefit bases and other program standards can be altered. But these changes are infrequent, and they tend to be fairly limited. The factors that determine the extent to which indexing provides a stabilizing force in programs—clientele strength, flaws in the indexing

1. Quoted in Jonathan Rauch, "Congress, Worried About Huge Budget Deficits, Eyes an UNCOLA Strategy," *National Journal*, vol. 17 (January 19, 1985), p. 153.
2. Of course, it is possible that clientele might have done better through ad hoc adjustments, especially before the onset of serious fiscal stress.
3. Benjamin Bridges, Jr., and John C. Hambor, "The New CPI and Cost of Living Increases for OASDI and SSI," *Social Security Bulletin*, vol. 45 (August 1982), pp. 15–17.

mechanism, the degree of automaticity in the mechanism—were outlined in chapter 11.

Fourth, indexing softens differences in the political strength of strong and weak clienteles when programs aimed at both are indexed. This is especially true in a period of fiscal stress and retrenchment, when programs with politically weak clienteles would otherwise be particularly vulnerable. Although politically weak clienteles are still more susceptible to having favorable indexing provisions cut than are strong ones, indexing of program benefits equalizes outcomes somewhat, by creating a strong bias for the status quo independent of clientele strength. Proponents of cutbacks must get those cuts over the many hurdles of the American policy process. In addition, indexing increases blame-generating opportunities for program advocates, who can accuse their opponents of lacking compassion and a sense of fairness.

Finally, in a period of fiscal stress, indexing strengthens differences between the clientele of indexed programs and those of nonindexed ones. The former are in a strong position to protect their position against cutbacks. In unindexed programs, program advocates have fewer blame-generating opportunities because cutbacks occur gradually and silently with inflation. They must win a change from the status quo simply to keep up with inflation. They are therefore likely to be politically easier targets for cutbacks. A comparison of changes in benefit standards for food stamps and supplemental security income (both indexed) with those for AFDC (unindexed) suggests that unindexed programs are indeed more susceptible to cuts.

Consequences for the Budget

Two claims are usually made about the effects of indexing on the federal budget. The first is that it freezes priorities, preventing government from responding to changing public needs.[4] The second is that it raises budget deficits.

The simplest way to examine these hypotheses is to compare changes in expenditures for indexed and nonindexed programs. But this approach implies what may be a spurious causal relationship. Just

4. See, for example, Jonathan Rauch, "The Fiscal Ice Age," *National Journal,* vol. 19 (January 10, 1987), pp. 58–64.

because programs that are indexed grow faster does not mean that they do so because they are indexed. Demographic changes, notably increases in the elderly population, may lead to spending growth in the social security program that has little to do with indexing. An increase in unemployment levels can have a major effect on food stamp expenditures. Improvements in medical technology may lead to higher—and more expensive—quality of care financed by medicare and medicaid, which will be affected only indirectly by whether user charges and reimbursement are indexed. And the fact that one program is indexed and another is not may reflect underlying differences in political support that are the true cause of variations in expenditure patterns.

Keeping these caveats in mind, data on federal expenditures suggest that widespread indexing inhibits but does not eliminate policymakers' ability to change budget priorities. Figure 12-1 shows several categories of federal spending as a share of GNP. Expenditure variations in income transfer programs have reflected economic cycles, but there have also been some long-term trends. Indexed income transfers (notably social security, SSI, food stamps, and government retirement programs) continued to grow until 1983, due in part to overindexing. But all of the secular growth in indexed transfers' share of GNP is accounted for by social security and federal employee retirement programs. The GNP share of means-tested indexed income transfer programs actually fell between 1975 and 1988, as did that of nonindexed income transfer programs (AFDC, unemployment insurance, and the earned income tax credit). Both of these categories of programs were affected by policy changes that restricted eligibility and benefits. In any case, indexed income transfers' overall share of GNP was relatively stable when compared with other sectors: growth rates were higher for health entitlements (medicare and medicaid) and, after 1979, defense spending. Domestic discretionary spending, on the other hand, fell precipitously, while interest payments rose.

In short, indexing can coexist with a substantial rearranging of priorities, but it makes such a shift much more difficult by giving additional protection to a major portion of the budget. Hence a change in priorities is most likely to occur by raising revenues, cutting other spending, or increasing government deficits. The United States has chosen the last two methods.

Overall spending data and the case studies also suggest that the current mix of indexed and nonindexed programs increases the fed-

FIGURE 12-1. *Selected Federal Expenditure Categories as a Percentage of Gross National Product, 1975–88*

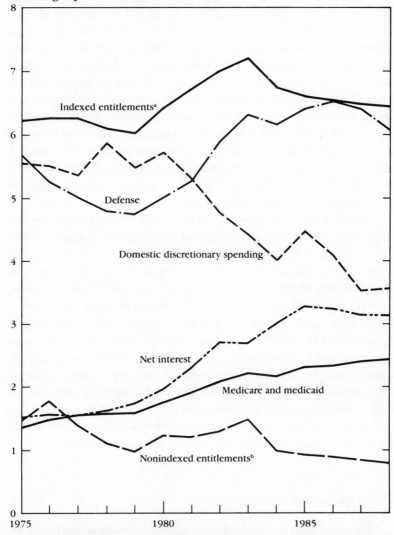

SOURCE: *The Budget of the United States Government, Fiscal Year 1989*, p. 6g–40, *Historical Tables, 1989*, table 11-3; and *Background Material and Data on Programs within the Jurisdiction of the Committee on Ways and Means, 1987 Edition*, Committee Print 100-4, House Committee on Ways and Means, 100 Cong. 1 sess. (Government Printing Office, 1987), p. 424. All 1988 figures are estimated.

a. Old age survivors insurance, social security disability insurance, civil service retirement, military retirement, coal miners' disability, child nutrition and special milk programs, supplemental security income, railroad retirement, veterans' pensions, food stamps, and low-income energy assistance.

b. Aid to families with dependent children, veterans' service-connected compensation, earned income tax credit, and unemployment insurance.

eral deficit and inhibits efforts at deficit reduction. In periods of fiscal stress, the agenda-limiting effect of indexing acts primarily to keep deficit-reduction initiatives—such as freezes in nominal benefit levels—off the agenda. Indexing also strengthens the bargaining position of program clienteles in their efforts to resist cuts in the status quo. The deficit-increasing effects of indexing in federal spending programs should not be overstated, however: the indexed programs with the highest expenditures are those with very strong clienteles—notably social security—that would be in a strong position to protect themselves even without indexing. In short, indexing in spending programs makes a significant, although unquantifiable, contribution to the federal deficit. But to say that indexing is *the* deficit problem overstates both the effect of indexing and the ease of making real cuts in popular programs in the absence of indexing.

In examining the effects of indexing on the federal budget it is also important to note that some forms of indexing (for example, of user charges) can at least in theory help in reducing deficits. But explicit efforts to use indexing to avoid blame for imposing losses (the pass-the-buck and scarcity-driven strategies) have usually failed. Among scarcity-driven proposals, for example, President Nixon's proposal to index social security benefits was enacted only with a huge benefit increase that set benefits at unprecedentedly high levels. The Reagan administration's proposals for an indexed cap on medicaid grants, indexed medicaid vouchers, and indexed veterans' compensation all went nowhere. These efforts have failed because they attracted the opposition of organized clienteles. Thus efforts to index to save money have succeeded only where the interests of those affected were placed against one another—as in the case of medicare providers and patients.

Consequences for the Economy

One of the most common charges against indexing is that it actually fuels inflation. There are several supposed mechanisms at work. First, individuals whose wage or social security income is indexed are immunized from inflation; as a result, they are less likely to punish policymakers who permit high inflation rates. Second, indexing (especially of wages, the minimum wage, and payroll tax bases) drives up business expenses, fueling the inflationary cycle. Finally, indexing fuels inflationary expectations.

Economists have done a great deal of research on the relationship between inflation and indexing. However, most of this research concerns wage indexing rather than indexing of government benefit programs, which are the most important indexed sector in the United States. The research generally draws upon data from societies suffering from hyperinflation (Brazil, Israel) rather than from the United States, where inflation has rarely hit double digits. And it deals with countries where indexing is far more pervasive than it is in this country.[5] Moreover, there are serious problems of reciprocal causation in the inflation-indexation relationship.

As a result, existing research can reveal only a limited amount about the effect of indexing of government programs on inflation in the United States. But there are strong reasons to believe that it is relatively modest, at least at current levels of inflation and indexing. The record of the Reagan administration certainly suggests that a firm monetary policy and a deep recession are more than adequate to overcome any inflationary effects of current indexing practices: inflation in the United States is far lower currently than in 1980 despite very modest cuts in indexing of expenditures and the addition of tax bracket indexing. Although there almost certainly is a point beyond which indexing does reinforce inflation, the United States does not appear to be near that point.

Conclusion

The record of indexing in the federal policy process is a mixed one at best. It has provided more stable income—and often a rising real income—to the beneficiaries of many federal benefit programs. But it has done so at substantial cost. Clienteles of some programs have been given a differential privileged status. The policy agenda has been skewed, with some programs forced to bear increased scrutiny because others are excluded from reconsideration. Government has lost flexibility in its spending priorities. Indexing has placed simultaneous upward pressure on government spending and downward pressure on revenues. Deliberation, discretion, and accountability for responsible policymaking have declined.

5. See, for example, Rudiger Dornbusch and Mario Henrique Simonsen, eds., *Inflation, Debt and Indexation* (MIT Press, 1983); Jagdeep S. Bhandari, "Indexation, Deficit Finance and the Inflationary Process," *Southern Economic Journal*, vol. 49 (April 1983), pp. 1077–93; and John Williamson, ed., *Inflation and Indexation: Argentina, Brazil, and Israel* (Washington, D.C.: Institute for International Economics, 1985).

That these trade-offs exist should not be surprising. What is distressing to many, however, is that indexing of federal programs has progressed so far. Moreover, the latitude for change is limited: blame-avoiding pressures appear to have frozen most indexing procedures in place. Can anything be done to improve the balance between automaticity and discretion in federal decisionmaking? It is to this difficult task that I now turn.

13

The Future
of Indexation

This study has attempted to weave together a theoretical argument about the objectives that guide policymakers' decisions with an empirical study of a policy problem: automaticity in government programs. For the most part, this examination has been retrospective. This chapter will project these twin themes into the future, with both predictive and prescriptive ends in mind. A first set of questions concerns how politicians' objectives—especially their desire to avoid blame—are likely to affect indexing policy choices in the future. Will indexing have a similar scope to that of today? Will it function in the same way?

A second set of questions concerns how, if at all, an understanding of politicians' objectives can be used to promote better policy choices. Should the scope and functioning of indexing be changed? And can changes be made that will simultaneously meet politicians' electoral objectives while promoting deliberative, comprehensive decisionmaking and policy outcomes that are responsible and equitable?

Prospects

Answering the first of the two questions about the future of indexing is relatively simple: its scope and functioning are unlikely to change greatly in the forseeable future. Mollie Orshansky, the Social Security Administration statistician who created the "poverty standard," pointed out that "the poverty line we've developed did not come from God. It came from me."[1] The bases and mechanisms used to index federal programs are not of divine origin. They are the result of

1. Quoted in Janet Hook, "Debate Rekindled on Defining Poverty Level," *Congressional Weekly Report,* vol. 42 (May 19, 1984), p. 1175.

political maneuvering and compromise rather than omniscient judgments, but all too often they have seemed to be omnipotent and immutable in guiding program growth. The reasons for this rigidity are entirely human and political: namely, politicians' fear of imposing losses and incurring blame, and the relative ease of blocking change in the American governmental system.

Most of the politically easy changes in indexed programs have been made. Automatic adjustments of greater-than-annual frequency in benefit programs have been eliminated (for example, in civil service retirement, food stamps, and dairy price supports). Elimination of semi-annual COLAs was relatively easy because they violated widespread perceptions of fairness: the clientele of some programs were receiving a greater protection that those in other programs. Most of the obvious flaws in indexing mechanisms (for example, in the Consumer Price Index, social security wage history adjustments, and dairy price support levels) have been removed as well. Correction or elimination of flawed indexing mechanisms was possible because the enormous financial drains they created eliminated their plausibility and increased their budget share at the expense of others.

Future changes will have a tougher time clearing the plausibility hurdle, and they will almost always run contrary to the interests of clienteles and policymakers. With respect to the major benefit programs, the only constituencies for change in indexing—at least a change that involves contraction—are the executive and legislative budget guardians. Nor is there a constituency for extending indexing to more regulatory, revenue and user charge, or other types of programs.

In the current situation of high budget deficits, an appropriate policy response might seem to be a "circle-the-wagons" strategy toward indexed programs, in which policymakers recognize that loss imposition is inevitable and unite on a policy to diffuse the resulting blame. But such a strategy has severe problems, because disagreements about what to do about the budget problem are so intense. There are also great incentives for some politicians to refuse to join in an agreement and to cast blame for the program cuts that would result from a modification of current indexing policies. In the past, a circle-the-wagons strategy has succeeded only in times of crisis in a program (such as social security in 1977 and 1983). Marginal changes in indexing procedures remain by far the most likely ones.

Rethinking Automatic Government

Global statements about the efficacy of indexing (or lack of same) are not very helpful. Indexing is not good or bad in itself. It is appropriate in some programs and inappropriate in others. Some indexing formulas that have been utilized are reasonable; others are less so. In some cases indexing needs checks or caps to prevent undesirable consequences; in other cases, this is less necessary.

It must also be recognized that neither the presence or absence of indexing nor its form fully determines policy outcomes. But they can have a major effect on agendas, strategies, and bargaining positions, especially insofar as they affect issues' blame-generating and blame-avoiding potential. Thus they do have a powerful effect on policy.

The inefficacy of global statements about indexing is particularly true with respect to the goal of deficit reduction. For example, purging benefit programs of automatic mechanisms would lead to lower expenditures only if, in the ad hoc changes that would inevitably follow, pressures to cut the deficit overwhelmed pressures to increase benefits. For many of the most important programs, like social security, it is far from clear that they would. Eschewing indexing entirely is one way to attack deficits. But in some cases it may be more appropriate—and more politically viable—to follow the path suggested by the Gramm-Rudman-Hollings budget initiative, that is, to create new automatic mechanisms and modify existing mechanisms so that they contribute to rather than detract from a responsible fiscal policy.

Guidelines for the Future

Rather than global prescriptions about indexing, what is needed is a set of guidelines to govern its use. These guidelines will of necessity be controversial. People's lives and billions of dollars are involved. Often the two—dollars and quality of individuals' lives—come into direct conflict.

Guidelines for the future use and modification of indexing should include the following. First, policy changes that further reduce open decisionmaking and direct accountability should be undertaken only with great caution. Second, indexing should be used only when the alternative—ad hoc adjustments—is likely to produce less efficacious outcomes and entail significantly higher decisionmaking costs. Third, indexing should be employed only when a reasonable mechanism is available and is used. The dairy price support case shows all too well the dangers of an inappropriate index. Fourth, indexing mechanisms should not be expected to serve as a surrogate for the marketplace, as they were, for example, in the cases of medicare reimbursement and dairy price supports. This approximation will be imperfect at best, horribly distortive at worst. Fifth, indexing provisions should be sensitive to the need to reduce the federal deficit, but that should not be the only goal. Thus the combination of unlimited indexing with entitlement status or an open-ended spending requirement should be avoided or limited whenever possible. Finally, any reforms should take into account politicians' need to avoid blame. To do otherwise is to doom the proposals to defeat. For example, changes in indexed programs can be made either in the indexing mechanism or in the base. Both types of changes will be discussed here, but making the indexing mechanism less generous is usually easier than shrinking the base; the latter is far more visible because it usually imposes nominal as well as real losses.

Specific Policy Options

There are obviously conflicts between these guidelines; trade-offs must be made. But they do suggest a number of specific options for policy change.

COLAs could be increased less than inflation. Proponents of reduced federal spending have suggested a variety of alternative indexing schemes to achieve that end. For example, inflation adjustments can be pegged to the increase in wages or the increase in prices, whichever is lower. Such a plan was enacted as part of the social security reform of 1983, although it takes effect only if trust fund reserves fall to dangerously low levels. Another option would cap the inflation adjustment at a particular level—for example, a 2 percent increase— with beneficiaries absorbing any inflation above that level. Variants on this option call for indexing only for a fixed share of inflation, or skipping the first 2 or 3 percent of the inflation rate in COLA adjustments. A method that has been used in Europe is to deny COLA protection for some or all of the inflation caused by developments that portend a permanent decline in the society's standard of living (for example, devaluations or the oil price increases of the 1970s).[2] Other methods

2. See Daniel Wartonick and Michael Packard, "Slowing Down Pension Indexing: The Foreign Experience," *Social Security Bulletin,* vol. 46 (June 1983), pp. 9–15.

focus on the base as well as the index—for example, indexing benefits only up to a maximum amount, with the remainder over that cap being unindexed or only partially indexed.[3] Obviously, this approach would affect high-income clientele of indexed programs most heavily.

If COLA cuts are to be successful, they must be designed in ways that allow politicians to minimize blame. One method that has proven somewhat successful in reducing blame was the COLA "delay" incorporated into the 1983 social security rescue package. This permanent cut for current retirees succeeded in large part because it was cleverly disguised as a delay, which is far more politically palatable than an outright cut. This opportunity for cutting benefits is an artifact of the way that social security COLAs are designed: instead of using the initial retirement benefit as a base and adjusting benefits for inflation since that time, the benefit established every year becomes the new base. If the period over which inflation is measured is moved forward in time but not stretched out to incorporate the period of delay, there will be a permanent decline in benefits for individuals already retired when the delay took effect. (Permanent cuts do not result from COLA delays when there is a fixed rather than a moving base for COLAs—for example, in the thrifty food plan.) But disguising cuts as delays is not an inexhaustible technique: after one or two applications, clientele groups will become more adept at explaining its true implications to their members and mobilizing them against it. In the budget negotiations that followed the 1987 stock market crash, for example, advocates for the elderly firmly rejected a social security COLA delay, and the idea was quickly dropped.

Given that benefit cuts inevitably impose losses vis-à-vis the status quo, this failure is not surprising. It is unlikely that proponents of various cutback schemes will be any more successful in the future at designing proposals that can clear the hurdles of the policymaking process than they have been in the past.

Even if political obstacles to cutting COLAs can be overcome, there are also very real problems of designing cutbacks that distribute losses equally across recipients. For example, a five-year program of capping social security COLAs at 2 percent below the rate of inflation would

3. See, for example, the proposals by Representative John Erlenborn for limiting federal pension COLAs, outlined in *Options for Changing Indexation of Entitlement Programs,* Hearing before the Task Force on Entitlements, Uncontrollables, and Indexing of the House Committee on the Budget, 98 Cong. 1 sess. (Government Printing Office, 1983), pp. 6–10.

leave those who retired before that period more than 10 percent behind in purchasing power. But people who retired just after that program ended, with a similar real wage history, would not suffer such a decline unless their initial benefit was also adjusted downward. In short, COLA cutbacks have great potential for creating new inequities as they solve budgetary problems: the social security "notch generation" is a good example.

This is not to say that such cutbacks should not be considered. They certainly should be, especially as part of a bigger package of deficit reduction. But tremendous care must be used to design cuts that are equitable as well as politically acceptable.

More use could be made of specialized indexes and bases. Given the wide variety of programs in which automatic adjustment mechanisms are employed, there are in fact relatively few indexes in use in federal programs. The Consumer Price Index is used in the vast majority of cases despite important shortcomings.

The major reason for the widespread use of the CPI is its familiarity and its perceived fairness—that is, its political neutrality. It has a known—if somewhat besmirched—track record. Using the CPI assures a clientele that their program will be treated equally with other programs. New, more specialized indexes are often viewed with suspicion by legislators and clienteles as subject to manipulation by the executive. But these same groups have sometimes favored new indexes if they believe that a change will work to their advantage: a new CPI specifically for the elderly, for example, has been proposed to give more adequate consideration to the ostensibly unique needs of the social security constituency.[4]

In some cases, such as medicare reimbursement, inflation trends for particular sectors or groups are so different from overall trends that measures such as the CPI cannot and should not be used. In general, however, a proliferation of specialized bases and indexes, such as a specialized CPI for the elderly, should be resisted. Use of these indexes breeds further demands for special treatment, reinforces clienteles' belief that they should be permanently entitled to complete insulation from the effects of inflation, and, of course, increases spending. This is an era where none of these phemonena may be sustainable. Certainly none of them should be encouraged.

---

4. See Macon Morehouse, "Measuring Inflation: Is a New Index Needed?" *Congressional Quarterly Weekly Report,* vol. 45 (August 22, 1987), pp. 1948–49.

Indexing linkages with perverse consequences could be broken or modified. Perhaps the clearest case of an indexing linkage with negative consequences is that of congressional pay increases to those for the executive and judiciary. The desire of legislators to maintain the link, and thus make their own pay increases more politically palatable, is understandable. If legislators had the courage not to block pay increases for all three branches, it might even be reasonable. But the pay linkage process has in fact become a hostage-taking process, with Congress holding up executive and judicial pay increases because they cannot strike a ransom bargain with themselves. The effects of this hostage taking on morale and retention in the other two branches are no longer tolerable. This linkage should be broken, with pay levels for the other two branches adjusted to be closer to private-sector equivalents.

Additional discretion could be built into indexing provisions for entitlements that are not means-tested. Automatic adjustment procedures for the major entitlement programs (social security, civil service and military retirement) are now embedded in statute. The barriers to any alternative adjustments being adopted, or even considered, are quite high. Additional discretion could be built into the process by allowing the president to submit an alternative plan, much as he does with civil service pay and congressional pay. The alternative plan would become law unless Congress enacted another plan in its stead. Although it would require a courageous president to use this provision to cut benefits (and a less courageous one would be tempted to use it to propose increases that outpaced inflation), this provision might at least give alternative adjustments a place on the agenda.

Increased use could be made of "pass-the-buck" indexing in a number of revenue, lending, and user charge programs. Two obvious candidates for indexing are the taxable wage base for unemployment insurance and deductibles in medicare supplementary medical insurance (SMI). The federal wage base (that is, wages on which a payroll tax is paid) used to finance unemployment insurance is now set at $7,000 a year, a level that has been changed only three times from the $3,000 level set in 1940.[5] Because benefits tend to increase with wages, the lack of wage-base indexing has required high payroll taxes and increased funding problems in the unemployment insurance sys-

---

5. Congressional Budget Office, *Reducing the Deficit: Spending and Revenue Options, A Report to the Senate and House Committees on the Budget—Part II* (CBO, 1987), pp. 109–10.

tem. In the SMI program, deductibles have been increased only twice (a total of 50 percent) in the twenty years since the program was created. The SMI deductible has fallen relative to the average per capita benefit from 70 percent in 1967 to less than 8 percent in 1987.[6] Increasing and indexing the SMI deductible, as has been proposed by the Congressional Budget Office, would of course cause hardship for many recipients. But the unemployment insurance and SMI cases do illustrate that a failure to index can create distortions in a program as much as it can eliminate them.

The same distortions have occurred in federal lending activity, whether it be direct loans or loan guarantees with interest subsidies. Several of these loan programs (such as for rural electrification) contain statutory lending rates that were close to the market rate when they were established, but now carry a subsidy that not only is substantial but changes markedly with the level of interest rates. A more responsible policy would include both a shift upward in the interest rate base and a linkage of the loan rate to the Treasury borrowing rate, creating a more stable interest subsidy.[7]

Indexing could also be employed in many user charge programs. It need not be fully automatic, however. In many programs where user charges are now set by statute or regulation as a fixed amount, statutes could be changed so that inflationary cost increases would establish a "zone of reasonableness" for agency price increases. Within this zone, administrators would have discretion to raise prices or not to do so if, for example, they felt that market conditions did not allow them. Agencies, which are usually reluctant to impose fee increases on their clienteles, would be required to report their rationale to the Office of Management and Budget if they took less than the full inflation adjustment. Congress could still intervene to overturn these increases by statute or to make ad hoc changes (which would then alter the base from which the "zone" would be calculated). Price increases within the zone that administrators chose not to make in a given year could be used in later years.

Critics may argue that indexing of revenue and user charge programs would artificially insulate the federal government from the effects of inflation. But this misses the point. Government is already very

6. Ibid., p. 89.
7. See Barry P. Bosworth, Andrew S. Carron, and Elisabeth B. Rhyne, *The Economics of Federal Credit Programs* (Brookings, 1987); and CBO, *Reducing the Deficit,* pp. 135–36.

sensitive to the political effects of inflation. One of the forms this sensitivity takes is a reluctance to raise fees commensurate with inflation trends. The reform proposed here would attempt to provide a little more insulation from these political effects, making the public sector more rather than less comparable with the private sector.

Indexing procedures could have fail-safe mechanisms to limit the effect of poorly designed adjustment mechanisms. Price and income changes always affect markets. Higher rather than lower social security benefits encourage workers to retire rather than stay in the work force; higher dairy prices encourage farmers to increase production; higher wage costs for unskilled labor cause employers to substitute capital for labor and to seek other sources of supply. None of these effects is necessarily bad in itself, but if they exceed expected magnitudes, any of them can be extremely costly to the budget, the economy, or both. The dangers are especially severe when the market effects of indexed price or income changes have a dominant effect in particular markets. This is especially likely in purchase and regulatory programs.

One way to address the problem is to include negative triggers in indexing procedures: if a program goes off track on a specified dimension, scheduled inflation adjustments would be eliminated or scaled back. Such triggers (relating to the quantity of government purchases of dairy products) are currently used to cut dairy price supports, but many other uses for them are possible. For example, if the minimum wage is indexed, as is currently being suggested by some legislators, there could be a negative trigger linked to an appropriate indicator— for example, the teenage unemployment rate. If the effects of past increases on teen unemployment become too pronounced, later increases would be canceled or cut back. These fail-safe mechanisms even have some attractions for politicians, since they eliminate the embarrassment of having to repair obviously faulty policies after they have failed.

Including fail-safe triggers is obviously no substitute for correcting the flaws through an open decisionmaking process. But it must be recognized that there are always beneficiaries from such distortions. These beneficiaries are likely to fight to prevent those distortive mechanisms from being repealed. And once the distortions are imbedded in law, their task is made easier; they need only prevent policy change. Including fail-safes may lower their windfall benefits and make correcting the mechanism easier.

Increased use could be made of contingent triggers for deficit reduction in indexed programs. Contingent cuts, it was argued in chapter 11, make it somewhat easier to impose losses because they obscure the relationship between the act of cutting and the loss of benefits. Several contingent mechanisms exist now, such as the one limiting social security benefit increases to the lower of wage or price increases if the social security trust fund runs low.

Perhaps the most important contingent mechanism already in place is the Gramm-Rudman-Hollings deficit reduction procedure. Even before Congress repaired the budget-cutting mechanism that had been overturned by the Supreme Court, Gramm-Rudman-Hollings had some effect: most budget makers in both parties now feel constrained to come close to the procedure's targets in their own proposals.[8] To do otherwise in the current budgetary climate would be seen as irresponsible. Thus policymakers have two kinds of reasons to meet the targets: policy (they want their proposals to be taken seriously) and blame avoiding (they want to avoid being labeled as budget-busters).

Several changes could make the Gramm-Rudman-Hollings statute a far more effective tool for deficit reduction, however. First, the automatic cutback provisions could be expanded to include entitlement programs that are not means-tested, notably social security. While this provision would be extremely difficult to sell politically, the extent of the cutback could be limited (for example, to a maximum of 1 percent below the full COLA) to make it slightly more tolerable, especially if it were included in a broader package with spending reductions attractive to liberals.

A second change would be to add certain revenue provisions to the Gramm-Rudman-Hollings process. The most appropriate starting point would be to make income tax bracket indexing dependent on meeting deficit reduction targets, just as indexing mechanisms for some expenditure programs are (in theory) treated under the current law. The personal exemption and standard deduction should continue to be fully indexed, however, to prevent tax increases for America's poorest citizens. Adjustment of tax brackets at a rate lower than the change in the CPI would then be part of a "three-legged stool," along with defense and domestic expenditure reductions, with each expected to contribute one-third of the required deficit reduction. Tax brackets

8. Joe White, "Order within Disorder: The Informal and Formal Structures of Federal Budgeting," paper prepared for the 1987 annual meeting of the American Society for Public Administration.

would be lowered no further than the previous year's level. For example, if bracket adjustments equal to one-half of the past year's inflation rate produced the necessary one-third of the deficit reduction, the brackets would be set at that level. If complete cancellation of bracket adjustments was insufficient to yield one-third of deficit reduction, the remainder would have to be made up by expenditure cuts.

The concept of a contingent tax increase, which this would be in effect, is not a new one. In 1983 President Reagan proposed a 5 percent tax surcharge on federal income tax bills if deficits did not reach specified targets. The idea was immediately rejected by congressional leaders, in part because the poor economic conditions at the time made a tax increase of any kind seem undesirable on policy grounds. But that does not mean that it would fail under current conditions. Including revenues in the Gramm-Rudman-Hollings process might even improve the popularity of the process among Democratic lawmakers. Or even better, it might prod policymakers of both parties and governmental branches to work toward an open compromise for deficit reduction.

In considering these and other proposals to modify indexing, policymakers and the public should acknowledge that a substantial degree of automaticity in government has become politically inevitable. It is foolish to think that indexing can be eliminated from government: the political costs to policymakers of doing so would be too high. Nor is it clear that eliminating indexing from most federal programs would produce superior policy outcomes. The challenge of the coming decades will be to make indexing more compatible with more responsible policymaking and a more responsible fiscal policy, and wherever possible to harness indexing to achieve those goals.

Index

270